Getting the Job
You Really Want

Fifth Edition

A Step-by-Step Guide to Finding a Good Job in Less Time

* Discover your best skills.

* Define and land your ideal job.

* Get the job you want in less time.

* Get ahead on your new job.

Michael Farr
America's Career Expert

jist
Works
America's Career Publisher

Getting the Job You Really Want, Fifth Edition
A Step-by-Step Guide to Finding a Good Job in Less Time
© 2007 by JIST Publishing

Published by JIST Works, an imprint of JIST Publishing
7321 Shadeland Station, Suite 200
Indianapolis, IN 46256-3923

Phone: 800-648-5478   Fax: 877-454-7839
E-mail: info@jist.com   Web site: www.jist.com

Note to instructors: This book has substantial support materials, including a thorough instructor's guide, an instructor's resources CD-ROM, and videos. Call 800-648-5478 or visit www.jist.com for details.

About career materials published by JIST: Our materials encourage people to be self-directed and to take control of their destinies. We work hard to provide excellent content, solid advice, and techniques that get results. If you have questions about this book or other JIST products, call 800-648-5478 or visit www.jist.com.

Quantity discounts are available for JIST products: Call 800-648-5478 or visit www.jist.com for a free catalog and for more information. Have future editions of JIST books automatically delivered to you on publication through our convenient standing order program.

Visit www.jist.com: Find out about our products, get free sample pages, order a catalog, and link to other career-related sites. You can also learn more about JIST authors and JIST training available to professionals.

Associate Publisher: Susan Pines
Associate Product Line Manager: Barb Terry Howe
Contributing Editor: Dave Anderson
Production Editor: Karen A. Gill
Cover Designer: Aleata Howard
Interior Designer: Marie Kristine Parial-Leonardo
Proofreaders: Linda Seifert, Jeanne Clark
Indexer: Tina Trettin

Reviewers

Thank you to the following career educators and trainers who reviewed the content of this book. This edition is based on your feedback.

Ken Price, Everest College, Portland, OR; Debbie Fleming, Ouachita Parish Alternative Center, West Monroe, LA; Maurice Stevens, President, The Career Consulting Group, LLC., Stow, OH; Sean McGrellis, Career Education Corporation, Chicago, IL; George Gomoll, Director of Career Development, Taylor Business Institute, Chicago, IL; Brenda A. Siragusa, Director of Applied & Social Sciences, Corinthian Colleges, Inc., Santa Ana, CA; Janie Stewart, Picka-wayross, Chillicothe, OH

Printed in the United States of America

12 11 10 09 08 07   9 8 7 6 5 4 3 2

We have been careful to provide accurate information throughout this book, but it is possible that errors and omissions have been introduced. Please consider this in making any career plans or other important decisions. Trust your own judgment above all else and in all things.

ISBN 978-1-59357-399-7

about this book

Almost everyone who looks for a job eventually finds one. This book, however, helps you find a better job or the one you really want—and find it in less time. These two points—how "good" the job is and how long it takes you to find it—are the only things that really matter in your job search.

My interest over many years has been to develop career planning and job search methods that get results. This award-winning book presents approaches that have been proven to help people identify career possibilities. It also presents proven methods that reduce the time it takes to find a job.

Career planning and job seeking are not easy. Luck plays a part, but you also have to work at it. The rewards are there if you do the work.

This world holds an important place for you, and you will find it eventually if you try. Trust yourself. I wish you good "luck" in your career and your life.

contents

introduction

This is the fifth edition of this book. Thousands of people have used earlier editions of *Getting the Job You Really Want*, so you are in good company. I have made a variety of changes to this edition to keep up with the rapid changes in technology and our economy. For example, the Internet is an increasingly important source of career information and job leads, and the computer plays a major role in the workplace, so I have added details throughout to assist you. This edition also includes an index so you can find what you are looking for more easily.

But the basics of finding and keeping a good job haven't changed all that much. You still need a clear sense of what you want to do, and you still need to convince an employer that you are worth hiring.

While career planning and job seeking can be complicated topics, only two things are truly important in planning your career and in looking for a job:

1. If you are going to work, you might as well do something you enjoy, are good at, and want to do.

2. If you want to find or change your job, you might as well do it in less time.

This book is about these topics—and about getting results.

Through examples and worksheets, *Getting the Job You Really Want* helps you identify a powerful new language to describe your skills and teaches you to use that language in interviews. If you don't have a job objective, it helps you define one. If you already know what sort of job you want, you learn how to find out more about it and about other jobs that use similar skills.

The techniques you learn here have been proven to cut the time it takes to get a job—and help you get a better one. There is even a chapter on keeping a job once you get it that includes tips for moving up and leaving a job if you have to. I have tried to cover all the basic issues you should know in defining, getting, and keeping a good job.

In many ways, this is more than a job search book. It encourages you to learn more about yourself. It helps you identify what you enjoy and are good at—and to include these things in your search for meaningful work. This book asks you to consider how you want to live your life. I hope that it helps you make better decisions and shows you techniques to be far more effective in your career planning and search for a job.

Getting the Job You Really Want is designed to be *used* and not just read. Make it your own by writing in it, jotting notes in margins, and completing the activities. I do hope that you enjoy it—and that it helps you get the job you really want in less time.

I wish you well.

Mike Farr

chapter 1

Get the Life You Really Want

Wile this book is mostly about getting a good job in less time, it is important for you to consider some related matters.

For example, just what sort of life do you want to live? What are you really good at? Or what is more important to you: doing something you love to do, or earning more money?

Thinking about these and other questions will help you make better career decisions—and get a job that more closely matches what you really want. This chapter asks you to consider your long-term goals so that you can include them later in your career planning.

KNOW THAT THERE IS MORE TO LIFE THAN WORK

Most people work about 40 hours a week. But a week has 168 hours in it, so work takes up only about one-fourth of that time. While work is an important part of life, it is just one way to spend time. This chapter will help you put work in its place.

To prepare for the future, you need to think about more than the type of job you want. You also need to consider what is important to you in your life.

The following exercises will give you information about yourself and your goals. This insight will help you make better career and life plans and put you on the path to getting the job you really want.

> *Hold fast to dreams*
> *For when dreams go*
> *Life is a barren field*
> *Frozen with snow*
>
> *Langston Hughes*

What Do You Want to Be Doing Five Years from Now?

Imagine yourself five years from now. If you could choose exactly what your life would be like, what would you be doing? Be realistic but positive. It's okay to dream! Take your time and answer the following questions. Use extra sheets of paper as needed.

1. Where would you be living—in what sort of area, in what sort of home or apartment?

   _____

   _____

   _____

2. How would you be making a living, doing what sorts of things?

   _____

   _____

   _____

3. With whom or with what sorts of people would you be sharing your time?

   _____

   _____

   _____

4. How would you spend your leisure time, doing what sorts of things?

   _____

   _____

   _____

5. Any other important details?

   _____

   _____

   _____

It might help to do another worksheet like this one but for 10 years or even more in the future. Would you write different answers if your time frame were longer?

THE WORKING WORLD

How Many Jobs Will You Have?

Gone are the days of gold watches when people worked for the same company 50 years until retirement. Today's high school graduates will hold an average of 10–15 jobs and change careers 3–4 times during the course of their lives. Thus, job search skills are not onetime-use-only but are good for a lifetime. Who knows, 10 years from now, you may be getting the job you really want...again.

An Inheritance from Uncle Harry

This activity is similar to the previous one, but it allows you to be "less practical" and will more likely help you think without restrictions. Do this activity quickly. Just write down whatever comes to you.

Imagine you've inherited $20 million from an uncle you didn't know you had. If you didn't want to, you would never have to work again. But there are a few catches! Uncle Harry put the money with a group of bankers, and these people will give the money to you only after you have met certain conditions. Answer the following questions as honestly as you can.

1. For two years, the bankers will give you $75,000 annually for expenses. You can do anything you want, but you must spend your time learning about something that interests you. How would you spend this time, doing what sorts of things?

   _____

   _____

   _____

   _____

2. After the first two years, Uncle Harry requires you to spend half of your money ($10 million dollars) on a project that would help others. What would this project be?

   _____

   _____

   _____

   _____

3. What sort of lifestyle would you have after the two years are over? Where would you live, with whom, and how would you spend your time?

   _____

   _____

   _____

   _____

   _____

The two preceding activities help you to look at your life creatively. In the next worksheet, you use those creative thoughts to assess what you really want to accomplish with your life.

THE WORKING WORLD

The Value of Higher Education

Individuals with a four-year college degree will typically earn an average of $16,000 more a year than those with only a high school diploma. Yet only a quarter of working adults have a bachelor's degree or higher. Getting more education not only sets you apart from the crowd, it also pays for itself in the long run. Something to think about as you imagine your future.

What Do You Want to Accomplish?

In 10 or 15 years, what three things would you most like to have accomplished? Don't think of all the reasons you might not succeed. Concentrate on the things you really would like to accomplish. You can list things from work or from your personal life.

1. _____
   _____
   _____
   _____
   _____

2. _____
   _____
   _____
   _____
   _____

3. _____
   _____
   _____
   _____

SET GOALS

The questions you just answered help you think about the future. They let you reflect on what you want to do or accomplish. These dreams can give you ideas for your work and your life goals.

While you may not be able to do everything you want, good planning can help you get closer. You need to ask yourself what you can do now to start making your dreams come true.

MONEY MATTERS

Your Financial Future

Although there are probably some people out there who love what they do enough to do it for free, most of us want to be paid for our work. Pay isn't the only consideration in accepting a job, but it often is the prime motivation to getting one. As such, getting the job you really want is as much about planning your financial future as it is paying for the present. To help ensure that future, it is important to consider several factors as you pursue the job of your dreams, including job security, long-term benefits like retirement and adequate health care, and the opportunity for advancement. Create financial goals now, and consider them as you move through your job search.

Your Three Most Important Goals

Look over the exercises you just completed. Pick the three work or life achievements or goals that seem most important to you and write them here. Be realistic about what you could accomplish if you worked at it. Think in terms of five years or more into the future.

Goal 1: _____
_____
_____

Goal 2: _____
_____
_____

Goal 3: _____
_____
_____

For the first goal, complete the following. (If you want to continue with the other two goals, you may copy the worksheet or just write the answers to the questions on a separate piece of paper.)

Goal 1:

1. Give details about this goal. What specifically would you like to accomplish?

* _____
_____
_____
_____
_____

* _____
_____
_____
_____
_____

* _____
_____
_____
_____
_____

(continued)

(continued)

2. Within the next two years, what three things could you do to move closer to this goal?

* _____

   _____

   _____

* _____

   _____

   _____

* _____

   _____

   _____

3. List at least three things you could do in the next six months to begin working toward this goal.

* _____

   _____

   _____

* _____

   _____

   _____

* _____

   _____

   _____

4. List at least three things you could do in the next 30 days to begin working toward this goal.

* _____

   _____

   _____

* _____

   _____

   _____

* _____

   _____

Innovation

Aisha has been working at her new job for three months now. In that time, she has noticed several processes and procedures that strike her as inefficient. In fact, in the back of her mind, she has thought up a new production method that could save the company lots of money. Being a relatively new employee, however, she is afraid of pointing out possible flaws and sharing her suggestions for improvement. What advice would you give her?

DREAMS CAN COME TRUE IF YOU ARE WILLING TO WORK AT THEM

I hope the activities in this chapter have helped you think about your long-term dreams and goals. But, as you already know, dreaming is not enough. While some of your dreams may not seem reachable, you can reach many of them if you are willing to work toward them.

As you continue with this book, keep your long-term career and other dreams and goals in mind. And remember that you have 168 hours a week to work toward your dreams!

TIP: Take action! Be clear about your goals and set up steps you can take to meet them. The activities throughout this book will help you move closer to your dreams. The rest, of course, will be up to you.

CASE STUDY: DREAMS, GOALS, AND SUCCESS

Donna Helms, one of only approximately 1,000 women in the 26,000-member Professional Golfer's Association (the PGA, not LPGA), believes in setting goals. Donna took up golf in college. She loved the game so much that she decided to become a golf professional (a teacher, not a player). At the age of 30, she earned a full golf scholarship, eventually passed a Player Ability Test, and completed the courses required for certification.

In the book *Firestarters* (JIST Publishing), Donna gives this advice about how to achieve a personal goal like hers: "Write it down. Even if you're 16 or 60, you're going to forget. You're going to be diverted by life. Know what you want and go after it."

chapter 2

Meet Your Employer's Expectations

To succeed as a job seeker and worker, you need to understand an employer's point of view. Many people believe that an employer thinks differently than they do. But employers are just like you and me. Try to think like an employer. Consider what you would want your employees to do, and you can figure out what is expected of you as a worker. Knowing what employers want will help you present yourself successfully when you look for a job.

> *If you work for someone, then work for them. Speak well of them, and stand by the institution they represent.*
>
> *Remember, an ounce of loyalty is worth a pound of cleverness.*
>
> *Ebert Hubbard*

AN EMPLOYER'S POINT OF VIEW

If you were an employer, how would you select people to work for you? The activity "Ten Reasons for Screening Job Applicants In or Out" will help you learn to think like an employer. Imagine that you run a company. Give your company a name and decide whether you make products or provide a service. Then choose the products or services you offer. Next, imagine you have been asked to help others in your company decide which people to hire—or not hire.

Ten Reasons for Screening Job Applicants In or Out

In the following spaces, see how many reasons you can list for screening applicants in or out of a job. You can list negatives, such as "sloppy appearance," or positives, such as "good communication skills." Think of at least 10 reasons.

1. _____

   _____

2. _____

   _____

3. _____

_____

4. _____

_____

5. _____

_____

6. _____

_____

7. _____

_____

8. _____

_____

9. _____

_____

10. _____

Now go back and put check marks by the five reasons you think are the most important to use when screening people in or out.

In the following worksheet, you prioritize your reasons even more by selecting your top three reasons for screening job applicants in or out.

Your Top Three Reasons for Screening Job Applicants In or Out

From those five, choose the three reasons you think are the most important to use in screening job applicants. List them in order of importance. Put the most important one first.

1. _____

_____

2. _____

_____

3. _____

_____

The reasons you listed are probably similar to those most employers would list. Keep in mind, however, that employers often have different opinions about what is most important.

SKILLS FOR SUCCESS

Appearance

Cyndi comes to work on time every day and does her job well. But despite being told about it before, she continues to dress in a manner that doesn't fit company policy, including wearing T-shirts with sometimes offensive logos and blue jeans instead of slacks. Is this a problem, or should Cyndi just be allowed to do her job?

WHAT EMPLOYERS LOOK FOR

Studies have been done to find out what employers look for in the people they hire. Check your list against the following findings. In deciding to hire one person over another, employers consider

* First impressions

* "Soft skills," especially dependability and other personality traits

* Job-related skills, experience, and training

Let's look at why this is true.

Expectation 1: First Impressions

First impressions are important because negative ones are hard to change. For example, one survey of employers found that more than 40 percent of the people they interviewed had a poor personal appearance. These job applicants created a negative first impression based on the way they dressed or groomed. It may not be fair, but it is a fact. First impressions are also based on things like how well you speak or whether you are friendly.

Did you put first impressions on your list? Why or why not?

_____

_____

Expectation 2: "Soft Skills," Especially Dependability and Other Personality Traits

Few employers will hire someone they think will be a "problem"—even if they have excellent credentials. Poor communication skills, unfriendliness, dishonesty, and other personality characteristics are all reasons for being screened out. You probably considered one or more of these things in your reasons for screening someone in or out.

One of the most important things an employer will consider is whether someone will be dependable. Most employers will not hire someone unless they think the person will be dependable.

This is often true even if the person has good experience or training for the job. Being dependable means being on time, having good attendance, and working hard to meet deadlines. It also may mean that you are likely to stay at the job a while. If you convince an employer that you are dependable and hard working, you may get the job over someone who has better credentials.

How do employers decide who will be dependable? They look at your past experience as well as your present situation. If you have been dependable in the past, they know you are likely to be dependable in the future. The information you or your references provide about previous jobs, schooling, and personal accomplishments will be important in helping an employer decide if you will be dependable. If employers are not convinced they can depend on you, they probably will not hire you.

> *Being dependable means being on time, having good attendance, and working hard to meet deadlines. It also may mean that you are likely to stay at the job a while.*

Did you put dependability on your list? Why or why not?

_____

_____

BUSINESS ETIQUETTE

Cell Phones Rule or Cell Phone Rules

Imagine that you are in a meeting with a potential employer and your cell phone starts blurting out the latest ring tone you downloaded. The situation is not unusual, but what is striking is the number of people—about 40 percent—who choose to answer the call. Cell phones are a necessity for many, but answering them during an interview could result in a lost job. Follow these steps for cell phone etiquette:

* Use your phone's silent or vibrating feature when you are in a business situation.
* Let the call go to voice mail and return the call as soon as possible.
* Let those you are in a meeting with know if you are expecting an urgent call.
* If you *must* answer a call, politely excuse yourself to a corner or another room and use your normal speaking voice.

Expectation 3: Job-Related Skills, Experience, and Training

Most employers will interview only those people who have at least the minimum requirements for a job. For example, for an office job, they will quickly screen out applicants who cannot use word-processing software. But employers often will hire a person with less training or experience over another applicant with more. Why? Many employers will hire the less experienced worker if that worker convinces the employer he or she will work harder or be more reliable.

In fact, most decisions are not based only on job-related skills, experience, and training. If the employer thinks you can do the work or that you can quickly learn to do it, you may be considered for the job. If the employer thinks you will fit right in, be dependable, and work hard, you may get the job over someone with more experience!

> Did you put job-related skills, experience, and training on your list? Why or why not?
>
> _____
>
> _____

Which Leads Me to This Conclusion

It is not always the most qualified person who gets the job—it's the best job seeker!

THE WORKING WORLD

Making an Impression

Just how long does it take to make a first impression? Some say thirty seconds, others say four minutes. Whether it's a matter of seconds or a matter of minutes, nearly everyone agrees that this is the most important stretch of time when networking or interviewing. Just remember, while you may have anywhere from one to five minutes to make a good impression, you have all the minutes afterward to maintain it. So whatever you do, try to be yourself.

EMPLOYERS ARE PEOPLE, TOO

Employers are people, just like you. Wouldn't you want to hire people who

* Look as if they can handle the job

* Appear to be good, dependable workers

* Convince you that they have enough job-related skills and training to handle the job or could learn it quickly

THE GOOD NEWS: EMPLOYERS WILL GIVE YOU A CHANCE OVER MORE EXPERIENCED APPLICANTS

Many employers *will* take a chance on hiring a less experienced worker *if* that worker convinces the employer that he or she can do the job. This is good news for you because

* You can learn to create a positive first impression.

* You can emphasize why you can be counted on as a dependable worker.

* You can present your strengths in a way that convinces an employer that you can do the job.

You can learn to do all of these things as part of your job search preparation. You can learn to meet an employer's expectations. Keep in mind that it is often the most prepared job seeker who gets the job, not the best qualified. This book will help you to identify skills you have and enjoy using and to decide what job you can do well and enjoy. You will also learn how to get and succeed on that job, even over more experienced workers.

It is not always the most qualified person who gets the job—it's the best job seeker!

CASE STUDY: A GOOD FIRST IMPRESSION

Raphael, owner of his own software design firm, would agree that first impressions can last a lifetime. His first job out of college was with a company he had interned with his junior year. Although he had worked at the company for only eight weeks over the summer, he impressed the owners enough that they promised to hire him when he finished his degree. While there, he learned all the skills he needed to start his own company.

Now, as a CEO, Raphael stays personally involved in all hiring decisions and often conducts interviews himself. He says it usually takes only five minutes to decide if a job candidate is a good fit and only a few weeks on the job to verify that decision. Raphael gives this advice to job seekers: "A good attitude can often overcome a lack of experience. A lot of the necessary training can be done on the job if the person is motivated. Be confident and flexible, and convince an employer that what you don't know already you are eager to learn."

chapter 3

Develop Your Skills Language

You have hundreds of skills. Most people do. You probably take for granted things you do well that others would find hard or even impossible to do. And no computer can yet handle simple things like riding a bike or getting across town.

Because we take our many skills for granted, most people are not good at explaining the skills they have. One study of employers found that three out of four people who interviewed for a job did not present the skills they had to do the job. Most people just don't have the language or interview training to spell out their skills.

Use the talents you possess. The woods would be silent if no birds sang except those who sang best.

Henry Van Dyke

In planning your career and in looking for a job, knowing what you can do well is important. Knowing your skills can help you decide what kind of work is right for you. It makes a lot of sense to do the things you do best. If you do, you will probably be more successful.

It is also important to do things you enjoy. If you enjoy what you do and are good at it, your job and your life will be more satisfying.

This chapter provides activities to help you identify what you are good at and enjoy doing. Through these activities, you will develop a powerful "skills language" that can help you plan your career and get the job you desire.

THE THREE TYPES OF SKILLS

To help you identify your skills, let's begin by organizing them into the three groups shown in the triangle here. Each skill group is explained briefly in the following sections.

Adaptive Skills/Personality Traits

These skills can be defined as personality traits or personal characteristics. They help a person adapt to or get along in many situations. Examples of adaptive skills valued by employers include punctuality, honesty, enthusiasm, and the ability to get along with others. While many job seekers do not emphasize these skills in an interview, they are important to employers.

Transferable Skills

Job-Related Skills

Adaptive Skills

Three Types of Skills

Transferable Skills

You can use these skills in many different jobs because they can transfer from one job to another. For example, the ability to write clearly, speak well, and organize things would be desirable skills in many jobs.

Job-Related Skills

You need these skills for a specific job. An auto mechanic, for example, needs to know how to tune engines, repair brakes, and use a variety of tools. An office worker needs to know how to do word processing, use a spreadsheet, and perform other office tasks. Most people think of job skills when they are asked what skills they have. While these skills are important, other skills are just as significant.

Understanding that you have different types of skills is essential. However, it is even more essential to know what skills you have. Most job seekers think job-related skills are their most important skills. They *are* important. But employers often select job seekers with less experience who present their adaptive and transferable skills well in interviews. For this reason, we will analyze your adaptive skills first, then your transferable skills, and finally your job-related skills. Knowing and being able to describe those skills can often give you a big advantage in getting the job you want.

BUSINESS ETIQUETTE

Business Etiquette Is a Skill

In a business environment, your manners can make you stand out, for better or for worse. Knowing how to properly introduce yourself, interact in a meeting, or answer the phone at work are skills that can be learned easily. Business etiquette is about making the people around you comfortable and making them feel like you are friendly, capable, and confident.

DISCOVER YOUR ADAPTIVE SKILLS

This section will help you discover your many adaptive skills.

Your Good-Worker Traits

List five things about yourself that you think make you a good worker. Take your time. Think about what an employer might like about you or the way you work.

1. _____
2. _____
3. _____
4. _____
5. _____

Most people will list a variety of skills here. Often, one or more of these skills are adaptive, such as "get along well with others" or "work hard." If you were an employer, would these skills be important for you to know about? Would knowing a job seeker's adaptive skills help you decide to hire one person over another?

In most cases, it would. Yet many people do not mention their adaptive skills in an interview! Use the checklist that follows to learn more about your adaptive skills.

Adaptive Skills Checklist

The following checklist shows the adaptive skills that most employers find important. Read each skill carefully. If you have or use that skill some of the time, put a check mark in the first column. If you have or use that skill most of the time, put a check mark in the second column. Don't mark either column if you don't use that skill very often.

Critical Skills

All employers highly value these skills. They often won't hire a person who does not have or use some of these skills.

Skill	Some of the Time	Most of the Time	Skill	Some of the Time	Most of the Time
Display honesty	❑	❑	Get things done	❑	❑
Arrive on time	❑	❑	Get to work every day	❑	❑
Follow instructions from supervisor	❑	❑	Meet deadlines	❑	❑
Get along well with others	❑	❑	Work hard, productively	❑	❑

Other Adaptive Qualities

Employers look for many other adaptive qualities or skills. Here are some of the more important ones. Use the spaces at the end to write adaptive qualities that are important to you but that are not included in the list. Also, write in adaptive qualities you included in the "Your Good-Worker Traits" activity earlier.

Quality	Some of the Time	Most of the Time	Quality	Some of the Time	Most of the Time
Able to coordinate things	❏	❏	Modest	❏	❏
Ambitious	❏	❏	Motivated	❏	❏
Ask questions	❏	❏	Open-minded	❏	❏
Assertive	❏	❏	Optimistic	❏	❏
Capable	❏	❏	Original	❏	❏
Cheerful	❏	❏	Patient	❏	❏
Competent	❏	❏	Persistent	❏	❏
Conscientious	❏	❏	Physically strong	❏	❏
Creative	❏	❏	Practice new skills	❏	❏
Dependable	❏	❏	Pride in doing a good job	❏	❏
Discreet	❏	❏	Reliable	❏	❏
Eager	❏	❏	Resourceful	❏	❏
Efficient	❏	❏	Responsible	❏	❏
Energetic	❏	❏	Results-oriented	❏	❏
Enthusiastic	❏	❏	Self-confident	❏	❏
Expressive	❏	❏	Self-motivated	❏	❏
Flexible	❏	❏	Sincere	❏	❏
Formal	❏	❏	Solve problems	❏	❏
Friendly	❏	❏	Spontaneous	❏	❏
Good-natured	❏	❏	Steady	❏	❏
Have a sense of humor	❏	❏	Tactful	❏	❏
Helpful	❏	❏	Take pride in work	❏	❏
Highly motivated	❏	❏	Tenacious	❏	❏
Humble	❏	❏	Thrifty	❏	❏
Imaginative	❏	❏	Thorough	❏	❏
Independent	❏	❏	Trustworthy	❏	❏
Industrious	❏	❏	Versatile	❏	❏
Informal	❏	❏	Well-organized	❏	❏
Intelligent	❏	❏	Willing to learn new things	❏	❏
Intuitive	❏	❏	Other		
Lead others well	❏	❏	_____	❏	❏
Learn quickly	❏	❏	_____	❏	❏
Loyal	❏	❏	_____	❏	❏
Mature	❏	❏	_____	❏	❏
Methodical	❏	❏			

SKILLS FOR SUCCESS

Leadership

A new position has opened for department head, and the two most eligible candidates for promotion are André and Shieka. André has been there longer—nearly 12 years—and has a proven track record of personal success, but he isn't well liked by other employees, who say he is hard to work with and sometimes has questionable business practices. Shieka has been at the company for seven years and has a similar record of success, yet she is well respected by everyone in the company, and group projects she's involved in often come in ahead of time and under budget. Who do you think should get the promotion?

In the following worksheet, you identify your top three adaptive skills.

Your Top Three Adaptive Skills

Review the "Adaptive Skills Checklist" carefully. Select three skills you checked that you think are the most important to an employer. List these skills here.

1. _____

2. _____

3. _____

The words you just listed are some of the most important in this book! Emphasize these adaptive skills, or personality traits, in job interviews. Employers will find them central to their decision about hiring you over someone else. Later in this book, you will learn to emphasize these skills in interviews, resumes, and other career planning and job search activities.

Employers will find [your adaptive skills] central to their decision about hiring you over someone else.

DISCOVER YOUR TRANSFERABLE SKILLS

Remember that you can transfer transferable skills from one job to another. You have *hundreds* of these skills. You've learned and used them at home and in school, hobbies, leisure activities, and volunteer and paid jobs.

The "Transferable Skills Checklist" that follows will help you identify some of these skills. It includes skills that employers are looking for and that will lead to job success.

Transferable Skills Checklist

Review each entry carefully. If you have that skill and are good at it, put a check mark in the first column. If you want to use the skill in your next job, put a check mark in the second column. Add any other skills you want to include in the "Other" sections. When you are finished, you should have checked 10 to 20 skills in both columns.

Critical Skills

People who use these skills in their jobs tend to get higher levels of responsibility and pay. If you have these skills, they are worth emphasizing in an interview!

Skill	Strong Skill	Next Job	Skill	Strong Skill	Next Job
Accept responsibility	❑	❑	Organize or manage projects	❑	❑
Deal with the public	❑	❑	Plan activities or events	❑	❑
Increase sales or efficiency	❑	❑	Solve problems	❑	❑
Instruct others	❑	❑	Speak well in public	❑	❑
Manage money or budgets	❑	❑	Supervise others	❑	❑
Manage people	❑	❑	Work well as part of a group	❑	❑
Meet deadlines	❑	❑	Write well	❑	❑
Meet the public	❑	❑	Other _____	❑	❑
Negotiate	❑	❑	_____	❑	❑

Other Transferable Skills

Using Your Hands/Dealing with Things

Skill	Strong Skill	Next Job	Skill	Strong Skill	Next Job
Assemble or make things	❑	❑	Repair things	❑	❑
Build, observe, inspect things	❑	❑	Use complex equipment	❑	❑
Construct or repair buildings	❑	❑	Use your hands	❑	❑
Drive or operate vehicles	❑	❑	Other _____	❑	❑
Operate or use tools and machinery	❑	❑	_____	❑	❑

Dealing with Data

Skill	Strong Skill	Next Job	Skill	Strong Skill	Next Job
Analyze data or facts	❑	❑	Compare, inspect, or record facts	❑	❑
Audit records	❑	❑	Count, observe, compile	❑	❑
Calculate, compute	❑	❑	Notice details	❑	❑
Check for accuracy	❑	❑	Evaluate	❑	❑
Classify data or things	❑	❑			

(continued)

(continued)

Skill	Strong Skill	Next Job	Skill	Strong Skill	Next Job
Investigate	❏	❏	Record facts	❏	❏
Keep financial records	❏	❏	Research	❏	❏
Locate answers or information	❏	❏	Set up budgets	❏	❏
Manage money	❏	❏	Synthesize	❏	❏
Negotiate	❏	❏	Take inventory	❏	❏
Observe or inspect	❏	❏	Other _____	❏	❏
			_____	❏	❏
			_____	❏	❏

Working with People

Skill	Strong Skill	Next Job	Skill	Strong Skill	Next Job
Administer	❏	❏	Negotiate	❏	❏
Care for others	❏	❏	Persuade	❏	❏
Confront others	❏	❏	Show empathy	❏	❏
Consider others	❏	❏	Socialize well with others	❏	❏
Counsel people	❏	❏	Supervise	❏	❏
Demonstrate	❏	❏	Teach	❏	❏
Handle criticism	❏	❏	Tolerate others	❏	❏
Have patience	❏	❏	Trust	❏	❏
Help others	❏	❏	Understand	❏	❏
Interact well with others	❏	❏	Use tact	❏	❏
Interview others	❏	❏	Other _____	❏	❏
Listen	❏	❏	_____	❏	❏
			_____	❏	❏

Using Words/Ideas

Skill	Strong Skill	Next Job	Skill	Strong Skill	Next Job
Articulate clearly	❏	❏	Reason	❏	❏
Communicate verbally	❏	❏	Remember information	❏	❏
Correspond with others	❏	❏	Research	❏	❏
Create new ideas	❏	❏	Speak in public	❏	❏
Design	❏	❏	Use resources wisely	❏	❏
Edit	❏	❏	Write clearly	❏	❏
Invent	❏	❏	Other _____	❏	❏
Research information	❏	❏	_____	❏	❏
			_____	❏	❏

Leadership

Skill	Strong Skill	Next Job	Skill	Strong Skill	Next Job
Act confidently	❑	❑	Make decisions	❑	❑
Arrange social functions	❑	❑	Make things happen	❑	❑
Compete with others	❑	❑	Manage or direct others	❑	❑
Control self	❑	❑	Mediate problems	❑	❑
Create solutions	❑	❑	Motivate people	❑	❑
Delegate	❑	❑	Motivate self	❑	❑
Direct others	❑	❑	Negotiate agreements	❑	❑
Explain concepts to others	❑	❑	Plan	❑	❑
Get results	❑	❑	Run meetings	❑	❑
Influence others	❑	❑	Solve problems	❑	❑
Initiate new tasks	❑	❑	Take risks	❑	❑

Creative/Artistic

Skill	Strong Skill	Next Job	Skill	Strong Skill	Next Job
Appreciate music	❑	❑	Paint	❑	❑
Dance, use movement	❑	❑	Perform, act	❑	❑
Draw, create	❑	❑	Play instruments	❑	❑
Express feeling artistically	❑	❑	Present artistic ideas	❑	❑
Invent	❑	❑	Other _____	❑	❑
			_____	❑	❑

Other Skills

Skill	Strong Skill	Next Job
_____	❑	❑
_____	❑	❑
_____	❑	❑
_____	❑	❑
_____	❑	❑

THE WORKING WORLD

Do You Need More Computer Skills?

It used to be that being proficient in computer software was a skill that set one apart from other applicants. Nowadays computer use is so widespread that basic proficiency is a must. In fact, *not* being able to use word-processing, spreadsheet, and database programs could *decrease* your employability. If you feel you need some help learning your way around computers, consider taking a class at a local college or attending free workshops at your local library.

In the following worksheet, you identify your top five transferable skills.

Your Top Five Transferable Skills

Carefully review your list of transferable skills. Then select the top five skills you want to use in your next job and list them here.

1. _____

2. _____

3. _____

4. _____

5. _____

It is important to use these transferable skills in your job. Doing so will allow you to use some of your best skills. Later, you will learn more about how to discuss these and other skills in interviews.

The Top Skills That Employers Want

To illustrate that employers highly value adaptive and transferable skills, here is a list of the top skills that employers look for in the people they hire. This information came from a study of employers conducted jointly by the U.S. Department of Labor and the American Association of Counseling and Development. Note that all skills are either adaptive or transferable.

* Learning to learn
* Basic academic skills in reading, writing, and computation
* Listening and oral communication
* Creative thinking and problem solving
* Self-esteem and goal setting
* Personal and career development
* Interpersonal skills, negotiation, and teamwork
* Organizational effectiveness and leadership

DISCOVER YOUR JOB-RELATED SKILLS

Knowing your adaptive and transferable skills is important. But many jobs require skills that are specific to the occupation. For example, an airline pilot obviously must know how to fly an airplane. Being "good with people" or "well organized" would not be enough.

While it takes years to learn to be an airline pilot, you can learn the job-related skills for many jobs in just a few days, weeks, or months. You may have more job-related skills than you realize, and you may have other skills that will help you learn a job quickly.

This section will help you consider your education and accomplishments, identify job-related skills, and develop specific examples of when and where you used those skills. This thorough review of your history will prepare you to plan your career, answer interview questions, and write a good resume.

When possible, give numbers to describe your activities and their results. For example, saying, "organized a trip for 30 people" has more impact than "planned trip." Use an erasable pen or pencil on the worksheets to allow for changes.

Pay particular attention to experiences you really enjoyed and to the skills you liked using. You should try to use these skills in your next job.

Education and Training

If you're a recent grad, you'll find the following information helpful. However, the longer you're out of high school, the less important this experience is to employers. Even if you've been in the work-force for some time, complete this section since it will help you remember what you liked and did well in.

1. Names of schools and years attended (including high school[s], vocational training, and colleges) _____

   _____

   _____

   _____

2. Courses you did well in, especially those that relate to jobs you might want _____

   _____

   _____

   _____

3. Extracurricular activities/hobbies/leisure activities/travel experiences you have had _____

   _____

   _____

   _____

4. Accomplishments, awards, recognitions you have had both in and out of school _____

   _____

   _____

   _____

Employers will also be interested in your work and volunteer history. For your own purposes, list as many experiences as you can.

Work and Other Life Experiences

Use the following worksheet to list a major job, military experience, or volunteer position you have had and its related information. Try to include numbers to support what you did: number of people served over one or more years, number of transactions processed, percent sales increased, total inventory value you were responsible for, payroll of the staff you supervised, total budget you were responsible for, and other data. As much as possible, mention results using numbers.

You will want to photocopy this form to create additional worksheets for each of your significant jobs, military experiences, and unpaid experiences. Begin with your most recent experience, followed by previous ones. (Military experience and unpaid work both count as work and are important if you do not have much paid civilian work experience.) If you have been promoted, consider treating it as a separate job with its own worksheet.

Job or Unpaid Experience

1. Organization name _____

2. Address _____

3. Worked from the date of _____ to _____

4. Job title or role _____

5. Supervisor's name _____

6. Phone number with area code _____ E-mail address _____

7. Machinery and equipment you used _____

_____

_____

_____

_____

8. Data, information, and reports you created or used _____

_____

_____

_____

_____

9. People-oriented duties and responsibilities you completed for co-workers, customers, and others

_____

_____

_____

_____

10. Services you provided and products you produced _____

_____

_____

_____

_____

11. If promoted, given pay increases, or given more responsibilities, list reasons _____

_____

_____

_____

_____

12. Descriptions of how you helped the organization, such as increased productivity, simplified or reorganized job duties, or decreased costs. Quantify results when possible—for example, "Increased order processing by 50 percent, with no increase in staff."

_____

_____

_____

_____

_____

13. Specific things you learned and can do that relate to the job you want _____

_____

_____

_____

_____

_____

14. What would your supervisor say about you? _____

_____

_____

_____

_____

MONEY MATTERS

The Ability to Budget

According to the Federal Reserve, about 43 percent of Americans spend more money than they earn. Living within one's means is difficult, but by creating a monthly or weekly budget, you can stay out of debt and ahead of the game. Simply compare your net pay to your total expenses. Identify those expenses you *can't* do without (needs like rent or mortgage, heat, water, electricity, and groceries) and those you *can* (wants like movies, dining out, or new shoes). Then cut down on the second category until it balances out. Besides, the ability to control spending and stay in budget is a valuable transferable skill.

IDENTIFY YOUR POWER SKILLS

In your life, certain activities have given you a great sense of accomplishment. These could be things you did long ago—or yesterday—that may not mean much to anyone else. An example might be the first bike ride you made by yourself. Or the delicious bread you baked last week. Or that award you received. You may not have obtained recognition, but you did it well and enjoyed doing it.

The things you remember as accomplishments can be another source for discovering your skills. For example, riding a bike requires working by yourself, not giving up, and taking chances. To bake bread, you need to plan, organize and measure ingredients, and follow directions.

Skills that you use in your special accomplishments are "power skills." These are skills that you are good at and enjoy using. They can be adaptive, transferable, or job-related skills. If you can identify them and use them in your next job, you will have a much better chance of career success and satisfaction.

In the following worksheet, you identify and prioritize your top five power skills.

Your Top Five Power Skills

Review the lists of your adaptive, transferable, and job-related skills. From those lists, select the five skills you would most enjoy using in your next job, and list them in the order of their importance to you.

1. _____
2. _____
3. _____
4. _____
5. _____

You are likely to enjoy and do well in a job that allows you to use all or most of your power skills. It is important for you to look for jobs that allow you to use these skills. Mentioning your power skills in an interview or resume can often help you get jobs over those who have better credentials.

Write a Story for Your Accomplishments

Select one of your top five power skills or an accomplishment that means the most to you—the one you truly feel proud of or enjoy. Write a detailed story about it on the following lines. Use your own paper if you need more space.

If you have more than one skill or accomplishment that makes for a good story to share with employers, consider writing it on a separate piece of paper.

Here is one person's story:

I wasn't the best student in high school. I goofed off most of the time. But I took a class in political science with a teacher I really liked. I participated more in that class than in any other, and the teacher got me involved in the student elections. I used the existing rules to create a new political party. We even used the rules to block the dominant party from shutting us down. I learned to speak in public and work within the existing framework to make changes. We got a lot of people involved in school politics and in voting for the first time. We even came close to winning the election. It was lots of fun, and it helped me realize that I can lead. I also gained self-confidence. I got one of the few A grades in my high school career and discovered that I could get good grades if I worked at them.

Your Story

_____

_____

_____

_____

_____

_____

_____

_____

_____

_____

_____

_____

_____

_____

_____

_____

_____

USE YOUR SKILLS LANGUAGE AND STORY THROUGHOUT YOUR JOB SEARCH

You now have the basis for describing your key adaptive, transferable, and job-related skills. You have a new skills language. However, like any new language, you need to use it. As you develop your skills language and stories, you will get better at explaining what you are good at and how you can best use your skills. Later chapters will teach you to use your skills language in interviews, applications, resumes, and job advancement.

CASE STUDY: THE SKILLS TO DO JUST ABOUT ANYTHING

Shelly never discovered the one thing she wanted to do with her life. In 30 years, she has worked as a teacher, tutor, florist, baker, landscaper, server, secretary, publicist, bank teller, housekeeper, and retirement home activities coordinator. She has also worked independently as a wedding planner and has run her own daycare center. To the best of her memory, she has had well over 30 jobs, some for only a day, others for years—all which she left voluntarily to do something different.

For Shelly, getting the job you really want means having the flexibility to change what you want to do every day. It means learning new skills and taking risks. She has never been unemployed for more than a month in her life and has acquired the skill and experience to succeed at dozens of careers. Her advice is simple: "Do what you like, and when you stop liking it, find something else to do."

chapter 4

Identify Your Job Objective

You may be exploring your career options or already know the sort of job you want. You may have taken a separate career interest inventory or be enrolled in a career education program leading to a specific type of job. Whatever your situation, this chapter will help you identify job titles to consider in your career planning and job search.

If you have not decided on your career path, this chapter will help you identify clusters of jobs to explore in more detail. If you already know what type of job you want, it will help you identify one or more job titles that use your skills but that you may not know much about. For example, if you are enrolled in a medical technology program, you probably have a good idea of the job title or titles you will seek. But are you familiar with the many related jobs with different titles and the industries where these jobs can be found? Selecting the right job, in the right industry or setting, can result in better pay and more satisfaction.

Whatever your situation, knowing more about your job options will help you in your long-term career planning. It will also help you find the job that best suits your personality and needs.

I am only one,
But still I am one.
I cannot do everything,
But still I can do something;
And because I cannot do everything
I will not refuse to do the something that I can do.

Edward Everett Hale

THINK CREATIVELY ABOUT YOUR JOB OPTIONS

There are more job titles than you probably realize. Any major job has a variety of more specialized jobs that are related to it. For example, I've selected one major job title—accountants—and listed the more specific job titles related to it as listed in one of the major career references that I'll explain later—the O*NET.

Major Job Title: Accountants

Related job titles from O*NET: accountants; treasurers; controllers; chief financial officers; cost estimators; auditors; budget analysts; credit analysts; tax examiners; collectors; revenue agents; actuaries; economists

The fact is that any major job title has dozens or even hundreds of specialized job titles—many you probably don't know much about. For example, here is a partial list of related job titles for "accountant" from www.ajb.gov, a job posting site run by the federal government. The entire list was too long to provide here, but notice the many specialties by industry, level of responsibility, or those that require specific areas of experience or knowledge.

> account executive; account executive–sales consultant; accountant–construction; accountant–construction/manufacturing; accountant–manufacturing; accountant–tax; accountant 1 (a government designation); accountant clerk–manufacturing; accountant IV; accountant MAS 90–service (MAS 90 is an accounting software program); accountant–hospitality; accountant–CPA (CPA refers to passing exams required of "certified public accountants"); accountant with collections/credit analysis experience; accountant, cost; accountant, senior; accountant, staff; accountant/bookkeeper; accountant/CPA contract; accountant-fixed assets; accountant-general ledger; accounting analyst; accounting clerk; accounting clerk–AP, AR, collections; accounting clerk/payroll; accounting clerk–manufacturing; accounting clerk–business; accounting clerk–computer software industry; accounting clerk/AP/AR; accounting coordinator–advertising; accounting generalist; accounting manager; accounting manager–advertising; accounting manager–CPA required; accounting manager–distribution; accounting manager–healthcare; accounting manager–technology; accounting manager/supervisor; accounting manager/office manager; accounting specialist; accounting supervisor/manager; accounting support; accounting technician; accounting/financial analyst I; accounting/accounts payable clerk; accounts analyst–financial; billing specialist; chief financial officer (1402sp) (the number refers to a government opening with specific duties); chief financial officer-psych (1354sp); controller (1379sp); controller (1386sp); financial consultant; hedge fund accountant; international accountant; patient account rep; senior accountant; system analyst III; voucher examiner/accounting clerk... and many, many other related titles—too many to list here.

Career references describe major jobs, but they can't describe all of the more specialized ones because there are so many of them. For example, one of the jobs in the previous list requires knowledge of a software program, "MAS 90," that is used by that employer.

While job posting boards do list a variety of related job titles, they don't list self-employment jobs, jobs posted under a different title, and military and other jobs that are not typically posted on these sites. Here are a few such examples that are related to "accounting" but not likely found in Internet employment listings:

> partner, accounting firm; consultant, computerized accounting systems; accounting software sales specialist; owner, accounting, bookkeeping, or tax preparation firm; federal or state budget director; purchasing or procurement specialist; teacher, high school business course; professor, college accounting, business, or related field; instructor, post-secondary; finance and accounting specialist, military; finance and accounting manager, military; financial services representative; banker, business and commercial; systems analyst, accounting and finance specialist; tax auditor, federal and state; airlines finance specialist...

As you can see, accountants have a bewildering number of job options to consider. And so do you.

THE 1,000+ JOBS LIST

This chapter includes a list of more than 1,000 job titles. You can find descriptions for all these jobs in standard career reference sources, covered later in this chapter. The jobs are organized into 16 major interest areas developed by the U.S. Department of Education followed by a brief description. Each interest area is then subdivided into work groups of related jobs. Within each work group are jobs from the *Occupational Outlook Handbook (OOH)* in italic type and related job titles from the O*NET. When the *OOH* and O*NET job titles are the same, the list includes only the *OOH* title. The *OOH*, O*NET, and other career references are explained later in this chapter.

Steps for Using The 1,000+ Jobs List

Follow these five steps to get the most out of the list:

1. Scan the major groups to find the one or more that most likely contain the jobs that interest you, and put a check mark by each.

2. Underline the one or more work groups that interest you most within that major group.

3. Underline *OOH* or O*NET job titles that interest you within these work groups.

4. Quickly review the other major groups for similar jobs within those groups, and underline any that interests you.

5. Review the jobs you underlined, and circle up to five jobs that interest you most.

TIP: *If you are enrolled in a career training program or know the sort of job you want:* If you are pretty clear about the sort of job you want, it will usually be easy to locate the jobs that most closely fit your objective. For example, if your training is in accounting, you will find most of the related jobs in the major group titled Business and Administration. After you underline the most closely related work groups and job titles, scan the other major groups for jobs requiring similar skills, training, and experience. For example, someone who has training in accounting might be interested in a related job in the Arts and Communication group, such as those found in the Managerial Work subgroup there.

If you have not decided on a job objective yet and are exploring career options: If this is your situation, plan to spend more time browsing the major groups and looking at the subgroups and job titles within them. Some of the major groups will interest you more than others, so try to select two or three major groups that interest you most and focus more of your attention on jobs in these groups. But also look over all the major groups; you may find jobs within them that also interest you.

The 1000+ Jobs List

AGRICULTURE AND NATURAL RESOURCES
An interest in working with plants, animals, forests, or mineral resources for agriculture, horticulture, conservation, extraction, and other purposes

Managerial Work in Agriculture and Natural Resources: *Conservation Scientists and Foresters*–Park Naturalists•*Farmers, Ranchers, and Agricultural Managers*–Agricultural Crop Farm Managers; Farmers and Ranchers; Fish Hatchery Managers; Nursery and Greenhouse Managers•*Grounds Maintenance Workers*–First-Line Supervisors and Manager/Supervisors—Landscaping Workers; Lawn Service Managers•*Purchasing Managers, Buyers, and Purchasing Agents*–Purchasing Agents and Buyers, Farm Products

Resource Science/Engineering for Plants, Animals, and the Environment: *Agricultural and Food Scientists*–Animal Scientists; Plant Scientists; Soil Scientists•*Biological Scientists*–Zoologists and Wildlife Biologists•*Conservation Scientists and Foresters*–Foresters; Range Managers; Soil Conservationists•*Engineers*–Agricultural Engineers; Environmental Engineers; Mining and Geological Engineers, Including Mining Safety Engineers; Petroleum Engineers

Resource Technologies for Plants, Animals, and the Environment: *Agricultural and Food Scientists*–Food Scientists and Technologists•*Science Technicians*–Geological Sample Test Technicians; Agricultural Technicians; Environmental Science and Protection Technicians, Including Health; Food Science Technicians; Geological Data Technicians

General Farming: *Agricultural Workers*–General Farmworkers; Farmworkers, Farm and Ranch Animals; Agricultural Equipment Operators

Nursery, Groundskeeping, and Pest Control: *Agricultural Workers*–Nursery Workers•*Grounds Maintenance Workers*–Landscaping and Groundskeeping Workers; Pesticide Handlers, Sprayers, and Applicators, Vegetation; Tree Trimmers and Pruners•*Pest Control Workers*

Forestry and Logging: *Forest, Conservation, and Logging Workers*–Fallers; Forest and Conservation Workers; Log Graders and Scalers; Logging Tractor Operators•*Science Technicians*–Forest and Conservation Technicians

Hunting and Fishing: *Fishers and Fishing Vessel Operators*–Fishers and Related Fishing Workers

Mining and Drilling: *Material Moving Occupations*–Loading Machine Operators, Underground Mining; Shuttle Car Operators; Wellhead Pumpers; Excavating and Loading Machine Operators

ARCHITECTURE AND CONSTRUCTION
An interest in designing, assembling, and maintaining components of buildings and other structures

Managerial Work in Architecture and Construction: *Construction Managers*

Architectural Design: *Architects, Except Landscape and Naval*•*Landscape Architects*

Architecture/Construction Engineering Technologies: *Construction and Building Inspectors*•*Drafters*–Electrical Drafters; Architectural Drafters; Civil Drafters•*Surveyors, Cartographers, Photogrammetrists, and Surveying Technicians*–Surveyors

Construction Crafts: *Boilermakers*•*Brickmasons, Blockmasons, and Stonemasons*•*Carpenters*–Boat Builders and Shipwrights; Brattice Builders; Construction Carpenters; Rough Carpenters; Ship Carpenters and Joiners•*Carpet, Floor, and Tile Installers and Finishers*–Floor Sanders and Finishers; Tile and Marble Setters; Floor Layers, Except Carpet, Wood, and Hard Tiles; Carpet Installers•*Cement Masons, Concrete Finishers, Segmental Pavers, and Terrazzo Workers*–Segmental Pavers; Terrazzo Workers and Finishers; Cement Masons and Concrete Finishers•*Construction Equipment Operators*–Grader, Bulldozer, and Scraper Operators; Operating Engineers; Paving, Surfacing, and Tamping Equipment Operators; Pile-Driver Operators•*Drywall Installers, Ceiling Tile Installers, and Tapers*•*Electricians*•*Glaziers*•*Hazardous Materials Removal Workers*•*Insulation Workers*–Insulation Workers, Floor, Ceiling, and Wall; Insulation Workers, Mechanical•*Material Moving Occupations*–Crane and Tower Operators; Dragline Operators•*Painters and Paperhangers*–Painters, Construction and Maintenance; Paperhangers•*Pipelayers, Plumbers, Pipefitters, and Steamfitters*–Pipe Fitters; Pipelayers; Pipelaying Fitters; Plumbers•*Plasterers and Stucco Masons*•*Roofers*•*Sheet Metal Workers*•*Structural and Reinforcing Iron and Metal Workers*–Structural Iron and Steel Workers; Reinforcing Iron and Rebar Workers

Systems and Equipment Installation, Maintenance, and Repair: *Electrical and Electronics Installers and Repairers*–Electrical and Electronics Repairers, Powerhouse, Substation, and Relay•*Elevator Installers and Repairers*•*Heating, Air-Conditioning, and Refrigeration Mechanics and Installers*–Heating and Air Conditioning Mechanics; Refrigeration Mechanics•*Home Appliance Repairers*–Home Appliance Installers•*Line Installers and Repairers*–Electrical Power-Line Installers and Repairers; Telecommunications Line Installers and Repairers•*Maintenance and Repair Workers, General*–Maintenance and Repair Workers, General•*Radio and Telecommunications Equipment Installers and Repairers*–Telecommunications Facility Examiners; Station Installers and Repairers, Telephone; Central Office and PBX Installers and Repairers; Communication Equipment Mechanics, Installers, and Repairers; Frame Wirers, Central Office

Construction Support/Labor: *Carpenters*–Carpenter Assemblers and Repairers•*Construction Laborers*•*Material Moving Occupations*–Grips and Set-Up Workers, Motion Picture Sets, Studios, and Stages

ARTS AND COMMUNICATION
An interest in creatively expressing feelings or ideas, in communicating news or information, or in performing

Managerial Work in Arts and Communication: *Actors, Producers, and Directors*–Producers; Program Directors; Technical Directors/Managers•*Advertising, Marketing, Promotions, Public Relations, and Sales Managers*–Public Relations Managers•*Artists and Related Workers*–Art Directors

Writing and Editing: *Writers and Editors*–Technical Writers; Poets and Lyricists; Editors; Copy Writers; Creative Writers

News, Broadcasting, and Public Relations: *Interpreters and Translators*•*News Analysts, Reporters, and Correspondents*–Broadcast News Analysts; Reporters and Correspondents•*Public Relations Specialists*•*Writers and Editors*–Caption Writers

Studio Art: *Artists and Related Workers*–Sketch Artists; Sculptors; Painters and Illustrators; Cartoonists

Design: *Commercial and Industrial Designers*•*Fashion Designers*•*Floral Designers*•*Graphic Designers*•*Interior Designers*

Drama: *Actors, Producers, and Directors*–Actors; Directors—Stage, Motion Pictures, Television, and Radio•*Announcers*–Public Address System and Other Announcers; Radio and Television Announcers•*Barbers, Cosmetologists, and Other Personal Appearance Workers*–Makeup Artists, Theatrical and Performance

Music: *Actors, Producers, and Directors*–Talent Directors•*Musicians, Singers, and Related Worker*–Music Arrangers and Orchestrators; Music Directors; Musicians, Instrumental; Singers; Composers

Dance: *Dancers and Choreographers*

Media Technology: *Artists and Related Workers*–Multi-Media Artists and Animators•*Broadcast and Sound Engineering Technicians and Radio Operators*–Sound Engineering Technicians; Audio and Video Equipment Technicians; Broadcast Technicians; Radio Operators•*Photographers*–Professional Photographers•*Photographic Process Workers and Processing Machine Operators*–Photographic Hand Developers; Photographic Reproduction Technicians; Photographic Retouchers and Restorers•*Television, Video, and Motion Picture Camera Operators and Editors*–Camera Operators, Television, Video, and Motion Picture; Film and Video Editors

Communications Technology: *Air Traffic Controllers*•*Communications Equipment Operators*–Central Office Operators; Directory Assistance Operators•*Dispatchers*–Dispatchers, Except Police, Fire, and Ambulance; Police, Fire, and Ambulance Dispatchers

Musical Instrument Repair: *Precision Instrument and Equipment Repairers*–Keyboard Instrument Repairers and Tuners; Stringed Instrument Repairers and Tuners; Percussion Instrument Repairers and Tuners; Reed or Wind Instrument Repairers and Tuners

BUSINESS AND ADMINISTRATION
An interest in making a business organization or function run smoothly

Managerial Work in General Business: *Human Resources, Training, and Labor Relations Managers and Specialists*–Compensation and Benefits Managers; Human Resources Managers; Training and Development Managers•*Top Executives*–General and Operations Managers; Private Sector Executives

Managerial Work in Business Detail: *Administrative Services Managers*•*Building Cleaning Workers*–Housekeeping Supervisors; Janitorial Supervisors•*Meeting and Convention Planners*•*Office and Administrative Support Worker Supervisors and Managers*–First-Line Supervisors, Customer Service; First-Line Supervisors, Administrative Support

Human Resources Support: *Human Resources, Training, and Labor Relations Managers and Specialists*–Compensation, Benefits, and Job Analysis Specialists; Employment Interviewers, Private or Public Employment Service; Personnel Recruiters; Training and Development Specialists

Secretarial Support: *Secretaries and Administrative Assistants*–Executive Secretaries and Administrative Assistants; Legal Secretaries; Medical Secretaries; Secretaries, Except Legal, Medical, and Executive

Accounting, Auditing, and Analytical Support: *Accountants and Auditors*•*Budget Analysts*•*Engineering Technicians*–Industrial Engineering Technicians•*Management Analysts*•*Operations Research Analysts*

Mathematical Clerical Support: *Billing and Posting Clerks and Machine Operators*–Billing, Cost, and Rate Clerks; Statement Clerks•*Bookkeeping, Accounting, and Auditing Clerks*•*Brokerage Clerks*•*Payroll and Timekeeping Clerks*

Records and Materials Processing: *File Clerks*•*Human Resources Assistants, Except Payroll and Timekeeping*•*Meter Readers, Utilities*•*Office Clerks, General*•*Postal Service Workers*–Postal Service Mail Sorters, Processors, and Processing Machine Operators; Postal Service Clerks•*Procurement Clerks*•*Production, Planning, and Expediting Clerks*•*Shipping, Receiving, and Traffic Clerks*•*Stock Clerks and Order Fillers*–Marking Clerks; Order Fillers, Wholesale and Retail Sales; Stock Clerks, Sales Floor; Stock Clerks—Stockroom, Warehouse, or Storage Yard•*Weighers, Measurers, Checkers, and Samplers, Recordkeeping*

Clerical Machine Operation: *Billing and Posting Clerks and Machine Operators*–Billing, Posting, and Calculating Machine Operators•*Communications Equipment Operators*–Switchboard Operators, Including Answering Service•*Data Entry and Information Processing Workers*–Word Processors and Typists; Data Entry Keyers

EDUCATION AND TRAINING
An interest in helping people learn

Managerial Work in Education: *Education Administrators*–Education Administrators, Elementary and Secondary School; Education Administrators, Postsecondary; Education Administrators, Preschool and Child Care Center/Program•*Instructional Coordinators*

Preschool, Elementary, and Secondary Teaching and Instructing: *Teacher Assistants*•*Teachers—Preschool, Kindergarten, Elementary, Middle, and Secondary*–Secondary School Teachers, Except Special and Vocational Education; Preschool Teachers, Except Special Education; Vocational Education Teachers, Secondary School; Middle School Teachers, Except Special and Vocational Education; Elementary School Teachers, Except Special Education; Kindergarten Teachers, Except Special Education; Vocational Education Teachers, Middle School•*Teachers—Special Education*–Special Education Teachers, Middle School; Special Education Teachers, Preschool, Kindergarten, and Elementary School; Special Education Teachers, Secondary School

Postsecondary and Adult Teaching and Instructing: *Teachers—Adult Literacy and Remedial Education*–Adult Literacy, Remedial Education, and GED Teachers and Instructors•*Teachers—Postsecondary*–Mathematical Science Teachers, Postsecondary; Library Science Teachers, Postsecondary; Law Teachers, Postsecondary; Home Economics Teachers, Postsecondary; Nursing Instructors and Teachers, Postsecondary; Health Specialties Teachers, Postsecondary; Recreation and Fitness Studies Teachers, Postsecondary; History Teachers, Postsecondary; Philosophy and Religion Teachers, Postsecondary; Physics Teachers, Postsecondary; Psychology Teachers, Postsecondary; Forestry and Conservation Science Teachers, Postsecondary; Social Work Teachers, Postsecondary; Sociology Teachers, Postsecondary; Vocational Education Teachers Postsecondary; Geography Teachers, Postsecondary; Political Science Teachers, Postsecondary; Biological Science Teachers, Postsecondary; Agricultural Sciences Teachers, Postsecondary; Anthropology and Archeology Teachers, Postsecondary; Architecture Teachers, Postsecondary; Area, Ethnic, and Cultural Studies Teachers, Postsecondary; Foreign Language and Literature Teachers, Postsecondary; Atmospheric, Earth, Marine, and Space Sciences Teachers, Postsecondary; Business Teachers, Postsecondary; Chemistry Teachers, Postsecondary; English Language and Literature Teachers, Postsecondary; Art, Drama, and Music Teachers, Postsecondary; Environmental Science Teachers, Postsecondary; Communications Teachers, Postsecondary; Engineering Teachers, Postsecondary; Education Teachers, Postsecondary; Economics Teachers, Postsecondary; Criminal Justice and Law Enforcement Teachers, Postsecondary; Computer Science Teachers, Postsecondary; Graduate Teaching Assistants•*Teachers—Self-Enrichment Education*

Library Services: *Librarians*•*Library Assistants, Clerical*•*Library Technicians*

Archival and Museum Services: *Archivists, Curators, and Museum Technicians*–Museum Technicians and Conservators; Archivists; Curators

Counseling, Health, and Fitness Education: *Counselors*–Educational, Vocational, and School Counselors•*Fitness Workers*–Fitness Trainers and Aerobics Instructors

FINANCE AND INSURANCE
An interest in helping businesses and people be assured of a financially secure future

Managerial Work in Finance and Insurance: *Financial Managers*–Financial Managers, Branch or Department; Treasurers, Controllers, and Chief Financial Officers

Finance/Insurance Investigation and Analysis: *Appraisers and Assessors of Real Estate*•*Claims Adjusters, Appraisers, Examiners, and Investigators*–Claims Examiners, Property and Casualty Insurance; Insurance Adjusters, Examiners, and Investigators; Insurance Appraisers, Auto Damage•*Cost Estimators*•*Financial Analysts and Personal Financial Advisors*–Financial Analysts•*Insurance Underwriters*•*Loan Officers*•*Market and Survey Researchers*–Market Research Analysts; Survey Researchers

Finance/Insurance Records Processing: *Credit Authorizers, Checkers, and Clerks*–Credit Authorizers; Credit Checkers

Finance/Insurance Customer Service: *Bill and Account Collectors*•*Interviewers*–Loan Interviewers and Clerks•*Tellers*

Finance/Insurance Sales and Support: *Advertising Sales Agents*•*Financial Analysts and Personal Financial Advisors*–Personal Financial Advisors•*Insurance Sales Agents*•*Securities, Commodities, and Financial Services Sales Agents*–Sales Agents, Financial Services; Sales Agents, Securities and Commodities

GOVERNMENT AND PUBLIC ADMINISTRATION
An interest in helping a government agency serve the needs of the public

Managerial Work in Government and Public Administration: *Top Executives*–Government Service Executives

Public Planning: *Urban and Regional Planners*

Regulations Enforcement: *Agricultural Workers*–Agricultural Inspectors•*Fire Fighting Occupations*–Fire Inspectors; Forest Fire Inspectors and Prevention Specialists•*Inspectors, Testers, Sorters, Samplers, and Weighers*–Mechanical Inspectors•*Occupational Health and Safety Specialists and Technicians*–Occupational Health and Safety Specialists•*Police and Detectives*–Child Support, Missing Persons, and Unemployment Insurance Fraud Investigators; Fish and Game Wardens; Immigration and Customs Inspectors•*Science Technicians*–Nuclear Monitoring Technicians•*Tax Examiners, Collectors, and Revenue Agents*

Public Administration Clerical Support: *Court Reporters*

HEALTH SCIENCE
An interest in helping people and animals be healthy

Managerial Work in Medical and Health Services: *Medical and Health Services Managers*

Medicine and Surgery: *Medical Assistants•Medical Transcriptionists•Pharmacists•Pharmacy Aides•Pharmacy Technicians•Physician Assistants•Physicians and Surgeons*–Pediatricians, General; Psychiatrists; Surgeons; Internists, General; Family and General Practitioners; Anesthesiologists; Obstetricians and Gynecologists•*Registered Nurses•Surgical Technologists*

Dentistry: *Dental Assistants•Dental Hygienists•Dentists*–Dentists, General; Oral and Maxillofacial Surgeons; Orthodontists; Prosthodontists

Health Specialties: *Chiropractors•Optometrists•Podiatrists*

Animal Care: *Agricultural Workers*–Animal Breeders•*Animal Care and Service Workers*–Animal Trainers; Nonfarm Animal Caretakers•*Veterinarians•Veterinary Technologists and Technicians*

Medical Technology: *Cardiovascular Technologists and Technicians•Clinical Laboratory Technologists and Technicians*–Medical and Clinical Laboratory Technicians; Medical and Clinical Laboratory Technologists•*Diagnostic Medical Sonographers•Medical Records and Health Information Technicians•Nuclear Medicine Technologists•Opticians, Dispensing•Radiologic Technologists and Technicians*–Radiologic Technicians; Radiologic Technologists•*Science Technicians*–Biological Technicians

Medical Therapy: *Audiologists•Massage Therapists•Occupational Therapist Assistants and Aides•Occupational Therapists•Physical Therapist Assistants and Aides•Physical Therapists•Radiation Therapists•Recreational Therapists•Respiratory Therapists*–Respiratory Therapists; Respiratory Therapy Technicians•*Speech-Language Pathologists*

Patient Care and Assistance: *Licensed Practical and Licensed Vocational Nurses•Nursing, Psychiatric, and Home Health Aides*–Home Health Aides; Nursing Aides, Orderlies, and Attendants; Psychiatric Aides

Health Protection and Promotion: *Athletic Trainers•Dietitians and Nutritionists*

HOSPITALITY, TOURISM, AND RECREATION
An interest in catering to the personal wishes and needs of others, so that they may enjoy a clean environment, good food and drink, comfortable lodging away from home, and recreation

Managerial Work in Hospitality and Tourism: *Food Service Managers•Gaming Services Occupations*–Gaming Supervisors•*Lodging Managers*

Recreational Services: *Gaming Services Occupations*–Gaming and Sports Book Writers and Runners; Gaming Dealers; Slot Key Persons•*Recreation Workers*

Hospitality and Travel Services: *Building Cleaning Workers*–Janitors and Cleaners, Except Maids and Housekeeping Cleaners; Maids and Housekeeping Cleaners•*Flight Attendants•Hotel, Motel, and Resort Desk Clerks•Reservation and Transportation Ticket Agents and Travel Clerks•Travel Agents*

Food and Beverage Preparation: *Chefs, Cooks, and Food Preparation Workers*–Cooks, Fast Food; Food Preparation Workers; Cooks, Short Order; Cooks, Institution and Cafeteria; Chefs and Head Cooks; Cooks, Restaurant•*Food and Beverage Serving and Related Workers*–Dishwashers•*Food Processing Occupations*–Bakers, Bread and Pastry; Butchers and Meat Cutters

Food and Beverage Service: *Food and Beverage Serving and Related Workers*–Hosts and Hostesses, Restaurant, Lounge, and Coffee Shop; Bartenders; Combined Food Preparation and Serving Workers, Including Fast Food; Counter Attendants, Cafeteria, Food Concession, and Coffee Shop; Dining Room and Cafeteria Attendants and Bartender Helpers; Waiters and Waitresses; Food Servers, Nonrestaurant

Sports: *Athletes, Coaches, Umpires, and Related Workers*–Athletes and Sports Competitors; Coaches and Scouts; Umpires, Referees, and Other Sports Officials

Barber and Beauty Services: *Barbers, Cosmetologists, and Other Personal Appearance Workers*–Barbers; Hairdressers, Hairstylists, and Cosmetologists; Manicurists and Pedicurists; Shampooers; Skin Care Specialists

HUMAN SERVICE
An interest in improving people's social, mental, emotional, or spiritual well-being

Counseling and Social Work: *Counselors*–Rehabilitation Counselors; Substance Abuse and Behavioral Disorder Counselors; Mental Health Counselors; Marriage and Family Therapists•*Probation Officers and Correctional Treatment Specialists•Psychologists*–Clinical Psychologists; Counseling Psychologists•*Social and Human Service Assistants•Social Workers*–Child, Family, and School Social Workers; Medical and Public Health Social Workers; Mental Health and Substance Abuse Social Workers

Child/Personal Care and Services: *Child Care Workers*–Child Care Workers; Nannies•*Personal and Home Care Aides*

Client Interviewing: *Interviewers*–Welfare Eligibility Workers and Interviewers; Interviewers, Except Eligibility and Loan; Claims Takers, Unemployment Benefits

---

INFORMATION TECHNOLOGY
An interest in designing, developing, managing, and supporting information systems

Managerial Work in Information Technology: Computer and Information Systems Managers•Computer Support Specialists and Systems Administrators–Network and Computer Systems Administrators

Information Technology Specialties: Computer Operators•Computer Programmers•Computer Scientists and Database Administrators–Database Administrators•Computer Software Engineers–Computer Software Engineers, Applications; Computer Software Engineers, Systems Software•Computer Support Specialists and Systems Administrators–Computer Support Specialists; Computer Security Specialists•Computer Systems Analysts

Digital Equipment Repair: Coin, Vending, and Amusement Machine Servicers and Repairers•Computer, Automated Teller, and Office Machine Repairers–Automatic Teller Machine Servicers; Data Processing Equipment Repairers; Office Machine and Cash Register Servicers

---

LAW AND PUBLIC SAFETY
An interest in upholding people's rights or in protecting people and property by using authority, inspecting, or investigating

Managerial Work in Law and Public Safety: Correctional Officers–First-Line Supervisors/Managers of Correctional Officers•Fire Fighting Occupations–Forest Fire Fighting and Prevention Supervisors; Municipal Fire Fighting and Prevention Supervisors•Police and Detectives–First-Line Supervisors/Managers of Police and Detectives

Legal Practice and Justice Administration: Judges, Magistrates, and Other Judicial Workers–Judges, Magistrate Judges, and Magistrates; Administrative Law Judges, Adjudicators, and Hearing Officers; Arbitrators, Mediators, and Conciliators•Lawyers

Legal Support: Paralegals and Legal Assistants

Law Enforcement and Public Safety: Correctional Officers–Bailiffs; Correctional Officers and Jailers•Fire Fighting Occupations–Fire Investigators•Police and Detectives–Criminal Investigators and Special Agents; Highway Patrol Pilots; Police Detectives; Police Identification and Records Officers; Police Patrol Officers; Sheriffs and Deputy Sheriffs; Transit and Railroad Police•Science Technicians–Forensic Science Technicians

Safety and Security: Private Detectives and Investigators•Security Guards and Gaming Surveillance Officers–Gaming Surveillance Officers and Gaming Investigators; Security Guards

Emergency Responding: Emergency Medical Technicians and Paramedics•Fire Fighting Occupations–Forest Fire Fighters; Municipal Fire Fighters

Military: Job Opportunities in the Armed Forces–Command and Control Center Specialists; Special Forces; Radar and Sonar Technicians; Infantry Officers; Infantry; Armored Assault Vehicle Crew Members; First-Line Supervisors/Managers of Weapons Specialists/Crew Members; Special Forces Officers; First-Line Supervisors/Managers of Air Crew Members; Artillery and Missile Officers; Armored Assault Vehicle Officers; Aircraft Launch and Recovery Specialists; Aircraft Launch and Recovery Officers; Air Crew Officers; Air Crew Members; Artillery and Missile Crew Members; Command and Control Center Officers

---

MANUFACTURING
An interest in processing materials into intermediate or final products or maintaining and repairing products by using machines or hand tools

Managerial Work in Manufacturing: Industrial Production Managers•Material Moving Occupations–First-Line Supervisors/Managers of Helpers, Laborers, and Material Movers, Hand

Machine Setup and Operation: Bookbinders and Bindery Workers–Bindery Machine Setters and Set-Up Operators•Machine Setters, Operators, and Tenders—Metal and Plastic–Metal Molding, Coremaking, and Casting Machine Operators and Tenders; Sawing Machine Tool Setters and Set-Up Operators, Metal and Plastic; Rolling Machine Setters, Operators, and Tenders, Metal and Plastic; Punching Machine Setters and Set-Up Operators, Metal and Plastic; Nonelectrolytic Plating and Coating Machine Setters and Set-Up Operators, Metal and Plastic; Plastic Molding and Casting Machine Setters and Set-Up Operators; Milling and Planing Machine Setters, Operators, and Tenders, Metal and Plastic; Metal Molding, Coremaking, and Casting Machine Setters and Set-Up Operators; Shear and Slitter Machine Setters and Set-Up Operators, Metal and Plastic; Heating Equipment Setters and Set-Up Operators, Metal and Plastic; Grinding, Honing, Lapping, and Deburring Machine Set-Up Operators; Forging Machine Setters, Operators, and Tenders, Metal and Plastic; Press and Press Brake Machine Setters and Set-Up Operators, Metal and Plastic; Extruding and Drawing Machine Setters, Operators, and Tenders, Metal and Plastic; Electrolytic Plating and Coating Machine Setters and Set-Up Operators, Metal and Plastic; Drilling and Boring Machine Tool Setters, Operators, and Tenders, Metal and Plastic; Combination Machine Tool Setters and Set-Up Operators, Metal and Plastic; Casting Machine Set-Up Operators; Buffing and Polishing Set-Up Operators; Lathe and Turning Machine Tool Setters, Operators, and Tenders, Metal and Plastic•Painting and Coating Workers, Except Construction and Maintenance–Coating, Painting, and Spraying Machine Setters and Set-Up Operators•Printing Machine Operators–Screen Printing Machine Setters and Set-Up Operators•Textile, Apparel, and Furnishings Occupations–Textile Cutting Machine Setters, Operators, and Tenders; Textile Knitting and Weaving Machine Setters, Operators, and Tenders; Textile Winding, Twisting, and Drawing Out Machine Setters, Operators, and Tenders; Extruding and Forming Machine Setters, Operators, and Tenders, Synthetic and Glass Fibers•Welding, Soldering, and Brazing Workers–Soldering and Brazing Machine Setters and Set-Up Operators•Woodworkers–Sawing Machine Setters and Set-Up Operators; Woodworking Machine Setters and Set-Up Operators, Except Sawing

---

MANUFACTURING
An interest in processing materials into intermediate or final products or maintaining and repairing products by using machines or hand tools

Production Work, Assorted Materials Processing: *Assemblers and Fabricators*–Team Assemblers•*Food Processing Occupations*–Food Cooking Machine Operators and Tenders; Food Batchmakers; Slaughterers and Meat Packers; Bakers, Manufacturing; Food and Tobacco Roasting, Baking, and Drying Machine Operators and Tenders; Meat, Poultry, and Fish Cutters and Trimmers•*Machine Setters, Operators, and Tenders—Metal and Plastic*–Combination Machine Tool Operators and Tenders, Metal and Plastic; Electrolytic Plating and Coating Machine Operators and Tenders, Metal and Plastic; Heat Treating, Annealing, and Tempering Machine Operators and Tenders, Metal and Plastic; Heaters, Metal and Plastic; Metal-Refining Furnace Operators and Tenders; Nonelectrolytic Plating and Coating Machine Operators and Tenders, Metal and Plastic; Plastic Molding and Casting Machine Operators and Tenders; Pourers and Casters, Metal•*Painting and Coating Workers, Except Construction and Maintenance*–Coating, Painting, and Spraying Machine Operators and Tenders•*Textile, Apparel, and Furnishings Occupations*–Textile Bleaching and Dyeing Machine Operators and Tenders; Shoe Machine Operators and Tenders; Sewing Machine Operators, Non-Garment; Pressing Machine Operators and Tenders—Textile, Garment, and Related Materials; Sewing Machine Operators, Garment•*Woodworkers*–Sawing Machine Operators and Tenders; Woodworking Machine Operators and Tenders, Except Sawing

Welding, Brazing, and Soldering: *Assemblers and Fabricators*–Fitters, Structural Metal—Precision; Metal Fabricators, Structural Metal Products•*Welding, Soldering, and Brazing Workers*–Welding Machine Operators and Tenders; Welding Machine Setters and Set-Up Operators; Welders and Cutters; Welders, Production; Soldering and Brazing Machine Operators and Tenders; Solderers; Brazers; Welder-Fitters

Production Machining Technology: *Computer Control Programmers and Operators*–Numerical Control Machine Tool Operators and Tenders, Metal and Plastic; Numerical Tool and Process Control Programmers•*Machine Setters, Operators, and Tenders—Metal and Plastic*–Foundry Mold and Coremakers; Lay-Out Workers, Metal and Plastic; Model Makers, Metal and Plastic; Patternmakers, Metal and Plastic; Tool Grinders, Filers, and Sharpeners•*Machinists*–Machinists•*Tool and Die Makers*

Production Precision Work: *Assemblers and Fabricators*–Electrical and Electronic Equipment Assemblers; Timing Device Assemblers, Adjusters, and Calibrators; Electromechanical Equipment Assemblers; Engine and Other Machine Assemblers•*Bookbinders and Bindery Workers*–Bookbinders•*Jewelers and Precious Stone and Metal Workers*–Bench Workers, Jewelry; Gem and Diamond Workers; Jewelers; Model and Mold Makers, Jewelry; Pewter Casters and Finishers; Silversmiths•*Medical, Dental, and Ophthalmic Laboratory Technicians*–Precision Lens Grinders and Polishers; Dental Laboratory Technicians; Medical Appliance Technicians; Optical Instrument Assemblers•*Semiconductor Processors*

Production Quality Control: *Agricultural Workers*–Graders and Sorters, Agricultural Products•*Inspectors, Testers, Sorters, Samplers, and Weighers*–Electrical and Electronic Inspectors and Testers; Materials Inspectors; Precision Devices Inspectors and Testers; Production Inspectors, Testers, Graders, Sorters, Samplers, Weighers

Graphic Arts Production: *Bookbinders and Bindery Workers*–Bindery Machine Operators and Tenders•*Desktop Publishers*•*Photographic Process Workers and Processing Machine Operators*–Film Laboratory Technicians; Photographic Processing Machine Operators•*Prepress Technicians and Workers*–Photoengraving and Lithographing Machine Operators and Tenders; Strippers; Scanner Operators; Platemakers; Electrotypers and Stereotypers; Plate Finishers; Typesetting and Composing Machine Operators and Tenders; Photoengravers; Paste-Up Workers; Hand Compositors and Typesetters; Electronic Masking System Operators; Dot Etchers; Camera Operators; Job Printers•*Printing Machine Operators*–Embossing Machine Set-Up Operators; Printing Press Machine Operators and Tenders; Precision Printing Workers; Offset Lithographic Press Setters and Set-Up Operators; Engraver Set-Up Operators; Letterpress Setters and Set-Up Operators; Design Printing Machine Setters and Set-Up Operators; Marking and Identification Printing Machine Setters and Set-Up Operators

Hands-On Work, Assorted Materials: *Assemblers and Fabricators*–Coil Winders, Tapers, and Finishers•*Painting and Coating Workers, Except Construction and Maintenance*–Painters, Transportation Equipment; Painting, Coating, and Decorating Workers•*Textile, Apparel, and Furnishings Occupations*–Fabric and Apparel Patternmakers; Sewers, Hand

Woodworking Technology: *Woodworkers*–Furniture Finishers; Model Makers, Wood; Patternmakers, Wood; Cabinetmakers and Bench Carpenters

Apparel, Shoes, Leather, and Fabric Care: *Textile, Apparel, and Furnishings Occupations*–Shoe and Leather Workers and Repairers; Upholsterers; Spotters, Dry Cleaning; Shop and Alteration Tailors; Pressers, Hand; Pressers, Delicate Fabrics; Precision Dyers; Custom Tailors; Laundry and Drycleaning Machine Operators and Tenders, Except Pressing

Electrical and Electronic Repair: *Aircraft and Avionics Equipment Mechanics and Service Technicians*–Avionics Technicians•*Electrical and Electronics Installers and Repairers*–Electrical Parts Reconditioners; Transformer Repairers; Electronic Equipment Installers and Repairers, Motor Vehicles; Battery Repairers; Electrical and Electronics Installers and Repairers, Transportation Equipment; Electric Home Appliance and Power Tool Repairers; Electrical and Electronics Repairers, Commercial and Industrial Equipment; Electric Motor and Switch Assemblers and Repairers•*Electronic Home Entertainment Equipment Installers and Repairers*•*Radio and Telecommunications Equipment Installers and Repairers*–Radio Mechanics

Machinery Repair: *Electrical and Electronics Installers and Repairers*–Hand and Portable Power Tool Repairers•*Home Appliance Repairers*–Gas Appliance Repairers•*Industrial Machinery Mechanics and Maintenance Workers*•*Millwrights*

(continued)

(continued)

MANUFACTURING
An interest in processing materials into intermediate or final products or maintaining and repairing products by using machines or hand tools

Vehicle and Facility Mechanical Work: *Aircraft and Avionics Equipment Mechanics and Service Technicians–Airframe-and-Power-Plant Mechanics; Aircraft Body and Bonded Structure Repairers; Aircraft Engine Specialists•Assemblers and Fabricators–*Aircraft Rigging Assemblers; Aircraft Structure Assemblers, Precision; Aircraft Systems Assemblers, Precision; Fiberglass Laminators and Fabricators•*Automotive Body and Related Repairers–*Automotive Body and Related Repairers; Automotive Glass Installers and Repairers•*Automotive Service Technicians and Mechanics–*Automotive Specialty Technicians; Automotive Master Mechanics•*Diesel Service Technicians and Mechanics–*Bus and Truck Mechanics and Diesel Engine Specialists•*Heavy Vehicle and Mobile Equipment Service Technicians and Mechanics–*Farm Equipment Mechanics; Mobile Heavy Equipment Mechanics, Except Engines; Rail Car Repairers•*Small Engine Mechanics–*Motorboat Mechanics; Motorcycle Mechanics; Outdoor Power Equipment and Other Small Engine Mechanics

Medical and Technical Equipment Repair: *Precision Instrument and Equipment Repairers–*Camera and Photographic Equipment Repairers; Medical Equipment Repairers; Watch Repairers

Utility Operation and Energy Distribution: *Material Moving Occupations–*Gas Pumping Station Operators; Gas Compressor Operators•*Power Plant Operators, Distributors, and Dispatchers–*Power Generating Plant Operators, Except Auxiliary Equipment Operators; Power Distributors and Dispatchers; Auxiliary Equipment Operators, Power; Nuclear Power Reactor Operators•*Stationary Engineers and Boiler Operators–*Boiler Operators and Tenders, Low Pressure; Stationary Engineers•*Water and Liquid Waste Treatment Plant and System Operators•*Water Transportation Occupations–*Ship Engineers

Loading, Moving, Hoisting, and Conveying: *Material Moving Occupations–*Industrial Truck and Tractor Operators; Refuse and Recyclable Material Collectors; Pump Operators, Except Wellhead Pumpers; Tank Car, Truck, and Ship Loaders; Hoist and Winch Operators; Freight, Stock, and Material Movers, Hand; Conveyor Operators and Tenders; Packers and Packagers, Hand; Machine Feeders and Offbearers

---

RETAIL AND WHOLESALE SALES AND SERVICE
An interest in bringing others to a particular point of view by personal persuasion and by sales and promotional techniques

Managerial Work in Retail/Wholesale Sales and Service: *Advertising, Marketing, Promotions, Public Relations, and Sales Managers–*Advertising and Promotions Managers; Marketing Managers; Sales Managers•*Funeral Directors•Property, Real Estate, and Community Association Managers•Purchasing Managers, Buyers, and Purchasing Agents–*Purchasing Managers•*Sales Worker Supervisors–*First-Line Supervisors/Managers of Non-Retail Sales Workers; First-Line Supervisors/Managers of Retail Sales Workers

Technical Sales: *Sales Engineers•Sales Representatives, Wholesale and Manufacturing–*Sales Representatives, Agricultural; Sales Representatives, Chemical and Pharmaceutical; Sales Representatives, Electrical/Electronic; Sales Representatives, Instruments; Sales Representatives, Mechanical Equipment and Supplies; Sales Representatives, Medical

General Sales: *Real Estate Brokers and Sales Agents•Retail Salespersons•Sales Representatives, Wholesale and Manufacturing–*Sales Representatives, Wholesale and Manufacturing, Except Technical and Scientific Products

Personal Soliciting: *Demonstrators, Product Promoters, and Models*

Purchasing: *Purchasing Managers, Buyers, and Purchasing Agents–*Purchasing Agents, Except Wholesale, Retail, and Farm Products; Wholesale and Retail Buyers, Except Farm Products

Customer Service: *Cashiers–*Cashiers; Gaming Change Persons and Booth Cashiers•*Counter and Rental Clerks•Customer Service Representatives–*Adjustment Clerks; Customer Service Representatives, Utilities•*Order Clerks•Receptionists and Information Clerks*

SCIENTIFIC RESEARCH, ENGINEERING, AND MATHEMATICS
An interest in discovering, collecting, and analyzing information about the natural world; in applying scientific research findings and technology; and in imagining and manipulating quantitative data

Managerial Work in Scientific Research, Engineering, and Mathematics: *Engineering and Natural Sciences Managers*

Physical Sciences: *Atmospheric Scientists–*Atmospheric and Space Scientists•*Chemists and Materials Scientists•Environmental Scientists and Hydrologists–*Hydrologists•*Geoscientists–*Geologists; Hydrologists•*Physicists and Astronomers•Social Scientists, Other–*Geographers

Life Sciences: *Biological Scientists–*Microbiologists; Biophysicists; Biologists; Biochemists•*Environmental Scientists and Hydrologists–*Environmental Scientists and Specialists, Including Health•*Geoscientists–*Environmental Scientists and Specialists, Including Health•*Medical Scientists–*Epidemiologists; Medical Scientists, Except Epidemiologists

Social Sciences: *Economists•Psychologists–*Industrial-Organizational Psychologists; School Psychologists•*Social Scientists, Other–*Political Scientists; Sociologists; Historians; Archeologists; Anthropologists

---

SCIENTIFIC RESEARCH, ENGINEERING, AND MATHEMATICS
An interest in discovering, collecting, and analyzing information about the natural world; in applying scientific research findings and technology; and in imagining and manipulating quantitative data

Physical Science Laboratory Technology: *Photographers*–Photographers, Scientific • *Science Technicians*–Chemical Technicians; Nuclear Equipment Operation Technicians

Mathematics and Data Analysis: *Actuaries • Mathematicians • Statisticians*

Research and Design Engineering: *Engineers*–Electrical Engineers; Mechanical Engineers; Materials Engineers; Marine Engineers; Nuclear Engineers; Electronics Engineers, Except Computer; Civil Engineers; Chemical Engineers; Biomedical Engineers; Aerospace Engineers; Marine Architects; Computer Hardware Engineers

Industrial and Safety Engineering: *Engineers*–Industrial Engineers; Industrial Safety and Health Engineers; Fire-Prevention and Protection Engineers; Product Safety Engineers

Engineering Technology: *Drafters*–Mechanical Drafters; Electronic Drafters • *Engineering Technicians*–Electro-Mechanical Technicians; Mechanical Engineering Technicians; Environmental Engineering Technicians; Electronics Engineering Technicians; Electrical Engineering Technicians; Civil Engineering Technicians; Aerospace Engineering and Operations Technicians; Calibration and Instrumentation Technicians • *Surveyors, Cartographers, Photogrammetrists, and Surveying Technicians*–Cartographers and Photogrammetrists; Mapping Technicians; Surveying Technicians

TRANSPORTATION, DISTRIBUTION, AND LOGISTICS
An interest in operations that move people or materials

Managerial Work in Transportation: *Rail Transportation Occupations*–Railroad Conductors and Yardmasters

Air Vehicle Operation: *Aircraft Pilots and Flight Engineers*–Airline Pilots, Copilots, and Flight Engineers; Commercial Pilots

Truck Driving: *Truck Drivers and Driver/Sales Workers*–Tractor-Trailer Truck Drivers; Truck Drivers, Heavy; Truck Drivers, Light or Delivery Services

Rail Vehicle Operation: *Rail Transportation Occupations*–Locomotive Engineers; Rail Yard Engineers, Dinkey Operators, and Hostlers; Subway and Streetcar Operators

Water Vehicle Operation: *Material Moving Occupations*–Dredge Operators • *Water Transportation Occupations*–Ordinary Seamen and Marine Oilers; Pilots, Ship; Motorboat Operators; Mates—Ship, Boat, and Barge; Able Seamen; Ship and Boat Captains

Other Services Requiring Driving: *Bus Drivers*–Bus Drivers, School; Bus Drivers, Transit and Intercity • *Couriers and Messengers • Postal Service Workers*–Postal Service Mail Carriers • *Taxi Drivers and Chauffeur • Truck Drivers and Driver/Sales Workers*–Driver/Sales Workers

Transportation Support Work: *Cargo and Freight Agents • Material Moving Occupations*–Cleaners of Vehicles and Equipment; Stevedores, Except Equipment Operators • *Rail Transportation Occupations*–Train Crew Members; Railroad Yard Workers

The following worksheet can help you use the information in The 1,000+ Jobs List to find the careers and jobs that interest you.

Your Top Job Work Groups

Go back over the list and circle the five—and only five—work groups you underlined that interest you the most. List them here, beginning with the most interesting.

1. _____

2. _____

3. _____

4. _____

5. _____

As you looked through The 1,000+ Jobs List, you identified not only work groups but also the job titles that interest you the most.

Your Top Job Titles

Go back over the list and look at the five—and only five—job titles you underlined that interest you the most. List them here, beginning with the most interesting.

1. _____
2. _____
3. _____
4. _____
5. _____

THE WORKING WORLD

Why Consider Working for the Government?

With about two million employees, the federal government is the nation's largest employer for the widest variety of occupations. Government jobs often offer greater stability and better benefits packages to make up for sometimes lower pay. For more information about federal jobs, see www. usajobs.gov.

RESEARCH THE JOBS THAT INTEREST YOU THE MOST

You now have a list of work groups and job titles that interest you. Here is a list of some major sources of job descriptions and career information that you can use in your research.

* **The *Occupational Outlook Handbook (OOH)*:** Updated every two years by the U.S. Department of Labor, the *OOH* provides thorough descriptions for nearly 270 major jobs that account for about 90 percent of our workforce. The descriptions are well done and include information on the nature of the work; working conditions; training, qualifications, and advancement; employment projections; job outlook; earnings; related jobs; and sources of additional information. You can find the *Occupational Outlook Handbook* in most libraries and bookstores. A book with the same information titled *Top 300 Careers* is also available from bookstores and libraries. In addition, you can get the *OOH* job descriptions on the Web at www.bls.gov/oco.

* **The Occupational Information Network (O*NET):** The O*NET is an information database of more than 900 jobs. Maintained by the U.S. Department of Labor, it is one of the most important and up-to-date sources of career information available. Each *OOH* job description includes reference numbers for related O*NET jobs that allow you to look up related job descriptions in the O*NET database. You can also find the O*NET job titles related for each *OOH* job in The 1,000+ Jobs List provided earlier in this chapter.

* *O*NET Dictionary of Occupational Titles*: This book provides detailed descriptions of each O*NET job and arranges these jobs into groupings used in the O*NET system. This approach makes it easy to find job descriptions listed by O*NET number in the *OOH*, by job title, or just by browsing the table of contents. Each O*NET description also lists related job titles and numbers found in other career resources.

  Best use of the *O*NET Dictionary of Occupational Titles:* The O*NET descriptions in this book are thorough and useful, more so than other print and online sources. It's the best resource to use if you want solid O*NET job descriptions or want to browse O*NET jobs that are related to your primary job objective. This book also lists thousands of more specific *Dictionary of Occupational Titles (DOT)* job titles that are related to the various O*NET jobs.

* *Enhanced Occupational Outlook Handbook (EOOH):* This book presents more than 6,500 job descriptions from the three major sources (*OOH*, O*NET, and *DOT*) in a useful way. It first presents the full text of each *OOH* job description followed by a brief description for each related O*NET job. These are then followed by brief descriptions of related titles from the *DOT*. This approach allows you to quickly and easily identify all O*NET and *DOT* job titles that are related to each *OOH* job title, as well as get a brief description of each.

  Best use of the *Enhanced Occupational Outlook Handbook:* The complete text of each *OOH* job is included in the *EOOH,* so you don't have to use several references to look up related job titles. Just look up the major *OOH* jobs that interest you, and then find related job titles you want to explore in more detail. This is the simplest resource to use if you are starting with the *OOH* job title and want to quickly see related jobs.

* *EZ Occupational Outlook Handbook (EZOOH):* This easy-to-use reference takes all of the job descriptions from the *OOH* and condenses them into easy-to-read one-page overviews. Each job description contains information on the nature of the work, work environment, and sources of additional information. At-a-glance data gives facts and figures on the education and training required, job outlook, job openings, starting earnings, average earnings, related jobs, and even the personality type best suited to the job. Indexes help users search for jobs by personality type or education and training required.

  Best use of the *EZOOH:* When you want to explore potential job titles quickly and easily. Each job description contains most everything you need to know in order to make career decisions or to assist in your job search. If you feel you need more information, you can always use one of the other references mentioned above.

THE WORKING WORLD

Is There Still a Glass Ceiling?

There is no question that more women are earning higher salaries and rising to top executive jobs across the country, yet a substantial earnings gap remains between the sexes. In a report issued in 2003, the Bureau of Labor Statistics found that women earned 76 cents for every dollar men made. The gap is even higher for minority women. That's just more incentive to make sure you're being paid what you're worth.

✳ *New Guide for Occupational Exploration (New GOE):* Previously titled the *Guide for Occupational Exploration,* the newest edition of this book organizes more than 900 O*NET job descriptions into 16 major groups and then into many specialized work groups of similar jobs (the same structure used in The 1000+ Jobs List). The 16 major groups are based on interests by the U.S. Department of Education. Each major group includes useful information on jobs in that group, skills and knowledge required, education and training, and other details. This book also provides excellent O*NET job descriptions.

Best use of the *New Guide for Occupational Exploration:* The *New GOE* is the best resource if you are not sure which career field to pursue, are looking for more responsible jobs within your chosen career field, or are exploring education options.

✳ **Major Web Sources of Career Information:** The government provides an online version of the *OOH* at www.bls.gov/oco. If you want more detailed information on an O*NET job title, you can get it at the government-operated site at online.onetcenter.org. One element allows you to find jobs that match your responses to a list of skills you can check. It comes up with some odd responses but can be helpful in exploring options. You can also search for O*NET jobs based on various criteria including tasks, knowledge, skills, abilities, work activities, work context, job zone, education, training, experience, interests, work styles, work values, work needs, related occupations, wages, and employment projections.

Best use of the government's O*NET Web site: The O*NET job descriptions found in the print sources noted previously are more helpful than those provided on the government Web sites. So use those sources first, and then consider getting additional information on a specific O*NET job from the government's site to prepare for interviews or to get key words to use in your resume.

There are hundreds of other Web sites that provide career information. Some are better than others. Feel free to explore them, but keep in mind that much of the most reliable information is in one of the resources mentioned earlier.

Research on Job Titles

This worksheet will help you record specific job titles that are related to a major one. Start with writing in one job title from the *OOH* that most closely fits your current job objective. Use copies of the worksheet if more than one *OOH* job title interests you.

Major job title from the *OOH*: _____

Related job titles from the O*NET: (Use sources covered in this chapter to list the O*NET job titles that are related to the *OOH* job titles you listed earlier.) _____

_____

_____

_____

_____

Resource you used to obtain these titles: _____
_____
_____

Related job titles from a major online job-posting source: (Use a major Internet site that lists job openings to identify job titles that are related to the *OOH* job title you listed earlier. Because there can be many titles, list only those that interest you most as job objectives to consider.) _____
_____
_____
_____
_____

Resource you used to obtain these titles: _____
_____
_____

Circle job titles you want to pursue: Go back over the job titles you listed, and circle the ones that seem most practical as job objectives for you to pursue. Then underline one or more job titles that interest you greatly but that may require additional effort to obtain. These circled and underlined job titles are the ones to learn more about from career references and other sources.

MONEY MATTERS

A Penny Saved

Planning for your future can be difficult. Part of that planning involves saving money, which can also be hard. There are so many things we need or want that putting any of our paycheck away requires willpower and careful planning. But while we can predict (mostly) what our money will go to today, we can't always know what we will need it for in the future. Whether it's for unemployment, a family vacation, or a medical emergency, the key to having a sound financial future is saving as much as you reasonably can whenever possible. Most advisors recommend that you start saving young. The sooner you start, the more you'll earn. Of course, simply saving pennies won't get you very far, but if you saved just $100 a month for the next 30 years at 5 percent interest, you would have over $100,000 dollars to your name.

YOU CAN DELIBERATELY CHART YOUR CAREER

Many people wander into their career and then wonder why they are unhappy in it. Often their unhappiness comes from the fact that they didn't take the time to research that career. They didn't know what they were getting into when they began the career. They also didn't know that other options were available to them.

In the next chapter, I share questions you need to ask yourself about any job before you take it. You are the only one who can answer the questions, but you do have the answers inside of you.

CASE STUDY: WHAT YOU LOVE

Though he had worked as a shipping clerk since he was 22, Bruce had been climbing and leading tour groups up mountains since he was 16. He had always considered it to be his hobby—the thing that he did to relax and unwind after work. It helped keep him in shape and gave him the chance to socialize with people who shared his interest. Finally, it dawned on him that he was better at mountain climbing and leading tours than just about anything else. He found business partners and opened his own tour guide business. Now he guides tours throughout the spring, summer, and fall and travels to exotic locations to lead tours in the winter. He says he has finally found a career that he enjoys.

Bruce says that job seekers should not ignore their hobbies and interests when considering careers. "It's easy to say that something is just what you do for fun," he says, "but there's no reason you can't say that about your job as well."

chapter 5

Consider Important Preferences in Your Career Planning

M ost people jump into education, training, or a job search with a job objective that is poorly formed and that excludes many possibilities. In most cases, they look for a job similar to one they have had in the past or that is related to their education or training. Rather than analyze what they really want to do, they stick to what they believe they are "qualified for."

THERE IS MORE TO CONSIDER THAN JUST THE JOB TITLE

But good decision making about a job or career involves more than just deciding on a job title. For example, if you are looking for a job in the accounting area but have a great interest in fashion design, can you think of a job that might combine these? Or what if you have a general job objective as a computer repair technician but have also enjoyed selling in the past? Can you think of a job that would combine these? The fact is that a variety of jobs can combine computer repair and selling.

> *Success on any major scale requires you to accept responsibility... in the final analysis, the one quality that all successful people have... is the ability to take on responsibility.*
>
> *Michael Korda*

And there are other personal preferences to consider. For example, are you willing to move out of the area, or would you prefer staying where you live now? Your answer will make a big difference in how you conduct your job search.

Any job will require you to make some compromises, but it is important to consider your preferences in advance. Doing this will clarify what is most important to you in the job you eventually accept.

Many experts have given a lot of thought to the factors that someone should consider in selecting a job that suits them well. I've adapted research findings to the things that follow as important in defining your job objective. Complete each activity now, and use your responses to help define your ideal job objective.

What Transferable, Adaptive, and Job-Related Skills and Abilities Do You Prefer to Use?

Knowing what you are good at and what skills you would like to use in your next job are essential in developing a proper job objective. Chapter 3, "Develop Your Skills Language," gave you a good sense of what skills and abilities you want to use on your next job. Go back now and review that chapter as needed. Think about those skills and abilities that you enjoy using *and* are good at.

Your Top Five Skills and Abilities

List the five skills and abilities that you would most like to use in your next job.

1. _____
2. _____
3. _____
4. _____
5. _____

Which of Your Interests Do You Want to Use?

You should already have a good idea of the jobs that interest you based on the education and training you have. Even so, you probably have other interests, such as extracurricular activities, hobbies, leisure, family, or other areas you would like to work into a career if you could.

Your Top Five Interests

List five of your interests that you would most like to include in a future career.

1. _____
2. _____
3. _____
4. _____
5. _____

What Types of People Do You Prefer to Work With?

An important element in enjoying your job is the people you work with and for. If you have ever had a rotten boss or worked with people you did not get along with, you know exactly why this is so important.

If you haven't already given thought to the subject, the following worksheet will help you do just that. Think about all your experiences (school, work, military, volunteer, and so on) and your co-workers or the people you were with in each of those settings.

The People You Work With

Write down the qualities you didn't like about previous co-workers or supervisors, and then redefine them into qualities you'd like to see in the people you will work with.

Negative Qualities

_____

_____

_____

_____

_____

_____

Positive Qualities

_____

_____

_____

_____

_____

_____

When your list is complete, go back and identify the types of people you would really like to work with in your next job. Then select the five qualities that are most important to you.

Characteristics You Prefer in the People You Will Work With

From the preceding worksheet, list the five qualities that are most important to you, in their order of importance to you, with 1 being the most important and 5 the least.

1. _____

2. _____

3. _____

4. _____

5. _____

MONEY MATTERS

An Interest in Interest

Put simply, *interest* is the amount a borrower pays a lender for the use of the lender's money. A bank will charge you interest on the loan you took out to buy a house or car. Likewise, that same bank will pay you an interest rate for the use of your money as you keep it in your savings account. Credit card companies pay for the latest shopping spree, but with the promise that you will pay them back, and often with interest. The key to saving is getting the highest interest rate you can on your investments (savings) and the lowest rate possible on your loans (like a mortgage). Also, the frequency with which banks compound interest (that is, pay interest on the interest already earned) can make a big difference in the rate of return.

How Much Money Do You Want to Make—or Are You Willing to Accept?

It's easy to say that money isn't important, but it is. Earnings are particularly important for those starting out and for those with lower incomes. While money may not be everything, it is important to consider when planning your career or looking for a job. Doing so now will help you make a good decision later, when you receive a job offer and have to balance the money with other factors.

Your Acceptable Pay Range

Pay is important, but relative. You need to consider that some compromise on money is always possible, so you should know in advance the pay you would accept, in addition to what you would prefer. Following are a few questions to help you define your salary range.

1. If you found the perfect job in all other respects (or were desperate), what would be the very least pay you would be willing to accept (per hour, week, or year)? _____

2. What is the upper end of pay you could expect to obtain, given your credentials and other factors? _____

3. What sort of income would you need to pay for a desirable lifestyle (however you want to define this)? _____

4. How much money do you hope to make in your next job? _____

Many people will take less money if the job is great in other ways—or if they simply need to survive. And we all want more pay if we can get it. Realistically, your next job will probably be somewhere between your minimum and maximum amount.

How Much Responsibility Are You Willing to Accept?

In most organizations, those who are willing to accept more responsibility are also typically paid more. Higher levels of responsibility often require you to supervise others or to make decisions that affect the organization. When things don't go well, people in charge are also held accountable for the performance of their area of responsibility. Some people are willing to accept this responsibility, while others, understandably, would prefer not to. Answer the questions that follow to help you define how much responsibility you are willing to accept.

Your Preferred Level of Responsibility

Answer the questions that follow to help you define how much responsibility you are willing to accept.

1. Do you like to be in charge? _____

2. Are you good at supervising others? _____

3. Do you prefer to be part of a team, where you share responsibilities with others? _____

4. Do you prefer working by yourself, or under someone else's guidance? _____

5. Jot down where you see yourself, in terms of accepting responsibility for others, and in other ways within an organization. _____

_____

_____

_____

_____

_____

_____

_____

_____

_____

_____

_____

SKILLS FOR SUCCESS

Reliability

Sara has had to miss three days so far in the month of February after missing four in January. At this rate, she will have used up all her vacation time before summer comes. The reasons are legitimate—she had the flu, her car broke down, her daughter was sick, the cable repair man was coming—but her boss is starting to wonder if he can count on her. Sara has already missed one important meeting, and her boss is afraid the trend will continue. What would you do if you were Sara's boss? What can Sara do to try to be more reliable?

Do You Prefer to Work in a Larger or Smaller Organization?

What size organization would you prefer to work for? Larger employers (with 500 or more employees) often offer higher pay and better benefits. Smaller employers often allow you to learn more and move up more rapidly. Smaller employers also now employ about 75 percent of the nongovernment workforce and are an important source of job openings. But many larger employers have smaller work groups or local offices that may "feel" more like a small employer.

The Size of Organization You Prefer

In the space that follows, describe the size of organization you prefer to work with and why.

_____

_____

_____

_____

_____

In Which City or Geographical Region Do You Want Your Next Job to Be Located?

There are often good reasons for wanting to stay where you now live, although certain jobs and career opportunities may be limited unless you are willing to move. If you decide to stay where you are, there are still geographic issues to consider. For example, how far are you willing to commute, or would it be more desirable for you to work on one side of town than the other?

If you prefer to stay but are willing to move, a good strategy is to spend most of your job search time looking locally. If you are willing to relocate, don't make the common mistake of looking for a job "anywhere." Instead, narrow your job search to a few key geographic areas, and concentrate your efforts there.

If you are willing to move and are flexible regarding where, try to narrow your search by defining characteristics of the place you'd like to live. For example, suppose you would like to live near the ocean, in a mid-sized city, and in a part of the country that has mild winters but does have four seasons. That leaves out a large number of places, doesn't it? Or it may be as simple as wanting to live near your mom. As you add more criteria, there are fewer and fewer places to look, and your job search becomes more precise. The more precise you are, the more likely you will end up with what you want.

One way to do this is to consider the places you have already lived. Think about what you did and did not like about them.

The Places You Have Been

List the cities, regions, or countries you have lived or visited that left a strong impression on you. Next to each, list things you liked (on the left side) and did not like (on the right) about these places.

Place	**Liked**	**Did Not Like**

This worksheet may help you identify the things you would like to have in the place where you work. You should also go to your library or the Internet to research a particular location you are considering or just to learn about your options.

Your Preferred Geographical Location

1. What is the most interesting city, region, or country you have ever visited? _____

2. Do you prefer to be in an urban (inner city), suburban, or rural environment? _____

3. Would you rather work in the environment you grew up in or an entirely different one?

   _____

4. List areas where you prefer your work to be located. _____

   _____

   _____

   _____

THE WORKING WORLD

Where the Jobs Are

Over the past several decades, the U.S. economy has shifted from a goods-producing to a services-providing perspective. Thus, jobs in the service-providing industries are expected to grow much faster than their counterparts, especially in the education and health services fields. This also means that many skills, such as good customer service skills and strong written and verbal communication skills, will become even more valued by employers.

What Sort of Work Environment Do You Prefer?

Do you like to work inside or outside, in a noisy or quiet environment? In my case, I prefer to work in a building with windows, to have the ability to get up and move around occasionally, and to have a variety of tasks during the day. While most of us can put up with all sorts of less-than-ideal work environments, some work environment issues will bother us more than others.

Once again, defining the things you did not like about previous work environments is a good way to help you define what you prefer. Think of all the places you've gone to school or worked, and write down the things you didn't like about those environments. Then redefine them as positives, as in the following example. When you have completed the list for each job you've had (use extra sheets if necessary), go back and select the five environmental preferences that are most important to you. Here is one example of such a worksheet—what an accountant wrote about working for the Internal Revenue Service—to help you get started.

Place or Job	Things I Did Not Like	Environment I Would Like
Accountant for the Internal Revenue Service	Too noisy	Quiet workplace
	No variety in work	Lots of variety in work
	No windows	My own window
	No place to park	My own airstrip (just kidding)
	Too much sitting	More activity
	Not people-oriented	More customer contact
	Indoors all the time	More outside work
	Too large an organization	Smaller organization

Complete the following worksheet to get a clearer picture of the environments you do not like.

Environments You Have Experienced

List the places you've gone to school or worked or jobs you've had, and then write down the things you didn't like about those environments. Then redefine them as positives.

Place or Job	Things I Did Not Like	Work Environment I Would Enjoy

When you have completed the list, think about the five environmental preferences that are most important to you.

Your Preferred Work Environment

Write those things that are most important to have in your next job on the lines that follow. List your most important selection first, followed by others in order of importance.

1. _____
2. _____
3. _____
4. _____
5. _____

Do You Want to Start Your Own Business, or Work for an Existing Employer?

More than 10 percent of workers either own their own business or are self-employed. If this interests you, you could seek a job now that gives you skills and experiences to prepare you for self-employment or start-up of your own business.

Your Preference for Employment or Self-Employment

In the space that follows, describe your long- and short-term preferences for working for an employer or being self-employed.

_____
_____
_____
_____
_____

What Values Are Important to You?

What are your values? I once had a job where the sole reason for the existence of the organization was to make money. That's not necessarily wrong, but I wanted to be involved in things that I could believe in. For example, some people work to help others, some to clean up our environment, and others to build things, make machines work, gain power or prestige, care for animals or plants, or something else. All work is worthwhile if it's done well, so the issue here is just what sorts of things are important to you.

While money is important to most people, a study by the Gallup Poll found that people rated 10 work-related factors as being more important for satisfaction with their careers. People with low wages rate earnings as most important, but only 56 percent in this survey rated "high income" as being very important to them. Notice that 10 things were rated higher than "high income" in this study:

Importance in Job Satisfaction	Percent
Good health insurance and other benefits	80
Interesting work	78
Job security	78
Opportunity to learn new skills	68
Having a week or more of vacation	66
Being able to work independently	64
Recognition from co-workers	62
Regular hours—no weekends or nights	58
Being able to help others	58
Limited job stress	58
High income	56

The following table shows the results of another survey, this one by Louis Harris and Associates, asking people to rate those things they considered very important in their work. Again, money was not rated as important as some other things.

Importance in Job Satisfaction	Percent
A challenging job	82
Good benefits	80
Good pay	74
Free exchange of information	74
Chance to make significant contributions	74
The right to privacy	62

The following table presents the results of the survey taken by Research & Forecasts. The percentages indicate those who selected each item among their highest two work-related values. It makes sense that those with lower levels of education and earnings rate money as more important. But over 50 percent of the high school grads or those with less education picked other things as more important than pay alone.

Percent Selecting Factor Among Two Most Important	High School Grad or Less	Some College	College Graduate
Pay	46	42	29
Amount of independence	31	35	40
Pleasant working conditions	30	23	17
Liking the people at work	29	24	19
Gratifying work	25	32	43
Contribution to the public good	11	14	23
Important career step	10	15	19

The type of work you do and the people you work with are consistently more important to job satisfaction than pay. For this reason, you would be wise to spend some time considering what you want out of your work before you go out and look for it. The worksheet that follows lists some of the values that others have found important or satisfying to them in their work.

Your Top Work Values

Read each value and think about how important it is to you. Then put a check mark in front of those values that you consider important enough to include in your next job.

- ❑ **Advancement:** Find work that allows me to get training, experience, and opportunities to advance in pay and level of responsibility.
- ❑ **Adventure:** Do work that allows me to experience new things and take some risks.
- ❑ **Artistic creativity:** Do creative work in writing, theater, art, design, or any other area.
- ❑ **Be busy:** Have work that keeps me fully occupied so that I am not bored.
- ❑ **Beauty:** Have a job that allows me to enjoy or that involves sensitivity to beauty.
- ❑ **Change and variety:** Have job duties that often change or are done in different settings.
- ❑ **Competition:** Compete against a goal or other people, where there are clear outcomes.
- ❑ **Excitement:** Do work that is often exciting.
- ❑ **Free time:** Have work that allows me to have enough time for family, leisure, and other activities.
- ❑ **General creativity:** Create ideas, programs, or anything else that is new and different.
- ❑ **Help other people:** Help others directly, either individually or in small groups.
- ❑ **Help society:** Contribute to the betterment of the world I live in.
- ❑ **Influence people:** Be in a position to change other people's attitudes and opinions.
- ❑ **Knowledge:** Seek knowledge, truth, and understanding.
- ❑ **Make decisions on my own:** Have the power to set policy and determine a course of action.

(continued)

(continued)

❑ **Moral fulfillment:** Feel that my work is contributing to a set of moral standards that are important.

❑ **Physical challenge:** Have a job whose physical demands are challenging and rewarding.

❑ **Power and authority:** Have control over other people's work activities; be a manager or supervisor.

❑ **Public contact:** Have lots of daily contact with people.

❑ **Quality:** Do work that allows me to meet high standards of excellence.

❑ **Recognition:** Be recognized for the quality of my work in some visible or public way.

❑ **Security:** Be fairly sure of keeping my job and not having to worry much about losing it.

❑ **Sense of accomplishment:** Have work that allows me to feel I am accomplishing something worthwhile or important.

❑ **Stability:** Have job duties that are predictable and not likely to change over a long period.

❑ **Status:** Be looked up to by others at work and in the community or be recognized as a member of an organization whose work or status is important to me.

❑ **Teaching and instructing:** Have a job in which I teach or guide other people.

❑ **Teamwork/work with others:** Have close working relationships with a group; work as a team toward common goals.

❑ **Time freedom:** Have a flexible work schedule that allows me to have control of my time.

❑ **Other values or preferences:** Write other work values or preferences that are important to you and that you want to include in your career planning.

_____

_____

_____

Your Most Important Values

Look over the checklist you just completed, and select the five values you would *most* like to include in your career or job. List them in order of importance to you, beginning with the most important value.

1. _____

2. _____

3. _____

4. _____

5. _____

> **THE WORKING WORLD**
>
> ### Who Is Responsible for Your Health?
>
> Studies show that one in three Americans is chronically overworked and that many of them would gladly give up some of their pay to get more time off. Yet a good percentage of Americans still don't take the full vacation time they are allotted. While proving you are a hard worker is a key to landing your dream job, it's important that the job provides the right balance between pay and workload. Dying of a stress-induced heart attack at the age of 48 will definitely put a damper on your retirement plans.

Which Sector Do You Want to Work In?

If you want to work for an employer, consider what major sector you would prefer: government (including schools); not-for-profit organizations; business or for-profit companies; or the military.

The Sector You Prefer to Work In

In the space that follows, describe how you feel about working in each sector.

1. Government: _____

   _____

2. Not-for-profit organizations: _____

   _____

3. Business or for-profit companies: _____

   _____

4. The military: _____

   _____

Within What Industry Do You Want to Work?

While most of us understand the importance of selecting a specific career based on our skills, abilities, interests, experience, and values, some overlook the importance of considering various industries. Yet the industry you work in is often as important as the job you choose. Why? There are various reasons, but here are the primary ones:

* **Some industries pay better:** Let's say that you want to manage some sort of warehouse operation or work in a clerical position. If so, it might help you to know that you are more likely to be paid more in the drug manufacturing industry than in the department or grocery store industries. The jobs are basically the same, but one industry pays better. That could end up being an important difference to you over a long period.

* **Some industries present more risk or less stability:** Some industries routinely hire more people when the economy is strong and lay people off when it is weak. Some industries are growing rapidly, others are declining, and many are changing as a result of technology or other forces. If it is important for you to work in a stable situation in which you are less likely to be laid off, select a more stable industry.

* **Some industries will be more fun for you:** Some industries will simply appeal to you more for a variety of reasons. You could be interested based on your values, previous training or education, or a variety of other factors. Selecting an industry that appeals to you more than another could be as important as the job you select.

Use the following worksheet to think about the industries that appeal to you.

Checklist of Industries to Consider in More Detail

Following is a list of 45 major industries, covering most of the labor market. Place a check mark before any industry that sounds interesting to you.

Goods-Producing Industries

Agriculture and Natural Resources
- ❏ Agriculture, Forestry, and Fishing
- ❏ Mining
- ❏ Oil and Gas Extraction

Manufacturing, Construction, and Utilities
- ❏ Aerospace Product and Parts Manufacturing
- ❏ Chemical Manufacturing, Except Drugs
- ❏ Computer and Electronic Product Manufacturing
- ❏ Construction
- ❏ Food Manufacturing
- ❏ Machinery Manufacturing
- ❏ Motor Vehicle and Parts Manufacturing
- ❏ Pharmaceutical and Medicine Manufacturing
- ❏ Printing
- ❏ Steel Manufacturing
- ❏ Textile, Textile Product, and Apparel Manufacturing
- ❏ Utilities

Service-Providing Industries

Trade
- ❏ Automobile Dealers
- ❏ Clothing, Accessory, and General Merchandise Stores
- ❏ Grocery Stores
- ❏ Wholesale Trade

Transportation
- ❏ Air Transportation
- ❏ Truck Transportation and Warehousing

Information
- ❏ Broadcasting
- ❏ Internet Service Providers, Web Search Portals, and Data Processing Services
- ❏ Motion Picture and Video Fields
- ❏ Publishing, Except Software
- ❏ Software Publishers
- ❏ Telecommunications

Financial Activities
- ❏ Banking
- ❏ Insurance
- ❏ Securities, Commodities, and Other Investments

Professional and Business Services

❑ Advertising and Public Relations Services
❑ Computer Systems Design and Related Services
❑ Employment Services

❑ Management, Scientific, and Technical Consulting Services
❑ Scientific Research and Development Services

Education, Health Care, and Social Services

❑ Child Day Care Services
❑ Educational Services

❑ Health Care
❑ Social Assistance, Except Child Day Care

Leisure and Hospitality

❑ Arts, Entertainment, and Recreation
❑ Food Services and Drinking Places

❑ Hotels and Other Accommodations

Government and Advocacy, Grantmaking, and Civic Organizations

❑ Advocacy, Grantmaking, and Civic Organizations
❑ Federal Government, Excluding the Postal Service

❑ State and Local Government, Excluding Education and Hospitals

The preceding checklist will help you quickly identify industries you should explore in more detail. Review the industries you underlined, and in the space that follows, write the three industries that you most want to consider in your job search.

The Industries You Most Want to Learn About

1. _____
2. _____
3. _____

LEARN MORE ABOUT TARGETED INDUSTRIES

Details on each of the major industries are provided in the government publication "Career Guide to Industries." A bookstore version of the same publication, *40 Best Fields for Your Career,* is more readily available in libraries and bookstores. You can also find industry descriptions at the U.S. Bureau of Labor Statistics Web site at www.bls.gov under the Publications section.

The industry descriptions in the resources noted earlier are packed with information that any job seeker would find useful, including nature of the industry, working conditions, employment, occupations in the industry, training and advancement, earnings, outlook, and sources of additional information.

To help you see how useful this information is, following is selected text from several sections of the "Health Care" description. You can use this information to learn about how your job objective fits into the industry, how you might seek the job you want within this industry, and specific job targets where the jobs are found.

EXCERPT FROM *40 BEST FIELDS FOR YOUR CAREER*

Health Care

- ◎ Annual Earnings: $32,149
- ◎ Job Growth: 27.3%
- ◎ Size of Workforce: 13,062,102
- ◎ Self-Employed: 2.7%
- ◎ Part-Time: 20.0%

Significant Points

- As the largest field in 2004, health care provided 13.5 million jobs—13.1 million jobs for wage and salary workers and about 411,000 jobs for the self-employed.

- 8 out of 20 occupations projected to grow the fastest are in health care.

Nature of the Field

Combining medical technology and the human touch, the health care field administers care around the clock, responding to the needs of millions of people—from newborns to the critically ill.

About 545,000 establishments make up the health care field; they vary greatly in terms of size, staffing patterns, and organizational structures. About 76 percent of health care establishments are offices of physicians, den-[...] hospitals [...] establish-[...] ble 1).

Table 1. Percent distribution of wage and salary employment and establishments in health services, 2004

Establishment type	Establish-ments	Employ-ment
Health services, total	100.0	100.0
Hospitals, public and private	1.9	41.3
Nursing and r[...]		
Offices of phy[...]		
Offices of den[...]		
Home healthc[...]		
Offices of oth[...]		
Outpatient car[...]		
Other ambula[...]		
Medical and d[...]		

Working Conditions

Average weekly hours of nonsupervisory workers in private health care varied among the different segments of the field. Workers in offices of dentists averaged only 26.9 hours per week in 2004, while those in psychiatric and substance abuse hospitals averaged 36.4 hours, compared with 33.7 hours for all nongovernment fields.

Many workers in the health care field are on part-time schedules. Part-time workers made up about 20 percent of the workforce as a whole in 2004, but accounted for 39 percent of workers in offices of dentists and 33 percent of those in offices of other health practitioners. Students, parents with young children, dual jobholders, and older workers make up much of the part-time workforce.

Many health care establishments operate around the clock and need staff at all hours. Shift work is common

Important Characteristics of the Field

Skills: Social Perceptiveness; Service Orientation; Instructing; Time Management; Learning Strategies; Active Listening. **Abilities:** Speech Recognition; Problem Sensitivity; Arm-Hand Steadiness; Gross Body Coordination; Speech Clarity; Stamina. **Work-Related Values:** Social Service; Co-workers; Activity; Variety; Security; Achievement.

Employment

As the largest field in 2004, health care provided 13.5 million jobs—13.1 million jobs for wage and salary workers and about 411,000 jobs for self-employed and unpaid family workers. Of the 13.1 million wage and salary jobs, 41 percent were in hospitals; another 22 percent were in nursing and residential care facilities; and 16 percent were in offices of physicians. About 92 percent of

Occupations in the Field

Health care firms employ large numbers of workers in professional and service occupations. Together, these two occupational groups account for 3 out of 4 jobs in the field. The next largest share of jobs, 18 percent, is in office and administrative support. Management, business, and financial operations occupations account for only 4 percent of employment. Other occupations in health care made up only 3 percent of the total (table 2).

Professional occupations, such as *physicians and surgeons, dentists, registered nurses, social workers,* and *physical ther-api*[...] cial[...] fiel[...] ate[...] oft[...] dut[...] ma[...]

Table 2. Employment of wage and salary workers in health care by occupation, 2004 and projected change, 2004–2014 (Employment in thousands)

Occupation	Employment, 2004 Number	Percent	Percent change, 2004–2014
Total, all occupations	13,062	100.0	27.3
Management, business, and financial occupations	574	4.4	28.3
Top executives	101	0.8	33.3
Medical and health services managers	175	1.3	26.1
Professional and related occupations	5,657	43.3	27.8
Psychologists	33	0.3	28.1
Counselors	152	1.2	31.8
Social workers	169	1.3	29.3
Health educators	17	0.1	27.0

Training and Advancement

A variety of programs after high school provide specialized training for jobs in health care. Students preparing for health careers can enter programs leading to a certificate or a degree at the associate, baccalaureate, or graduate level. Two-year programs resulting in certificates or associate degrees are the minimum standard credential for occupations such as dental hygienist or radiologic technologist. Most therapists and social workers have at least a bachelor's degree. Health diagnosing and treating practitioners—such as physicians and surgeons, optometrists, and podiatrists—are among the most educated workers, with many years of education and training beyond college.

The health care field also provides many job opportunities for people without specialized training beyond high school. In fact, more than half of workers in nursing and residential care facilities have a high school diploma or less, as do a quarter of workers in hospitals.

Some health care establishments provide on-the-job or classroom training as well as continuing education. For example, in all certified nursing facilities, nursing aides

Outlook

Job opportunities should be excellent in all employment settings because of high job turnover, particularly from the large number of expected retirements and tougher immigration rules that are slowing the numbers of foreign health care workers entering the U.S. Wage and

Table 3. Employment in health care by field segment, 2004 and projected change, 2004–2014 (Employment in thousands)

Field segment	2004 Employment	Percent change, 2004–2014
All fields	145,612	14.0
Health services	13,062	27.3
Hospitals, public and private	5,301	13.1
Nursing and residential care facilities	2,815	27.8
Offices of physicians	2,054	37.0
Home health care services	773	69.5
Offices of dentists	760	31.7
Offices of other health practitioners	524	42.7
Outpatient care centers	446	44.2
Other ambulatory health care services	201	37.7
Medical and diagnostic laboratories	189	27.1

Earnings

Average earnings of nonsupervisory workers in most health care segments are higher than the average for all nongovernment fields, with hospital workers earning considerably more than the average and those employed in nursing and residential care facilities and home health care services earning less (table 4). Average earnings often are higher in hospitals because the percentage of jobs requiring higher levels of education and training is greater than in other segments. Those segments of the field with lower earnings employ large numbers of part-time service workers.

Table 4. Average earnings and hours of nonsupervisory workers in health services by field segment, 2004

Field segment	Earnings Weekly	Earnings Hourly	Weekly hours
Total, nongovernment	$528.56	$15.67	33.7
Health care	572.83	17.32	33.1
Hospitals	715.12	20.31	35.2
Medical and diagnostic laboratories	634.79	18.15	35.0
Offices of physicians	613.82	18.41	33.4
Outpatient care centers	631.38	18.57	34.0

Sources of Additional Information

For additional information on specific health-related occupations, contact

- American Medical Association/Health Professions Career and Education Directory, 515 N. State St., Chicago, IL 60610. Internet: http://www.ama-assn.org/go/alliedhealth

For information on physician careers and applying to medical school, contact

- Association of American Medical Colleges, 2450 N Street NW, Washington, DC 20037. Internet: http://www.aamc.org/students

THE WORKING WORLD

What Is Your Job's Safety Factor?

When searching for a job, most people consider salary, job growth, or its fit with their own skills and interests, but they may not always think about on-the-job hazards. Still, work environment—especially as it relates to one's health—is important in choosing the right career. Here are the top 10 most dangerous jobs according to the Bureau of Labor Statistics: timber cutters, fishers, pilots and navigators, structural metal workers, driver-sales, roofers, electrical power installers, farm occupations, construction laborers, and truck drivers.

Three Tips for Getting the Most Out of the Industry Descriptions

I know you will resist looking up the industry descriptions, but consider the advice that follows, and try to understand how useful the industry descriptions can be. Here are some things you can do to make the most out of these descriptions:

* **Mark up the descriptions:** Circle or underline anything in the description that is important to you, such as the pay rates, skills, education, or training required. (If you borrow the book from the library, write notes on a piece of paper instead of marking up the book.)

* **Include important requirements in your interviews and resume:** Later, when you are looking for a job in this industry, include things you learned that you want to emphasize to an employer. For example, do you have the skills or other characteristics that this industry requires? Do you have related interests, experience, training, or education? Can you mention any important industry trends to indicate your knowledge of what is going on in the industry? Jot notes in the margin of strengths you have that you could highlight in an interview or resume.

* **Consider the industry's pay, growth, and other factors:** I mentioned earlier that some industries pay better than others. Because this is so, consider working in an industry that pays better than average, particularly if you find it of interest. You should also, of course, consider other factors, such as industry growth and stability. For example, government jobs tend to be more stable than jobs in industries that are more sensitive to changes in the economy.

More Specific Industry Listings

More detailed listings of specialized industries are provided in the "North American Industry Classification System" (NAICS). The government developed this system to organize more than 1,100 industries within major groupings. The NAICS allows you to find a major industry group and then drill down to more and more specific industries that are within it. This can be helpful in showing you the many opportunities to specialize within a major industry that interests you. You can find NAICS listings online at www.census.gov/epcd/www/naics.html or at http://stats.bls.gov/bls/naics.htm.

Even if you already know the sort of job you want, it's likely there are related jobs that you haven't considered. For example, if you are enrolled in a medical technology program, you probably have a good idea of the job title or titles you will seek. But are you familiar with the many related jobs with different titles and the industries where you can find these jobs? Are you as sure of the work environment and people you prefer to work with or the size of the employer? Selecting the right job in the right industry or setting can end up paying you significantly more or be more satisfying in other ways.

Whatever your situation, you are likely to gain useful information from this chapter. Knowing more about your job options will help you in your long-term career planning. It will also help you find the job that best suits your personality and needs.

YOUR FIVE MOST IMPORTANT PREFERENCES OVERALL

From the job-related preferences you just completed, select the five that are *most* important to you to try to include in your next job. The preferences are

* Transferable, adaptive, and job-related skills and abilities
* Interests
* Types of co-workers
* Income
* Responsibilities
* Size of organization
* Geographic location
* Type of work environment
* Self-employment or employment by an organization
* Values
* Sector
* Industry

THE WORKING WORLD

What Is Self-Employment?

Self-employment means that you work for yourself rather than for an employer. Freelance editors, for example, are self-employed; they work by themselves to edit documents for other companies. About 10 percent of American workers are considered self-employed. In fact, nationwide there are at least 23 million individually owned companies. Maybe the job you really want is one working for yourself.

Your Five Most Important Preferences

List the five most important preferences that you will want to look for in a job.

1. _____

2. _____

3. _____

4. _____

5. _____

YOU'RE READY TO BEGIN YOUR JOB SEARCH

If you have completed this and the preceding chapter, you have a better idea of the career and job that you want. Knowing those two pieces of information can help you understand where to begin your job search. In the upcoming chapters, I share the most effective job search methods and the best ways to use the less effective methods.

CASE STUDY: MONEY DOESN'T EQUAL HAPPINESS

Money sometimes can buy happiness, but Alicia will tell you it works both ways. As an elementary school teacher for four years, she was already experiencing burnout from the stress of managing her own classroom. With disciplining 30 students, countless parent-teacher conferences, and the time spent grading and planning lessons, she was putting in well over 50 hours a week and often couldn't see the results of her efforts. She knew that she loved teaching, but she didn't realize how much stress, paperwork, and after-hours preparation was involved.

The next year, a position opened as a personal teaching assistant for a student she liked. The only problem: It paid 50 percent less than her current salary. She took the job anyway and never regretted the decision. Her 50 percent pay decrease came with innumerable benefits, including less stress, more free time, and more intrinsic rewards. Alicia cautions job seekers to consider all aspects of a career and to find some balance between what you earn—salary—and what you spend in terms of time, energy, and mental health to get it. As she is fond of saying, "Money can buy you happiness. Mine costs about $15,000 a year."

chapter 6

Use the Most Effective Job Search Methods

There are many job search methods, and each of them works for some people. One expert will tell you how to create the most effective electronic resume and then post it on lots of Web sites for employers to find. Another will advise you that the best approach is to contact people you know and ask them for job leads. And there are many other methods you can use during your search.

But the problem is that most job seekers use relatively ineffective methods in their job search. As a result, they too often remain unemployed longer than they should, or they end up taking a job that does not fit them well.

Teamwork is so important that it is virtually impossible for you to reach the heights of your capabilities...without it.

Brian Tracy

This chapter will help you identify the most effective job search methods. While some of these methods are not the easiest to use, you need to know which ones are most likely to identify job openings that others may be overlooking.

What Methods Are Most Effective?

Following is a list of job search methods that many people use. Read the list carefully. You may think of others not included on this list. If you do, write those methods in the blank lines provided. Later you will select the three methods you think are most effective.

* Placing or responding to help-wanted ads

* Posting your resume on major Internet job sites

* Following up on leads from friends and relatives

* Walking into an employer's workplace and asking for an interview

* Registering at a private employment service or agency

(continued)

(continued)

* E-mailing or mailing your resume to the human resources departments

* Filling out applications in person or online

* Asking people you know in your "network" of acquaintances for referrals to employers

* Following up on referrals provided by the public employment service

* Using school, union, or other employment center services

* _____

* _____

* _____

On line 1 that follows, write the job search method you think is *most* effective, and explain why you chose it. Then write the second and third most effective methods in the corresponding lines, and explain why you think they are effective.

1. _____

_____

2. _____

_____

3. _____

_____

You probably selected job search methods that have worked well for you in the past. But you also probably overlooked one or more of the most effective methods you will learn about in this chapter.

SOME JOB SEARCH METHODS WORK BETTER THAN OTHERS

Finding a good job often takes longer than most people think. The average job seeker spends two to three months looking for a new job. In some cases, luck helps someone get hired quickly. For most people, however, finding a job takes more than luck.

The truth is that almost everyone who wants a job will eventually find one. Because this is so, your task in the job search is to accomplish two simple things:

1. Reduce the time it takes to find a job.

2. Get a better job than you might otherwise.

Some job search methods have been proven to reduce the time it takes to find a job or to increase your chances of finding a job that meets your needs. These more effective methods tend to be active rather than passive and help you find jobs that are not advertised. As a result, people who use these methods often face less direct competition and are more likely to find jobs that closely match their skills.

USE A VARIETY OF METHODS, BUT EMPHASIZE THOSE THAT WORK BEST

The fact is that the job search methods you selected in the previous activity *do* work for some people. Even so, what research there is on job seeking indicates that some methods are more effective, on the average, than others. The research also suggests that successful job seekers use a variety of methods. What this means to you is that you should use a variety of job search methods but spend more time on the ones that tend to get better results.

I'll review the more effective job search methods later in this chapter, but here are three important concepts to consider as you decide which job search methods you will use:

* **Active approaches are typically more effective than passive ones:** Active job search methods are those where you don't wait around for someone to contact you. Instead, you go out and *make* things happen. For example, posting your resume on Web sites is passive, because it requires the employer to come to you. Should you post your resume on these sites? Sure, because doing so works for some people. But my point is that, while you are waiting for the perfect employer to contact you as a result of your Web posting, take action by contacting potential employers.

* **The objective is to get an interview with the people who are most likely to hire or supervise you:** Few people get job offers without having an interview first. Even in an increasingly electronic world, employers will often want to meet you in person before they decide whether to hire you. So your objective in your job search is to get interviews with the people who are *most* likely to hire or supervise you—*not* to put your resume on a dozen Web sites, create the perfect resume, fill out applications, put all your canned goods in alphabetical order, or other tasks.

> *As you go about your job search, repeatedly ask yourself: Is what I am doing now likely to result in my setting up an interview?*

* **Get more interviews to reduce your length of unemployment:** People who get one or two interviews per week tend to be unemployed much longer than those who get four or more. It makes sense. Sitting at home waiting for employers to call you or respond to your resume on the Web is *not* a good way to get interviews.

As you go about your job search, evaluate how you are spending your time. Repeatedly ask yourself: "Is what I am doing now likely to result in my setting up an interview?" If your answer is "no," you need to spend more of your time doing things that are likely to get interviews.

An Emergency Financial First Aid Kit

Emergencies come when we least expect them, and, while we may prepare food for a snowstorm or board windows to protect our homes from a hurricane, we do not think to prepare our financial records in advance. Everyone should create an Emergency Financial First Aid Kit (EFFAK), a simple form for identifying and organizing key financial records. It provides a quick reference file for your most important financial documents. To download the kit, go to http://www.ncua.gov/Publications/brochures/EmergencyFinancialFirstAidKit.pdf.

THREE ACTIONS YOU SHOULD TAKE AT THE BEGINNING OF YOUR JOB SEARCH

Here are three actions you should take as soon as you begin your job search:

* Use school, program, and other insider resources.

* Register with the public employment service.

* Post your resume with major Web sites, and then use more active methods.

In the next sections, I present information about these actions.

Use School, Program, and Other Insider Resources

Do you have access to a school or program that provides job search assistance? If so, consider yourself fortunate, and find out all you can about how the school or program can help you. Many such services provide a career and job search resource library, access to resume-creating software, computer and copy resources, and other services. Some provide individual assistance from trained staff or even referrals to job openings.

Be professional and friendly with program staff, because their opinion of you will make a difference in your getting good service. And *never* miss an appointment they schedule for you with an employer. Besides this being rude, you will not likely get another referral from them.

Register with the Public Employment Service

Every state in the United States and province in Canada has what is called the "public employment service." It goes by different names in different areas, but this is the agency where you register for unemployment checks and re-employment assistance. It's important to register right away with this agency so that you can collect any unemployment compensation you're due.

Some of these agencies provide job search classes, referrals to employers, access to computers and copy machines, and other services. So check out what is available as soon as practical, and use whatever resources they provide that will help you. I'll give you more tips on using this program in the next chapter.

Post Your Resume with Major Web Sites, and Then Use More Active Methods

If you want to post your resume or complete the information requested on one or more Web job posting sites, go ahead and do so. But don't wait by your computer for the job offers to roll in. Keep in mind that you will be posting your information along with millions of other job seekers, in a national market of more than 150 million workers. Employers do search these sites for qualified candidates, but they are often looking for people with specific job-related computer, technical, or other skills. Employers want to exclude as many candidates as possible so that they don't end up with hundreds of applicants. They typically set criteria for education, training, experience, and other fields in a way that excludes those without perfect credentials.

The following excerpt is from an article titled "Monster's Competitors Are Nipping at Its Heels" in *Workplace Magazine* (www.workforce.com) reviewing how employers are using job posting sites and evaluating their effectiveness.

> *"Monster.com and its job-board archrivals are fighting for resumes and listings. But all three face competition on another front, as corporate recruiters find that internal referrals, their own sites, and niche job boards are bringing them better candidates. Whether the frenzied fight for resumes and job listings by the big job boards means better-quality candidates for job openings is uncertain. Corporate recruiters complain that the big job boards flood the field with candidates, many of whom are inappropriate for the jobs they are advertising. As always, the name of the game in recruiting is finding the right candidate for the right job in the least expensive way in the shortest time possible. In most cases, that still means that most new hires come by word of mouth and employee referrals. 'Employee referrals are by far the most effective source of new hires in terms of return on dollar invested and quality of hire, especially if you track that 6 or 12 months out,' says Bertrand Dussert, Vice President of Global Services for Recruitmax, an applicant-tracking company that powers corporate career sites."*

Employers use the job posting sites, but they clearly prefer inside referrals. Chapter 9, "Write Effective Resumes, E-mail, and Cover Letters," helps you create a resume that will work well for electronic postings. Go ahead and put your information out there on the Web. Who knows, it might result in a good lead or two. But then use more active approaches to find out about jobs before they are advertised. I'll provide more information on using the Internet in your job search later in this chapter as well as throughout the book.

BUSINESS ETIQUETTE

Using First Names

When Henry Stanley met up with Dr. David Livingston in the African jungle, Stanley used a formal "Dr. Livingston, I presume." He did not say, "Is that you, David?" In most business situations, including interviews, first names are appropriate, but you should always follow the other person's lead. If you are addressed as a Mr. or Ms., be sure to respond likewise. Similarly, if you are addressed by your first name, you should feel free to do the same (unless it is the president, at which point Mr. President will do nicely).

Top 17 Internet Job Posting Sites

Here are the 17 "general" job posting Web sites with the highest number of visitors at the time I am writing this. You can get similar listings for college, specialized, foreign, and other jobs at www.topjobsites.com.

* www.monster.com
* www.careerbuilder.com
* www.hotjobs.com
* www.indeed.com
* www.jobing.com
* www.job.com
* www.vault.com
* www.simplyhired.com
* www.4jobs.com

* www.regionalhelpwanted.com
* www.jobster.com
* www.snagajob.com
* www.net-temps.com
* www.freelanceworkexchange.com
* www.jobs.com
* www.quintcareers.com (Quintessential Careers)
* www.employmentguide.com

WHAT WE KNOW ABOUT THE JOB MARKET

Before reviewing specific job search methods, consider the following important points about the job market and the job search.

At Any One Time, There Are Lots of Openings

There are about 150 million workers in the U.S. labor force. During the course of a year, there are about 30 million job openings. While no one knows how many jobs are available on any given day, the numbers are huge. And this number includes only formally open jobs. Employers without a formal opening may hire someone if they like the person and see a need for the person's skills. These potential openings are not counted anywhere.

There Is No Organized System for Finding Jobs or for Hiring People

Although millions of jobs are open today, the problem is that you don't know where they are. Yes, you can find some openings on the Internet, in want ads, through employment agencies, and via other sources. Still, if you put all these advertised sources together, they cover less than 35 percent or so of the jobs available. The fact is that there is no one place for finding out about all—or even most—job openings. This is an obvious problem for you, the job seeker.

SKILLS FOR SUCCESS

Teamwork

Luis is a hard worker and a driven employee who gets it right most of the time. The problem is that he thinks he's right *all* the time. When it comes time for group projects, he often takes the lead and sometimes takes over completely, refusing to listen to feedback and often alienating his co-workers as a result. The projects are completed, but they might have been done better or faster with more group involvement. What can Luis do to become a better team player?

Why Most Jobs Are Never Advertised

Most jobs are never advertised. Why not? Think about it and write three reasons here.

1. _____

2. _____

3. _____

Employers Don't Like to Advertise and Often Don't Need To

It would be nice if you could find out about all job openings from one source. Unfortunately, no such resource exists. One reason is that this is a free country, and employers can find their employees in any way they want. Employers don't advertise openings for many reasons. The most common ones are

* They don't like to.

* They often don't need to.

Why don't employers like to advertise job openings? When employers post an opening on the Internet or put an ad in the paper, they often get hundreds of responses, mostly from unqualified applicants. Screening and interviewing all these applicants takes time and can be very expensive. They also end up interviewing strangers, something few employers enjoy.

When unemployment is low, fewer people are available, and employers will use any method to find the people they need. This is most true for jobs that are hard to fill, such as entry-level, technical, and high-skills openings. Even in these situations, employers prefer to hire people recommended by someone they trust.

It makes sense that employers would rather hire people they know. This is why most jobs are filled before advertising is needed. The employer may know someone who seems to be right for the job. Or someone may hear about an opening through someone else and get an interview before the job is advertised.

The point to remember is that about 65 percent of all job openings are never advertised. These unadvertised jobs are often the best ones. Knowing how to find them can make a big difference to you.

What Employers Have Discovered About Finding Good Employees

Research suggests that hiring strangers is not the best way to find good employees. John Wanous, a researcher at The Ohio State University, analyzed data from 28 studies of 39,000 employees. He found that new hires are more likely to stay on a job if they are recruited through inside sources instead of ads and employment agencies. Long-term success increases by 25 percent or more when new employees are referred by former employees, current employees, or internal postings.

While most employers don't know about this research, they know that hiring strangers is not the best way to find good people. They have learned that interviews and background checks are not very reliable.

Smaller Employers Do Most of the Hiring

Most people don't realize that smaller businesses employ about three out of every four workers outside of government.

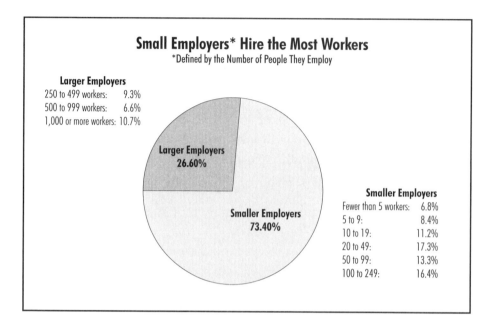

Small Employers* Hire the Most Workers
*Defined by the Number of People They Employ

Larger Employers
250 to 499 workers: 9.3%
500 to 999 workers: 6.6%
1,000 or more workers: 10.7%

**Larger Employers
26.60%**

**Smaller Employers
73.40%**

Smaller Employers
Fewer than 5 workers: 6.8%
5 to 9:   8.4%
10 to 19:   11.2%
20 to 49:   17.3%
50 to 99:   13.3%
100 to 249:   16.4%

At one time, large employers hired a much larger percentage of all workers. Even today, most job search approaches assume that you are interacting with a large employer. For example, online resume submission and application forms collect information to help large human resources departments review applicants more quickly. Many job search books are written by people who have experience in large corporations, and the authors recommend techniques from that point of view.

But things have changed, and most people now work for smaller employers. Many small employers don't even have human resources departments! What this means is that job seekers need different techniques to find openings in smaller organizations.

Small employers are even more important when you consider that they create most new jobs as well. The U.S. Small Business Administration found that very small employers—those with 20 or fewer workers—created about half of all new jobs. Small employers are simply too important to ignore in your job search.

The Clearer You Are About What You Want, the More Likely You Are to Find It

Job seekers often look for any job. They look through Web sites, want ads, and other sources and will apply for anything they think they might get. Instead, as I say in earlier chapters, I recommend that you be clear about the job you would most like to have. Then look for employers who are most likely to have that kind of work. Target your job search to these employers instead of all employers.

Most Job Seekers Don't Spend a Lot of Time Looking

Research has found that few unemployed people spend more than 15–20 hours per week looking for work. As a result, they get relatively few interviews and are unemployed longer than they need to be.

Looking for a job should be your full-time job when you are unemployed!

Looking for a job should be your full-time job when you are unemployed! It's a simple idea: The more time you spend looking, the more likely you are to get job offers, and the less time you will be unemployed.

Job Seekers Don't Spend Enough Time Using the Most Effective Methods

Looking for work is not easy, and using ineffective methods can quickly get discouraging. The reason is that using those methods too often puts you into fierce competition for advertised openings that anyone can find out about. More effective approaches often help you find jobs that are not advertised at all, where the chances of your getting an interview and job offer are much improved.

TAKE ADVANTAGE OF JOB MARKET "FRICTION"

A study done by the U.S. Department of Labor years ago found that many jobs are available at the same time that qualified applicants are looking for them. The problem is that the job seeker and the employer have not yet found each other.

This time between a job becoming open and being filled is responsible, the study found, for about 40 percent of total unemployment. The researchers called this inefficiency in the labor market *frictional unemployment*. What this means is that, today, an employer wants to hire someone with your skills. All you have to do is find that employer. That is where the five more effective job search methods I share in the sections that follow can help.

THE WORKING WORLD

Is Unemployment a Good Thing?

Generally, unemployment is not good for the person who doesn't have a job (unless, of course, that person doesn't want or need one). But a world without a certain amount of unemployment is not only impossible but unhealthy. Frictional unemployment represents people in between jobs—often those who are moving on to something better. This change is healthy for an economy. What isn't healthy are high rates of unemployment that come with recession or a weak economy (called *cyclical unemployment*), when the total number of job seekers far outnumbers the number of available jobs.

METHOD 1: FIND JOB OPENINGS BEFORE THEY ARE ADVERTISED

The job search, for most people, is a search for open positions. This seems obvious, and all conventional job search methods take that approach. The problem is that this results in your missing most of the best opportunities. Instead, I suggest that your job search should be a search for employers who need your skills, whether or not a job is open now.

> *Your job search should be a search for employers who need your skills, whether or not a job is open now.*

This is a *very* different approach to the job search. It allows you to talk to employers *before* a job is advertised and sometimes before it is even formally available. Of course, you can also look for openings that exist now and that may or may not be advertised. The fact is that jobs are always available, but getting them depends on the methods you use.

The Four Stages of a Job Opening

If you look just for advertised jobs, you will never know about the good jobs that are not advertised. Someone else will get them. But how do you find these openings if they're not advertised? You have to learn to find employers *before* they advertise the job you want.

Most jobs don't simply pop open; they are created over time. Carefully study the graphic on the next page. It shows how most jobs open up and become filled. Notice that about 50 percent of all jobs are filled by the third stage. That is why so few jobs are advertised—most are filled before they need to be.

All jobs open up in stages, creating opportunities for those who contact employers before a job is advertised. Your task in this chapter is to learn how to find job opportunities before they are advertised. Let's look at the four stages in more detail.

Stage 1: There Is No Opening Now

If you contact an employer at this stage and ask if there are any openings, the employer will say, "No." If you go about your job search in the traditional way, you would probably overlook this employer. Yet, should an opening come up in the future, this employer will first consider people he or she already knows. If you had gotten in to "interview" the employer during this stage, the company would already know you—a huge advantage. About 20–25 percent of all people get their jobs by becoming known to employers during this stage, *before* an opening exists.

Stage 2: No Formal Opening Exists, But Insiders Know a Job May Soon Be Available

As time goes on, someone inside an organization knows that a need exists for a new employee in the future. Perhaps business is picking up, or a new product or marketing plan is in the works. Maybe someone is getting ready to leave or will be fired. If you ask the boss if a job opening exists at this stage, you will probably be told "no" once again—unless you happen to ask the

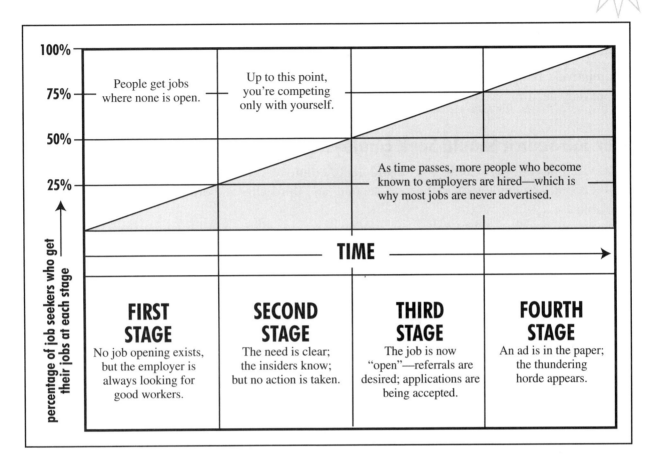

In the chart:

- **100%** / **75%** / **50%** / **25%** (y-axis labels)
- *percentage of job seekers who get their jobs at each stage* (y-axis title)

People get jobs where none is open.

Up to this point, you're competing only with yourself.

As time passes, more people who become known to employers are hired—which is why most jobs are never advertised.

TIME

FIRST STAGE	**SECOND STAGE**	**THIRD STAGE**	**FOURTH STAGE**
No job opening exists, but the employer is always looking for good workers.	The need is clear; the insiders know; but no action is taken.	The job is now "open"—referrals are desired; applications are being accepted.	An ad is in the paper; the thundering horde appears.

right person in that organization. And most job seekers will keep looking elsewhere, not seeing the job that was about to open up right before them.

About 50 percent of all jobs are filled by people who come to know an employer before the end of this stage, when no job is formally open but someone in the organization knows that a job is likely to become available soon.

Stage 3: A Formal Opening Exists, But It Has Not Yet Been Advertised

At some point, the boss says, "Yes, there is a job opening." Maybe someone suddenly resigned, or that big order just arrived. People who work for the company know about the opening, but it is often days or weeks before it is advertised. If you happen to ask if there is a job opening now, you will finally be told that, yes, there is. If you are fortunate to be at this place at this time (and with the right credentials), you will probably get an interview.

But the problem is that, for those who see the job search as a search for advertised openings, most jobs are filled before or at this stage. Those jobs never need to be advertised.

Stage 4: The Position Is Finally Advertised

If a job is not filled by insider referrals, by someone the boss knows, or by other informal means, it will finally be made known to the public. An employer might post the opening on the Internet or run an ad in the newspaper. A sign may be hung out front, the employment service notified, and people interviewed at job fairs. Because anyone looking for a job can now find out about this one, dozens or hundreds of people apply for it. That is why the competition for these relatively few advertised jobs is so fierce.

But relatively few jobs make it this far. All the others, including many of the best ones, are filled before they need to be advertised.

Your Job Search Should Seek Employers at All Stages of an Opening

To succeed in your job search, you should get to employers at all stages of an opening. This means contacting employers in the first, second, and third phases, before the position is publicly available.

Of course, you should also go after advertised openings—those in the fourth stage. But you must realize that most jobs will never be advertised. This is why the job search methods in this book can help you find better jobs, and they can help you find them in less time.

METHOD 2: NETWORK TO GET LEADS FROM PEOPLE YOU KNOW—YOUR WARM CONTACTS

You've probably heard of the sales method called "cold contacting." This is where someone contacts sales prospects they don't know in advance, one after another. They make their pitch and, every once in a while, they make a sale.

While this approach can be adapted to the job search, it is often much easier to contact people you already know and ask them for leads. Because these are not "cold contacts," I call them "warm contacts." If you use this technique properly, these people can be a *very* effective source of job leads.

Develop and Use Your Network of Contacts

A *network* is an informal group of people who have something in common. As a job seeker, your network is made up of all the people who can help you—and the people they know. Networking is the process you use in contacting these people. You may be surprised at how many people you can meet this way. Let's look at how networking works.

Start with the People You Know

Your friends and relatives are the people who are most willing to help you find a job. They can also provide valuable leads to the people they know. To see how networking can work for you, begin by writing the names of three friends or relatives on the following lines.

1. _____

2. _____

3. _____

Networking Can Result in Thousands of Contacts

Now take the first person on the list as an example. If you ask that person for the names of two people he or she knows who might help you in your job search, you will have two new contacts.

Continue the process, and your network will look like the following figure.

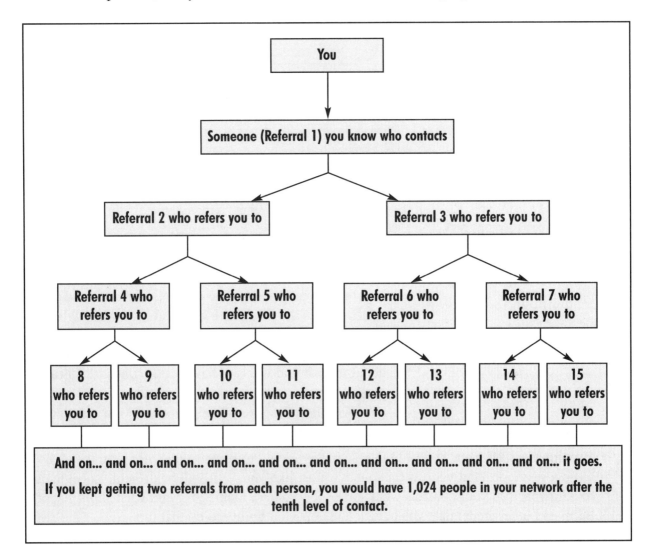

The number of people you could contact this way is amazing. For example, if you kept getting two referrals from each person, you would have 1,024 people in your network after the tenth level of contact. And that is starting with only one person!

You can network using e-mail, the phone, or face-to-face contact. Networking is a simple idea, and it works. It helps you meet potential employers you would not find through any other method. These potential employers are a friend of a friend of a friend. And they will be willing to see you for this reason.

Effective Networking Requires Clear Goals

Networking is a very effective job search method. If you do it well, it will help you contact many potential employers. To be effective, your networking must begin with clear goals. Think in advance what you want to accomplish when you contact someone in your network. Write your networking goals here.

_____

_____

_____

_____

Set Three Important Networking Goals

Following are three goals that experience shows are important to keep in mind for each networking contact.

> _It is possible to begin net-_
> _working with anyone who_
> _knows people and is willing_
> _to talk to you. But people_
> _who know and like you are_
> _often the best ones to use as_
> _your first contacts._

* **Select good contacts:** It is possible to begin networking with anyone who knows people and is willing to talk to you. But people who know and like you are often the best ones to use as your first contacts. Select friends and relatives who are likely to have good contacts or who know something about the type of work you want. The people they refer you to are likely to know even more about the job you want, or have better contacts. As each person in your network refers you to others, your contacts will more and more likely be those who hire people with your skills or those who know someone who does.

* **Present yourself well:** You need to convince your warm contacts that you have the skills to do a good job. And your warm contacts must like you, or it will be difficult to get them to help you. Tell your contacts what sort of job you are looking for and what skills, experience, and other credentials you have to support your ability to do that job.

* **Get two referrals:** Sometimes warm contacts know of an opening for someone with your interests, but more often they will not. Whatever the situation, your objective is to get the names and contact information of two people who could help you in your search.

Ask These Three Essential Questions to Get Good Referrals

To expand your network, it is important that you get names of other people to contact from each person in your network. Based on many years of experience, the three questions that follow are most likely to get you good referrals. Ask one question after another until you get the names of two more people to contact.

Three Essential Questions to Get Referrals

1. **Do you know of anyone who might have a job opening in my field? If no, then ask...**
2. **Do you know of anyone who might know of someone who would? If still no, then ask...**
3. **Do you know someone who knows lots of people?**

Most job seekers don't use their warm contacts in an organized way, but even then, these contacts still end up being one of the most effective sources of job leads. If you approach your warm contacts using the techniques I suggest, most will be very willing to help you. So ask the three questions throughout your job search. If you follow up on these leads carefully, this one technique may be the only one you need!

Networking Worksheet—Groups of People You Know

You already know many people who can help you. To identify them, think about the groups of people who have something in common with you. Following are some of the groups most often listed by other job seekers.

Look over my list of groups, and put a check mark to the left of each group you are in. Use the listed groups for ideas, and then add other groups that you are in. Be specific. For example, write "people in my aerobics class" or "members of the Association of Collectible Jelly Jars." Finally, when you finish your list, go back and write in the number of people who might be in each group.

✔	You Are in This Group	Number in Group	Your Other Groups	Number in Group
❑	Friends	_____	_____	_____
❑	Relatives	_____	_____	_____
❑	Friends of parents	_____	_____	_____
❑	Former co-workers	_____	_____	_____
❑	Members of my church or religious group	_____	_____	_____
❑	People who sell me things (store clerks, insurance agent, real estate agent, and so on)	_____	_____	_____
❑	Neighbors	_____	_____	_____
❑	People I went to school with	_____	_____	_____
❑	Former teachers	_____	_____	_____
❑	Members of social clubs or groups	_____	_____	_____

(continued)

(continued)

✔	You Are in This Group	Number in Group	Your Other Groups	Number in Group
☐	People who provide me with services (hair stylist, counselor, mechanic, and so on)	_____	_____	_____
☐	Former employers	_____	_____	_____
☐	Members of sports or hobby groups	_____	_____	_____
☐	Members of a professional organization I belong to (or could quickly join)	_____	_____	_____

List the People to Contact in Each Group

Most people never guess they have as many potential warm contacts as they do. The previous worksheet can help you identify many people you might overlook. You may not know some of these people well or at all, but you have something in common with them. Contacting them takes some courage, but you will find that most people are willing to help if you ask them to in a nice way.

You can use each group on the previous worksheet to create a list of names for your network. And these people can give you the names of others to contact. Following is a sample worksheet for just one of the groups on your list. Go ahead and complete it now. Later, you can do a similar list for each group you listed.

Networking Worksheet—Friends List

How many friends do you have? Don't limit yourself to close friends. Include anyone who is friendly to you. Think hard, and guess how many friends' names you might be able to list.

Write the number here _____

Now list all the names of friends you can think of. You can use additional sheets later if you need more space. You also can add phone numbers and e-mail addresses later.

Name	Phone Number and E-mail Address
_____	_____
_____	_____
_____	_____
_____	_____
_____	_____

Networking with Your Warm Contacts May Be the Only Approach You Need

Networking allows you to begin with people you know. They, in turn, will lead you to others you did not know previously. As each person refers you to others, you are more and more likely to get the names of people who are employers. You will quickly find that some of your referrals will supervise people with skills similar to yours, or they will give you names of others who do.

If you create lists for each group on your "Networking Worksheet—Groups of People You Know" list, you could end up with hundreds of names. Each person knows other people who will refer you to still others. If you keep at it, you will eventually meet someone who needs a worker with your skills, and that contact might very well lead to a job offer. Networking that begins with your warm contacts may be the only job search method you need. It is an effective technique for finding unadvertised jobs.

METHOD 3: MAKE DIRECT CONTACTS WITH EMPLOYERS— YOUR COLD CONTACTS

While it is less comfortable to do, it can be effective to directly contact potential employers you don't know and have not been referred to. Called *cold contacting*, this approach usually involves calling an employer on the phone without a referral or dropping in without an appointment. Both methods are covered here, along with tips to adapt these approaches for use on the Internet.

Develop a Prospects List of Potential Employers to Contact

I suggested in Chapter 5, "Consider Important Preferences in Your Career Planning," that it is best to target your job search to a specific geographic area. Even if you are willing to relocate, it will help you to know in advance what sort of place you'd like to live. One of the negatives of posting your information on Internet job search sites is that you may be contacted by employers from anywhere. While this can create an opportunity to consider, a similar job is probably available where you would rather be.

So let's assume, for the purpose of this chapter, that you know the area or areas where you would prefer to work. Your task then becomes to create a list of employers you can cold contact in that area. In any community, the best free listing of employers who need someone with your skills is an Internet or paper version of the yellow pages.

A variety of free Web-based yellow pages directories is available. I like MSN's service at www.yellowpages.msn.com because it allows you to browse by category and subcategory, whereas some others require you to know in advance the category name. This site also provides the related Web address, phone number, address, and other information of potential employers.

The printed yellow pages book is also helpful, particularly for its category listings, but it does not provide Web site addresses or other information. If you are looking in multiple locations, Web sources allow you to find information for anywhere, which is a big plus if you want to relocate.

Whatever source you use, the yellow page resources allow you to quickly create large lists of employers you can cold contact. You can use these sources to identify and contact 10–20 employers in one hour via phone or e-mail.

Many people, using the phone and the right techniques, have been able to set up one or more interviews per hour! Cold contacting people via e-mail typically takes longer but can also be effective if used in combination with follow-up phone calls.

You might be surprised at how many types of organizations could be job sources for you. Yellow page sources list virtually all small and large private employers in an area, including government and not-for-profit employers.

The Four-Step Process for Using the Yellow Pages

Here is the four-step process for using the yellow pages to find potential employers:

1. **Find the index:** The printed yellow pages book has an index in the front that lists organizations in general groupings, arranged in alphabetical order. Some online yellow pages also provide this, but others do not. For this reason, I suggest that you use your local printed yellow pages book as a convenient listing of organizations by type. If you use a Web source, you can then know what groupings to enter in this search field.

2. **Select likely targets:** Go through the printed yellow pages index and, for each entry, ask yourself this question:

   Could this type of organization use a person with my skills?

   If the answer is yes or maybe, put a check mark by that type of organization.

3. **Prioritize those targets:** For the types of organizations that you checked, go back and put a number next to each type based on how interesting it sounds to you. Use the following scale:

   1 = Sounds very interesting

   2 = Not sure if interested

   3 = Does not sound interesting at all

4. **Contact specific organizations:** Once you have identified target groups, you can turn to the section of the yellow pages where those organizations are listed, or you can look them up online. Use the phone numbers provided to call directly and ask for an interview. If the online yellow pages provides a Web site address, try to find an e-mail address for the person most likely to hire you, and send that person an e-mail.

I include part of a real page from a yellow pages index in this section to show you how this process works. The person using it is looking for a job as an electrical engineer. The check marks are for those types of organizations that might need these skills, and the numbers refer to the job seeker's interest level.

E

Ear Piercing———————461	Electric Heating Elements———469	✓Elevators Install, Maintenance &	Engravers Metal, Plastic, Wood,
Early Childhood Intervention Servs	Electric Heating Equip &	Repair————————③—470	Etc.————————————481
See	Systems————————469	Emblems & Insignia————470	Engravers Stationery————481
Health Agencies————590	Electric Motor Controls Whsle &	Embossing————————470	Engrossers See Calligraphy Servs—280
Physical Therapists——869-871	Mfrs————————————469	Embossing Equip & Supplies—470	Entertainer Family & Business—481
Social Serv & Welfare	Electric Motors————————469	Embroidery——————470,471	Entertainment Adult———481,482
Organizations————1101,1102	Electric Motors Serv & Repair—469	Embroidery Equip & Supplies—471	Entertainment Agencies &
Speech & Language Pathologists—1104	Electric Motors Used————469	Emission Testing Serv & Repair See	Bureaus————————————482
Tutoring————————1194,1195	Electric Motors Whsle, Distrs &	Auto Diagnostic Serv————183	Envelopes————————————482
Eating Disorders Information &	Mfrs————————————469	Auto Repair & Serv———201-217	Environmental, Conservation &
Treatment Centers——461,462	Electric Poles Installed See Electric	Auto & Truck Inspection Serv——219	Ecological Organizat————482
Ecological Organizations See	Contractors——————462-469	Service Station Gasoline &	Environmental & Ecological
Environmental, Conservation &	Electrical Discharge Machines &	Oil————————1080,1081	Consultants—————————482
Ecological Organizat————482	Supplies————————469	Employee Assistance Programs—471	Environmental & Ecological Equip &
Environmental & Ecological Equip &	✓Electrical Power Systems	Employee Benefit Consulting	Servs—————————————482
Servs—————————————482	Maintenance————②—469	Servs——————————471	Environmental Testing Equip See
Economic Development Authorities,	Electrical Surge Suppressor See	Employee Benefits & Compensation	Air Pollution Control—————20
Commissions, Cou————462	Electric Contractors————462-469	Plans—————————————471	Vacuum Equip & Systems———1199
Economic Research & Analysis—462	Electricians See Electric	Employment Agencies———471-475	Epoxy Flooring See
Editorial & Publication Servs—462	Contractors——————462-469	Employment Contractors Temporary	Floor Materials Retail———506,507
Educational Consultants————462	Electrologists————————470	Help—————————475,476	Floor Materials Whsle & Mfrs—507
Educational Research————462	Electrolysis See Electrologists——470	Employment Opportunities———476	Floors Industrial————————507
Educational Servs————————462	Electronic Equip & Supplies	Employment Screening Servs——476	Terrazzo———————————1150
Eggs————————————————462	Dealers————————470	Employment Servs Employee	Erecting Contractors See
Elderly Care Product & Services-462	Electronic Equip & Supplies Serv &	Leasing——————————476	Machinery Movers & Erectors——751
Electric Appliances See	Repair————————470	Employment Servs Non Profit——476	Riggers—————————————1018
Appliance Major-Repair & Serv——34	Electronic Equip & Supplies Whsle &	Employment Training———476,477	Steel Erectors————————1108
Appliances Major Dealers————41	Mfrs————————————470	Encyclopedias———————477	Erosion Control————————483
Appliances Major Used————42	Electronic Instruments———③—470	Energy Mgmt & Conservation	Errand Servs See
Appliances Small Dealers————42	Electronic Stores————————470	Consultants————————477	Delivery Serv—————381,382
Electric Companies————————462	Electronic Tax Filing See	✓Engineering Equip & Supplies ②—477	Messenger Serv—————————771
Electric Contractors———462-469	Accountants Certified Public————3-5	Engineering Reports————477	Personal Servs & Assistants———844
Electric Equip Serv & Repair—469	Tax Return Preparation———1135,1136	✓Engineers-Professional———①—477	Escorts-Personal—————483,484
Electric Equip & Supplies Retail—469	Electronic Test Equip & Supplies 470	Engineers-Professional Guide——479	Escrow Serv————————————484
✓Electric Equip & Supplies Whsle &	✓Electronics Consulting & Research	Engines Diesel————————480	Estate Appraisers See Appraisers—43
Mfrs————————————469	Development——————②—470	Engines Gas & Gasoline————480	Estate Consultants See
③	Elevator Consultants &	Engines Rebuilding &	Attorneys—————————52-108
Electric Heating Contractors See	Inspectors————————470	Exchanging—————480,481	Estate Sales————————————484
Electric Contractors————462-469	Elevators & Escalators————470	Engines Supplies, Equip & Parts-481	
Heating Contractors———597-610			

As you can see, this is a good process for identifying opportunities you might otherwise overlook—and this is only one page from the index!

Yellow Pages Prospects Worksheet

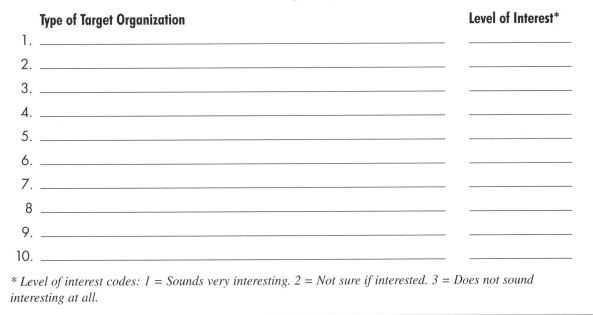

Use your local yellow pages index to identify at least 10 types of organizations you might contact. Then use this worksheet to write them down, along with your interest level number for each*.

Type of Target Organization   **Level of Interest***

1. _____   _____

2. _____   _____

3. _____   _____

4. _____   _____

5. _____   _____

6. _____   _____

7. _____   _____

8 _____   _____

9. _____   _____

10. _____   _____

Level of interest codes: 1 = Sounds very interesting. 2 = Not sure if interested. 3 = Does not sound interesting at all.

You now have a list of types of organizations that you can contact. All you need to do is use the print or online yellow pages sources to find specific names of organizations and their contact information. You can then call these places and ask to speak with the person in charge of the department or function that interests you. If you can get their Web site address, you can find out more about the organization there and see if it provides e-mail addresses of staff. If it does, try to identify the best person to contact and ask for an interview. If staff e-mail addresses are not provided, you can simply e-mail the Webmaster and ask for this, or even call and ask.

Although this process sounds easy, making effective cold contacts takes practice. You will learn much more about how to make effective phone calls and cold contacts in Chapter 10, "Use JIST Cards® to Get Interviews."

Drop In on Employers Without an Appointment

If you are creative, there are many opportunities to make direct contacts with employers during your job search. For example, on your way home from an interview, look for other places that might use someone with your skills, and then stop in and ask to see the person in charge. In smaller organizations, this will usually be the manager or owner. In larger organizations, ask for the person in charge of the department where you are most likely to work.

Many times, you can speak with the person in charge without an appointment. If so, tell the person you are looking for a position and would like to speak briefly about your qualifications. If you're told the company has no openings, say you would still like to talk about the possibility of future openings. If the boss seems busy, it is often best to set up a time when you can come back. Get his or her business card or name, and set a day and time for your appointment.

While this approach takes courage, it often works. If you make a good impression, you are likely to be considered for a future job—before it is advertised!

TIP: Nothing works all the time. Sometimes dropping in without an appointment will get you an interview. At other times, you will have to be more creative to overcome an initial rejection. For example, if the person you want to speak to is not in, ask if someone else can help you. Make friends with that person, and ask him or her to tell the boss you will follow up by phone or e-mail. Leave a JIST Card (see Chapter 10) for the boss and your new contact. Then contact the boss later and ask for an interview. Your new contact, if he or she likes you, will probably put in a good word for you. Be creative! Learn to follow up, and don't take an initial "no" as a final answer.

METHOD 4: USE THE INTERNET TO SUPPORT YOUR JOB SEARCH

I said earlier in this chapter that posting your resume or other information on job posting sites like Monster.com was unlikely to work well for you. However, I did suggest you do this anyway and then use other job search methods to actively develop job leads.

While I do warn you not to depend too heavily on getting employer responses from job posting sites, I *do* encourage you to use the Web throughout your job search. Following are some ways you can use the Web as an important tool to support your job search:

✳ **Use online directories for employer prospects:** I've already shown you how you can use online and print yellow pages resources to identify employers that you can cold contact. You can use online yellow page resources to get the Web site addresses of employers you learn about through networking. Some organization Web sites provide lists of staff and their e-mail addresses or direct phone numbers, allowing you to discover a specific person to contact and ask for an interview.

✳ **Research potential employers:** Check out an employer's Web site, if there is one, to get information on what that company does. You can also google a company to get additional information. This can be useful to help prepare for an interview.

✳ **Interact via e-mail before the interview:** E-mail is a time-efficient way for employers to get information. So make your initial contact by phone or e-mail, and then follow up with additional e-mail that includes your resume or other information you want them to know.

✳ **Say thank you after the interview:** You should always say thank you immediately following an interview. Sending an e-mail to do this is fine, but sending an e-mail and a mailed note, with a JIST Card enclosed, is better. For more information on thank-you notes, see Chapter 11, "The Seven Phases of an Interview—and How to Succeed in Each."

✳ **Find directions to interview locations:** It is essential that you arrive a bit early for an interview. Use www.mapquest.com or another mapping system to find specific directions to get there.

✳ **Access targeted sites for networking and uncovering job leads:** Many Web sites provide a community of people with similar skills or interests to your own. For example, try to find the sites of professional organizations that are related to the job you want. See if they have resources allowing you to post a message saying that you are looking for related work or that allows chat resources where others can provide advice. The point here is to be active, not passive, in using the Web to develop networking opportunities and to actively develop job leads.

The Internet is an important tool that you can use throughout your job search in a variety of ways. But keep in mind that it is a communication tool, not a job search method itself. Use it in sensible ways to support your active search for unadvertised job opportunities.

Four Tips for Using the Internet

Following are some other Web-related things you should do to use the Internet to support your job search:

✳ **Clean up your blogs and personal information that may be on the Web somewhere:** Have you written a journal, blog, or other personal things on the Web? If so, make sure you modify them to be acceptable if an employer finds that information.

A survey by collegegrad.com of online job seekers advised job seekers to beware of the image they project. "... job seekers should avoid anything that might cause a recruiter to say 'Yikes!' when they found you on the Web. Like it or not, MySpace and Facebook are public sites. Instead of posting information and photos from that all-night party, job seekers can stand out from the crowd by using these sites as an opportunity to generate a positive first impression. If you wouldn't put it in your resume, don't put it on the Web."

One question the survey asked was "Have you changed your content at MySpace or Facebook because of your job search?" Of those surveyed, roughly 40 percent said no, 25 percent said yes, 9 percent said no but that they planned to, and 25 percent said they did not use either MySpace or Facebook.

* **Check your e-mail often:** You may prefer to use instant messaging more than e-mail, but many employers will contact you via e-mail, so check your e-mail daily, and respond quickly to any employer messages.

* **Use more formal writing in your e-mail, and make sure it contains good grammar and correct spelling:** Text messages and e-mail are often informal, but using a casual writing style will not likely create a positive impression with employers. Write your e-mail carefully, and check for correct spelling, grammar, and other details before sending it to an employer.

* **Use instant messaging only if the employer interacts with you in this way:** Do not assume that an employer wants your instant messages, because many will see this as inappropriate from someone they don't know well. Instead, rely on e-mail unless the employer contacts you via instant messaging.

METHOD 5: SEND THANK-YOU NOTES, AND FOLLOW UP

Following up is an important part of the job search. Send a thank-you e-mail or note after you talk with an employer or anyone in your network. Mention that you will contact him or her again at a certain date and time to answer any other questions. Stay in touch in a friendly, polite way with everyone on your network list. Following up and thanking people who help you is good manners. It is also likely to help you in your job search.

> *Following up and thanking people who help you is good manners. It is also likely to help you in your job search.*

More Than Just Courtesy

Writing a thank-you letter after an interview doesn't just showcase a candidate's manners—it can also make or break someone's chances of landing a job. Nearly 15 percent of hiring managers say they would not hire someone who failed to send a thank-you letter after the interview. Thirty-two percent say they would still consider the candidate but would think less of him or her, according to the CareerBuilder.com "How to Get in the Front Door" survey.

YOU HAVE ALREADY LEARNED A LOT!

I hope this chapter has given you some ideas on using more effective methods in your job search. Other chapters will provide additional details on things like using e-mail, phone contacts, resumes, thank-you notes, and other topics. The chapter that follows will cover a variety of other job search techniques, with tips to make them more effective.

CASE STUDY: NETWORKING EARLY PAYS OFF

When Asha was 16, she asked her friend's father if his company—one of the world's leading building developers—was hiring summer help. He helped her get a position doing photocopying and filing in the architecture department—a job she kept every summer throughout high school. While earning an undergraduate and then a master's degree in architecture, Asha continued to intern in the summers with the same company. When she graduated, the company offered her a job.

Now, 13 years after starting out as a filing clerk, Asha is the lead architect and is still grateful for that first opportunity. She says that in the job market, it is often "who you know" that matters most, adding, "It doesn't hurt to get started early, making contacts and finding summer jobs or internships with the kinds of companies you might like to work for in the future." Asha sees herself sticking with this same company to retirement—an unusual circumstance in today's job market.

Increase the Effectiveness of Passive and Alternative Job Search Methods

In the previous chapter, I said that any job search method would work for some people some of the time. I also said that the most effective approach is to use a variety of methods. I covered the most effective job search approaches in the previous chapter, but in this one, I review how to get better results from other methods. I also cover some alternative job search methods you may not have considered.

GET THE MOST OUT OF LESS EFFECTIVE JOB SEARCH METHODS

Keep in mind that the more effective job search methods tend to be active rather than passive. For example, posting your resume online or filling out an application is passive, because it requires the employer to contact you back. More active approaches include contacting the employer directly and asking for an interview. You can do this by walking in and asking for the manager, using the phone and asking for an appointment, or sending an e-mail requesting an interview.

> *Ability is what you're capable of doing. Motivation determines what you do. Attitude determines how well you do it.*
>
> *Lou Holtz*

Passive job search methods may result in an employer not contacting you at all. Think about it. If you fill out an application and leave, you may never hear from that employer. But if you drop in and ask to talk to the person who does the hiring, you are more likely to get an interview right then.

Whatever job search methods you use, your objective is to get an interview. Be creative, and look for ways to make any method work better in getting you directly to the person who is most likely to hire or supervise someone with your skills.

THE MOST FREQUENTLY USED PASSIVE METHODS

Don't allow yourself to be passive in your search for a job. Even with passive job search methods, however, there are things you can do to increase your chances. Here are some of the more frequently used passive methods, along with tips to increase their effectiveness.

Employment Agencies

Private employment agencies are businesses that charge a fee either to you or to the employer who hires you. You often see their ads in the help wanted section of the newspaper and yellow pages. Fees can be from less than one month's pay to 15 percent or more of your annual salary.

Be careful about using fee-based employment agencies. Recent research indicates that more people use and benefit from fee-based agencies than in the past. But you need to realize that relatively few people who register with private agencies get a job through them.

Eight Tips for Using Employment Agencies

When should you use an agency and when shouldn't you? The following tips may be helpful in deciding:

* **If your skills are in demand and you have a clear job objective, an agency is more likely to help you:** For example, an experienced accountant, medical technician, or carpenter is more likely to get good results than a teacher wanting to change careers or a new graduate.

* **Request employer-paid job leads:** Ask the agency for job leads where the employer pays the fee. Unless the employer pays the fee, using a for-profit employment agency can be expensive and is not a good idea for most people.

* **Save money by doing your own job search:** Many agency workers find their clients jobs the same way you can—by calling employers. Agencies get at least some of their postings by calling employers and asking if they have any job openings. You can do the same thing yourself, so consider doing the work and saving a bundle.

* **Do not accept a job you do not want:** Some agencies will pressure you to accept any job they can talk you into so they can collect their fee. If you feel pressured to take a job, say that you want to think about it overnight, and then decide whether you want it.

* **Be wary of want ads placed by agencies:** The agencies advertise an enticing position in the newspaper. Then you find out that the advertised position is not available, and the agency may refer you to a less desirable job.

* **Check out the agency's Web site:** Most private employment agencies have Web sites. Many of the larger ones have Web sites that help you understand what they do, list their fee structures, and even offer available openings. Online yellow pages listings may include their Web site address.

Avoid Employment Agency Rip-Offs

While most employment agencies provide valid services, the industry does have some dishonest operations. Here is how you can avoid being ripped off:

* Do not pay fees up front, avoid hard-sell tactics, and disregard promises that the agency can get you a job.

* *Never* sign an agreement if you are pressured to do so. If the agency won't let you take the agreement home to study, just get up and walk out. An agreement should allow you to find jobs on your own without payment to the agency, and it should include service guarantees and refunds if you're not satisfied.

* Before you sign, check out the agency with the local Better Business Bureau or online sites like www.ripoffreport.com and scamwatch.com. More reputable firms belong to the International Association of Career Consulting Firms at www.iaccf.com.

---

* **Continue looking for a job:** If you decide to use a private agency, continue to look for jobs on your own. A legitimate agency should not require you to pay a fee for a job that you find yourself or limit your job search in any way. Look for an agency that specializes in the types of jobs you want. If you decide to use their services, continue to actively look for other openings at the same time.

* **Not all employment agencies are interested in helping the unemployed:** Executive search firms and headhunters are specialized agencies paid by employers to find already-employed people with excellent work histories. With few exceptions, they are not interested in unemployed people who are looking for jobs.

Government "Career One-Stop" Centers

Every state is required to process unemployment compensation claims and provide free employment assistance. I mentioned these centers in the previous chapter, suggesting that you should register with them at the beginning of your job search. Here are some additional details.

While services vary from site to site, many of these centers provide a wide range of services. Services can include career resources, access to computers and copy machines, career interest and skills testing, job search and job-readiness workshops, youth services, help with finding child care and other community services, GED and English proficiency assistance, training and education funding, help with resume preparation and Web posting, and many other things. These centers also list job openings from local employers and provide computer access to job listings placed anywhere in the country. And all their services are free!

There are about 2,000 comprehensive plus another 1,500 "affiliate" One-Stop programs nationwide. Because services can vary enormously by location, it is important to find out what your local center does and then use whatever services you can. You can locate the nearest centers these ways:

* **Online:** Log in to www.careeronestop.org and look for "Service Locator." Enter your zip code, and it will bring up the centers that serve your area. From there, you can find the services they provide, hours of operation, phone number, driving directions, and a map.

Other Programs from the Federal Government

You can find out about various programs provided by the federal employment service at www.doleta.gov/uses/. The site explains the programs and provides links to other useful sites.

* **White pages:** Most phone book white pages have a blue section listing government offices. Look up the state government listings. The name of the agency that operates the Career One-Stop programs varies from state to state, so the correct agency may not be easy to find if you don't know what it is called. If you have trouble finding it, call the state's information center and explain what you are looking for. (The state information center is usually listed at the beginning of the state government listings.)

After you find the program, plan to check out the services in person at the beginning of your job search. You may also be eligible for programs that help people with disabilities, veterans, laid-off workers, youth, older workers, women, the economically disadvantaged, and other groups.

Newspaper Help Wanted Ads

Most help wanted ads that appear in the newspaper are also now listed online. The larger newspapers jointly operate one of the major job posting Web sites, www.careerbuilder.com, and smaller newspapers use this or other sites to post their help wanted ads online.

Careerbuilder.com is not a good thing for you as a job seeker. It used to be that only about 15 percent of all people got their jobs through newspaper help wanted ads. This means that 85 percent found their jobs using other methods. Everyone who read the paper could find out about these openings, so competition for advertised jobs was fierce.

Because help wanted ads are now often on the Web, too, even more people can find out about them, making the competition for these jobs even greater. Still, some people do get jobs this way, so go ahead and apply for help wanted ads in the newspapers. Just be sure to spend most of your time using methods that are more effective.

Six Tips for Using Help Wanted Ads

Here are some tips to increase your effectiveness using this source of job leads:

* **Read help wanted ads on a regular basis:** The Sunday and Wednesday editions usually have the most ads. Look at every ad, because jobs of interest may not be listed in an obvious way. For example, an accounting job could be listed under "bookkeeper," "accountant," "controller," or some other heading.

* **Read the ads online:** If your newspaper lists its want ads online, it will probably tell you what Web site it uses. You may be able to get new ads there before they hit the print edition, and you can probably sort the ads for key words, date posted, and other criteria.

* **Respond to any ad that sounds interesting, even if you do not meet one or more of its requirements:** Employers sometimes list skills, educational requirements, or other credentials they do not require to screen out candidates. For example, they may say "college degree required" but end up hiring someone with good experience but no degree.

* **Try to contact the employer directly:** Instead of sending a resume like the ad requests, call and ask for the person who supervises the position you want. Then ask for an appointment to discuss the position. The ad may include the company name or Web site, and you can use either to get more information on the organization and perhaps contact the hiring authority directly via e-mail. These more direct approaches sometimes work and can reduce your chances of being screened out.

* **Look at old want ads:** Employers that are advertising for one job often have openings for others they have not yet advertised. Jobs advertised in the past may still be open or be filled by someone who is not working out, and you could be the only candidate at this point!

* **Read want ads and online ads during the evenings and weekends:** Save weekdays for making direct contacts with employers.

Posting Resumes or Seeking Job Leads on Job Posting Sites

I covered this topic some in the previous chapter, but here is some additional information and tips. The major national Web sites, such as www.monster.com and www.careerbuilder.com, have millions of jobs posted and hundreds of thousands to millions of resumes in their systems. This sounds *very* appealing to most job seekers, because it makes it seem that all you have to do is post your information on these sites, and employers will contact you.

I wish it were that easy. Every once in a while, these systems do link up an employer with the ideal candidate, and a job offer ends up being made. Unfortunately, this is the exception, most likely to occur with someone who has hard-to-find technical skills, experience, or other credentials. For the rest of us, it is simply a waste of time. The list on the next page offers some additional information that can help you decide whether to use a job posting site.

BUSINESS ETIQUETTE

E-mail Etiquette Is Economical

E-mail is an integral part of our economy. As such, it is a good idea to follow a few simple rules before you click the Send button:

* Type a specific and informative subject line to avoid your message being filtered.
* Although e-mail is often informal, begin with a greeting that uses the person's name.
* Use proper English. Don't use abbreviations or acronyms that you might use in your personal e-mail.
* Be sure to check the grammar and spelling. Many e-mail programs have a spell-check feature.
* Keep your message short and to the point.

---

* **Most Web sites limit access unless you register:** Most job posting sites require you to register with them and use a password to access more of the site's features. They will allow you to review job postings without registering but won't let you submit your resume, for example. Careerbuilder.com allows you to search job openings by industry or job type and then limit the search to openings in your zip code area. Once you find a job that looks interesting, it also allows you to click the employer's Web site to learn more about the company and see any other listed jobs. But you can't apply for one of these jobs through the Web site *unless* you register, give your name and e-mail address, and provide other information. This is the typical approach used by job posting sites.

* **Most sites have their own resume submission requirements:** Monster.com, for example, wants you to register and then fill in a series of fields for your name, address, education, and other fields. Doing this ends up submitting a resume (which they also allow), but in a format that allows registered employers to search their database of job seekers more efficiently. Most job posting sites will accept your resume in electronic format or allow you to cut and paste sections of your resume into their fields, but they prefer that you enter your information using their procedures.

* **There are some legitimate fee-based online services for job seekers:** While many are rip-offs, there are some legitimate services available online for a fee. For example, www.resumerabbit.com will post your resume on more than 70 job posting sites for a fee. Or you can buy personal help in writing your resume from members of the Professional Association of Resume Writers at www.parw.com or the National Resume Writers' Association at www.nrwa.com. And there are many others. While the services mentioned here are legitimate and can be well worth their fees, be careful about any online services you use.

I know you may want to post your resume on Web sites, so the following section offers information that can increase your chances of finding a good job.

Seven Tips for Using Internet Job Posting Sites

The following tips can be helpful if you plan to post your resume on the Web:

* **Modify your resume for better online results:** Many sites allow employers to search their resume database based on key words, level of education, location, and other criteria. What this means is that if you have a skill or credential that an employer is searching for but did not list it on your resume, yours will not be selected. Resumes searched by employers online are different from those you mail, so make sure you include things in your electronic resume that an employer might use in an automated search. I cover electronic resumes in more detail in Chapter 9, "Write Effective Resumes, E-mail, and Cover Letters."

* **Do not pay to post your information on a site:** If you spend enough time looking for job openings on the Web, you will probably come across some sites that charge you for posting your resume or for other services. While there are some legitimate fee-based online services for job seekers, you should *not* pay for posting your resume on a site. All the major job posting sites will accept your resume free, because employers are the ones who pay for posting their job openings.

❋ **Keep in mind that most employers who are using online job posting sites will look for ways to eliminate as many candidates as possible:** Why? Because the numbers of online candidates have become so huge that employers want to screen out all but the ones with the "best" credentials. That's one reason not to hold your breath too long after posting your resume online.

❋ **Get to the employer's site:** If you do find an interesting job on a national job posting site—and it lists the name of the employer—apply for it at the job posting site, and then apply for that same job through the employer's site. You can often find the employer's site by searching for its name on your browser, on www.google.com, or on a similar site. The employer's site often provides details missing from the job posting site, such as pay, benefits, working conditions, company philosophy, and staff e-mail addresses. The employer's site may even allow interaction with current employees via e-mail.

❋ **Seek out smaller and more specialized job sites:** You may have better results by posting your resume on smaller sites that specialize in your interest areas. Many professional associations and user groups, for example, allow members to post their resumes on their sites. So ask around and see if anyone can give you good sources of smaller and more specialized sites where you can post your resume.

❋ **Make sure that your e-mail messages are professional and error-free:** Be formal, and use correct language in the e-mail message you send to an employer that lists a job on the Internet. Errors in spelling and grammar will hurt you, so be careful about what you say and how you say it.

❋ **Be cautious about what you put online:** After you put your information online, you lose control of who has it. You may be contacted by scam artists trying to get your Social Security number, bank account number, or passwords; offering you a bogus job; or attempting to get more personal details so they can steal your identity. So please be careful what you put in your resume and how you respond to those who contact you.

Also, know that your resume may be floating around in cyberspace for months or even years after you find a job. This is even more true if you submit it to multiple sites. Some sites even use Web crawlers to gather resumes from other sites and then post them on sites you know nothing about. That's a problem, and there's no easy way to correct it. Just be careful in what you do and how you do it.

SKILLS FOR SUCCESS

Attitude

Mitch was hired only three months ago and seemed to have all the right qualifications: He was well educated and had a solid work history. Since he has started working, though, Mitch has been less than eager to take on new projects and hasn't come up with any new ideas on his own. He is often heard complaining about the job to co-workers or on the phone, and his dreary attitude is having a negative impact on company morale. If you were Mitch's boss, what would you say to him?

Interacting with Personnel and Human Resources Departments

There are several things to remember when dealing with human resources (HR) departments:

* **Only larger organizations have HR departments:** Few small employers have a separate person or department to handle employee screening. So, if your job search consists of submitting applications and/or resumes to a human resources or personnel department, you will miss out on three out of four job opportunities. Even very large organizations often have smaller local operations that do their own hiring without a formal human resources department.

* **The function of HR departments is to screen people out:** You may think that submitting a resume or application following a brief interview with someone in the HR department will result in your being considered for current or future openings. Not so. You might be referred to a department head if HR has a job posting that matches your skills. More likely, though, your resume will be put into a pile with just a few sent to the department head who will then make the hiring decision.

* **At best, HR departments can set up an interview:** Unless you want to work in an HR department, there is little advantage to your being interviewed by them. Many employers in larger organizations prefer hiring people who are referred to them by people they trust. And many jobs are filled in just this way, before the HR department even knows there is a job opening up. If you do get an interview from HR, the odds are good that the one making the decision will hire someone else who was personally referred or who got past the HR screening in some other way. It happens all the time.

If all this seems discouraging, think of the positives. While all the other job seekers are going through the HR screening process, you can be spending more of your time seeking out smaller employers or using methods that allow you to get past the HR department to the people who actually do the hiring.

Sending Unsolicited Resumes

Most people will not get good results by e-mailing or mailing resumes to people they don't know. Yes, I know that many resume books suggest this approach, but there is little evidence to suggest this method is effective. True, a good resume will help you in your job search, but it won't get you many interviews unless you use it in appropriate ways.

Three Tips for Sending Resumes

While I cover resumes in more detail in Chapter 9, here are some suggestions for using them:

* **Very few people get a job by sending resumes to people they do not know:** It is almost always better to contact the employer in person, through e-mail, or by phone first. Ask for an interview, and *then* send your resume.

* **Make sure you have a presentable resume as soon as you start your job search:** Write a simple one at first, and use it in your job search without delay. You can always write a better one later.

* **Give your resume to friends, relatives, and anyone else you can think of:** Ask others to pass your resume along to anyone they think might know of an opening for someone with your skills.

Filling Out Applications

Application forms, whether completed online or in paper form, have many of the same limitations of resumes. For example, the details that most job seekers provide—or leave off—their applications are far more likely to get them screened out than in.

Even so, research indicates that filling out applications is a reasonably effective approach, particularly for young people who are seeking entry-level jobs. I'll cover applications in more detail in Chapter 8, "Why Bother with Employment Applications?"

Five Tips for Submitting Applications

Following are some tips to increase the effectiveness of your applications:

* **Understand that application forms are designed to collect negative information:** If your application is not the best, you will often be screened out, even if you can do the job. For example, applications ask for education and training history. Employers are looking for the person whose answers best meet their needs.

* **Know that many employers require that you complete an application before you are hired:** The form collects information employers need that is often missing from a resume. You need to know how to complete applications carefully.

* **Be neat when filling out your application:** Read the instructions carefully before completing the application. For online applications, make sure your spelling and grammar are correct. If you're using a printed form, make it neat and error-free.

* **Do not include information that could get you screened out:** If necessary, leave a problem section blank. You can always explain it after you get an interview. Find a way to include reasons that an employer should hire you, even if this information is not requested.

* **Understand that your best approach is to ask to talk to the person who will make the hiring decision:** If you're required to fill out an application first, you should still ask for an interview. However, it's always better to ask to see the person in charge. Fill out an application if you're asked to, but don't expect it to get you an interview.

THE WORKING WORLD

How Has the Internet Changed Business?

If you tried naming all the ways the Internet has changed business, who knows how many pages you'd need to record them. Suffice it to say, the impact has been major. Companies like Amazon paved the way for small businesses to be run almost entirely over the Web. E-mail has changed the way businesses communicate and share data. Search engines like Google have made research easier and created new avenues for advertising. Knowing how to use the Internet has become a prerequisite for many positions, and for some business owners, it is their livelihood.

Other Job Search Alternatives to Consider

While most people will use one of the methods I've already covered in this chapter to find a job, here are others to consider:

* **Government civil service jobs:** Jobs with federal, state, and local government agencies are a major part of our labor market. About 8 percent of all workers are employed by the government; 2 percent are employed by the federal government, and another 6 percent are employed by state and local governments. And that does not include the 10 percent of people who work in educational services and other government-funded jobs. Applying for government jobs often requires you to follow specific procedures. It can take a long time to get an interview for one of these jobs and even longer before you get an offer. Even so, they may be worth looking into.

  Find out about local, state, and federal jobs by contacting the personnel divisions for each. State and local government agencies are often listed in the yellow pages, and many have Internet sites that provide information. Two sites providing federal government job information are www.ajb.dni.us and www.opm.gov. A book titled *Guide to America's Federal Jobs: A Complete Directory of U.S. Government Career Opportunities* (JIST Publishing) is another good information source.

* **Self-employment:** About 12 percent of all workers are self-employed. It's an option you might consider now or in the future. If you want to join the growing number of people who work for themselves, start by learning more about self-employment options. Libraries offer many helpful books and resource materials. The Small Business Administration provides free resources for entrepreneurs. You can find it in the phone book or at www.sba.gov. Another good idea is to work in a business like the one you want to start. There is no better way to learn how to run a similar business. If you work in your family business, get education, training, and work experience in a related business to help grow the family business when the time comes for you to take a leadership role.

* **Volunteer:** If you lack experience or are not getting job offers, consider volunteering to work free. Perhaps you could offer your services for a day or a week to show an employer what you can do. Promise that if things don't work out, you will leave with no hard feelings. This approach really does work, and many employers will give you a chance because they like your attitude.

* **Temporary agencies:** Temporary agencies offer jobs lasting from several days to many months. They charge the employer a bit more than you are paid and keep the difference, so you pay no direct fee. Many private employment agencies now provide temporary jobs as well. Temp agencies have grown rapidly in recent years for good reason. They provide employers with short-term help, and employers often use them to find people they may want to hire later. Temp agencies can help you survive between jobs and get experience in different work settings, and they may lead to a long-term job offer.

* **The military:** The military is one of the nation's largest employers, with 2.6 million people in the various branches, plus an additional 1.2 million in Reserve and National Guard units. It also provides free training, education, and tuition credits for college courses during and after service. Almost any kind of civilian job can also be found in the military. Increasingly, technical training can often be used to transition to civilian jobs after time spent in the service. You can find additional information on enlisting at www.todaysmilitary. com and on its many career and training options at www.militarycareers.com.

* **School employment assistance:** This is mentioned in the previous chapter but deserves emphasis again. If you are lucky enough to attend a school that offers help in career planning or job search, find out what is available. If the school offers job listings, follow the counselor's advice and go to any interviews he or she sets up. Never miss an interview that the school sends you to.

* **Professional associations:** Many career areas have associations for people who work in that field. These associations are often a good source of information and networking contacts. The *Occupational Outlook Handbook* lists major professional associations for each job it covers and gives contact information, including Web addresses. Consider joining one or more of these groups, and use their members as a source of networking for leads.

* **Apprenticeships:** An apprenticeship is a formal program that allows you to learn through on-the-job experience under the supervision of an experienced worker—and get paid. These programs often include formal classroom training related to the job. From actor, animal trainer, and baker to surveying technician, truck driver, and well and core drill operator, there are more then 800 registered apprenticeships, including one or more that may interest you. An excellent resource on this is *250 Best Jobs Through Apprenticeships* (JIST Publishing), or use the Web site at www.doleta.gov/OA/eta_default.cfm that is run by the federal government.

MONEY MATTERS

Check It Out

Checking and savings accounts are standards for entering the working world. Checking accounts allow you to write checks (which for many of us simply means "pay bills") against the balance in the account. They also provide the convenience of ATMs (automated teller machines). Savings accounts are interest-bearing accounts that often only charge a fee if you drop below a minimum balance. Banks also offer interest-bearing checking accounts, money market accounts, and certificates of deposit, all of which promise a more substantial return on your deposit, though the minimum balance is often much higher than a traditional checking or savings account.

Seven Additional Tips to Use During Your Job Search

You may need to be patient while you're working your way toward the job you really want. Follow these tips:

* **Start at the bottom:** If you are being told you do not have enough experience to get the job you want, take an entry-level job in the field that interests you. Look for ways to work your way up as quickly as possible. Learn as much as you can, let the boss know you want to move up, and take on difficult tasks.

* **Consider additional training or education:** If a job interests you, it is often worth getting the education it requires. Additional training and education often quickly pay off in earnings and advancement opportunities. For example, data from the Census Bureau shows that the average annual pay of a college graduate is about $23,000 more than a high school graduate. Many of the fastest growing jobs require education or training beyond the high school level. These jobs often pay better and have more potential for the future than jobs that do not require special training. While a college degree is required for more and more jobs, many good-paying jobs require training or education that lasts from six months to two years. Look into financial aid that is available through many schools. Even if you can't afford to go to school full-time, you can often go to night classes or work an evening job that allows you to take classes during the day. Once you are sure about what you want to do long-term, find a way to get the education or training it requires. Few people regret it.

* **Apply for benefits, but don't wait:** If you qualify—or might qualify—for unemployment compensation or other benefits, apply for them right away. Looking for a job and being out of work is stressful, so get what economic support you can, and then actively go about looking for your job.

* **Weigh the options in working with small versus large businesses:** I've already mentioned the importance of looking for jobs in smaller businesses. They employ almost three out of four workers and offer many opportunities to gain experience and skills needed for career advancement. Many of the job search methods I cover in this book are effective in getting interviews with small employers, but don't overlook larger employers in the process. Although many smaller employers offer competitive pay and benefits, larger employers tend to pay better and have better benefits. Larger employers often need people with specialized technical skills or entry-level workers. If you want to work for a larger employer, consider accepting a less-than-perfect job and then working your way up or over to another area that appeals to you more.

* **Don't be "unemployed" while looking:** Being "unemployed" for months will create a negative impression with employers. They will wonder why you have not been hired by someone or question your energy level. So look for some positive reason for being out of work, such as going to school, raising a family, being self-employed (even if it was working temporary jobs with a temp agency, painting houses, or mowing lawns), seeing the country (or whatever you were doing while you were unemployed), or some other reason. Did you learn new skills, work in different environments, use your talents, or gain anything you can apply to a new job? Probably so. Make certain you find a way to present what you were doing as an advantage to an employer who hires you.

* **Make looking for a job your full-time job:** Do you want to be unemployed for as short a time as possible? Then plan to spend 40 hours per week on your job search as soon as practical. You will need to organize your job search time so that looking for a job *is* your job. I'll cover how to do this in Chapter 13, "Getting a Job *Is* a Job," but it is important that you understand that spending more time on your job search is likely to result in getting a job in less time.

* **Send thank-you notes:** I covered this in the previous chapter, but it is important enough to review again here. Your mom was right: Send thank-you notes after an interview! It seems so simple an idea, but doing so creates a positive impression with employers. It separates you from the less appreciative and more self-centered applicants, which is a good thing. Doing so also helps to keep you in the employer's mind and gives you another opportunity to provide your contact information and JIST Cards®. The research indicates that doing this one thing well can make an enormous difference in getting a job offer or not. I'll cover this in more detail in Chapters 9 and 10.

BE CREATIVE AND WELL ORGANIZED IN YOUR JOB SEARCH

Your reading this book will help you be better prepared for the job search than most of your competition. This is good news, because employers will often be willing to hire those who present themselves well in the job search and interview over others with better credentials.

But how you spend your time in the job search and what techniques you use will be up to you. Those who get jobs in less time tend to use a variety of job search methods, not just one or two. You just never know what will end up working for you, so plan to use a variety of methods, and follow up quickly on any leads.

Spending full time on your job search will be difficult if you are going to school or working, but plan to spend as much time as you can. If you are in school or a training program now, start getting interviews *before* you finish. The best situation is to already have a job lined up soon after you graduate. If you don't have a position lined up before then, decide in advance that you *will* make getting a job your full-time job as soon as you complete your program.

While I have covered a variety of job search techniques in this and the previous chapter, you should look for creative opportunities throughout your job search. So feel free to adapt what I present in this book to suit your personality. Be willing to try new things that may intimidate you, and don't give up.

As you continue in this book, here are some key points to remember:

* Most jobs are not advertised.

* Use a variety of job-seeking methods.

* Some of your best leads will come from people you know.

* You don't have to wait for a job opening before contacting a potential employer.

* Always try to make direct contact with the person who will hire you.

* Follow up!

YOU ARE READY TO BUILD YOUR JOB-SEARCHING TOOLS

The chapters that follow build on what you have learned so far. There is a good job out there that will meet your needs and an employer who wants what you have to offer. All you need to do is go out and make it happen.

CASE STUDY: A TEMPORARY POSITION LEADS TO SUCCESS

When Reggie was laid off from his job as a social worker as an unexpected casualty of budget cuts, he struggled to find a job. Not willing to relocate, he eventually took a temporary position with a video game producer as a game tester, creating detailed reports on his experiences for the design team. The understanding was that once the game design was finished, he would be looking for work. Though the job paid only minimum wage, the months he spent on the project gave him the chance to show the company how dependable and quick learning he was. In the middle of the project, the company gave him a promotion and hired him permanently as a lead tester.

What started as a way to pay the bills for Reggie soon opened into a possible career choice. His advice: "Take advantage of any opportunities that come your way." There's no telling when something temporary will turn out to be something permanent.

chapter 8

Why Bother with Employment Applications?

I said in an earlier chapter that completing applications is not an effective job search method for most people. Even so, there are several reasons you need to know how to complete them. But before I get into this topic, you need to consider why many employers want you to fill out an application for employment.

> *"To be free is not merely to cast off one's chains, but to live in a way that respects and enhances the freedom of others."*
>
> *Nelson Mandela*

WHY EMPLOYERS WANT AN APPLICATION

Applications are forms to collect information about you that a company needs before deciding to interview or hire you. While most employers use paper application forms, more and more require you to complete their applications on the Internet or their in-house computers.

Some Reasons That Employers Use Applications

Why do employers want you to complete an application? List some of the reasons you think they do here.

1. _____
2. _____
3. _____
4. _____
5. _____

Employers use applications for several reasons. You probably listed several. Were the following on your list: to quickly screen applicants and to collect essential information?

To Quickly Screen Applicants

The major purpose of applications is to help employers screen people out. If your qualifications are not "right," you will not get an interview.

Even a qualified candidate often gets screened out based on his or her application. Maybe the application was too incomplete, had bad spelling or handwriting, or was messy. Some applicants are screened out because they do not have as much experience or as good of credentials as others. Some employers screen out those who were paid more than other applicants on their last job. Companies have many reasons for rejecting applicants. You might be able to do the job you're applying for, but you may never have the chance to prove it.

To Collect Essential Information

Most employers require you to complete an application. The application form is an efficient way for employers to collect essential information that may not have been included on your resume or covered in your interview. A complete application provides one more review of your situation, including things that may not have been asked in an interview. Some employers require you to complete an application before a formal interview to help them identify any problem areas to discuss.

Other employers require applications after an interview to help identify potential problem areas in the people they are considering hiring. For example, if the interview did not cover a previous felony conviction, the application may force you to either lie (grounds for future dismissal) or leave this section blank (allowing the employer to clarify this matter prior to employment).

A completed application is also typically needed for the employer's records, to meet legal requirements for documentation or to provide information the employer will need later. For example, the employer will be required at some point to prove you are a citizen or a legal alien or have certain credentials needed for the position. Also, an employer may want to have information on file regarding who to contact in an emergency.

Completing an Application Is Often Not the Best Way to Get an Interview

Some people do get interviews by filling out applications. Many young people, for example, get their jobs in this way. This is because employers are often less selective for the entry-level and lower-paying jobs that many young people apply for.

But, for most people, filling out applications is not an effective way to get an interview. As noted in an earlier chapter, it is almost always better to ask an employer directly for an interview.

ANOTHER IMPORTANT REASON FOR KNOWING HOW TO COMPLETE APPLICATIONS

This reason is all about you. Learning more about completing applications will also help you prepare for more effective interviewing and resume writing. An application will help you identify problem questions you will need to address in the interview and gather key facts that you will need throughout your job search.

WHAT SHOULD YOU KNOW ABOUT COMPLETING APPLICATIONS?

There are many reasons for you to know how to complete an application in the way that is the least likely to get you screened out—and the most likely to help you get a job offer.

Four Tips for Completing Online or Paper Applications

Here are some general suggestions for completing applications. Most of these tips apply to both paper and electronic applications. Keep these simple points in mind when completing your applications:

* **Complete at least one online and one paper application as practice before you submit the real things:** Your instructor may provide you with one or more paper applications to complete for practice, or you may be asked to get them from local employers.

  Many national companies, such as Sears, have Web sites that include an online application. If you can't easily find a company's employment information on its Web site, searching the site for key phrases such as "employment opportunities" or "human resources" will often get you what you want. For example, Sears' main site at www.sears.com has store products, but a keyword search for "employment opportunities" takes you to www.aboutsears.com/careers, where you can log in to search for job openings, complete an online application, and get additional information.

* **Follow directions:** Before you complete an application, review the entire form so you're familiar with what information is being requested and how. Read all directions carefully before you complete anything. For example, if you are asked to print all responses, do not write them! You can make a negative impression quickly if you don't follow directions.

* **Be neat and complete:** Carefully answer all sections of the application. A very incomplete application or one that has poor spelling, grammar, or appearance gives a negative impression. For paper applications, carry an erasable black or blue ink pen for completing applications, because it allows you to correct errors.

* **Provide only positive information:** Most applications are designed to collect negative information about you. But if you provide such information, it will be used to screen you out. If a question forces you to give negative information, leaving a space blank is better than giving information that will keep you from being considered. You can always explain your situation in the interview.

  Find a place to include important positives about yourself, even if the application does not ask for this information. This is an exception to my earlier advice to follow the application's instructions, but including this information is too important to you to exclude. For example, if you have limited work experience, list any important volunteer or extracurricular experience in the work experience section. List key skills, accomplishments, training credentials, or other things that support your doing the job well, even if there is no place on the application that asks for this information.

Seven Tips for Overcoming Problem Questions on Applications

Applications ask some difficult questions, and how you answer them could get you screened out. Remember that you should never give negative information. Never lie on an application, though. That could get you fired later.

A variety of laws limit the types of questions that employers can ask on application forms and in interviews. Even so, some employers may not know about these laws or may use out-of-date applications that include "illegal" questions. If so, you can leave these questions blank. Let's review typical problem questions and ways to handle them.

* **Gaps in employment:** Employers want your complete employment history. They will wonder what you did during the times you were not employed. If you have a good reason for an employment gap, be sure to list it. Examples include "raised children," "returned to school," and "helped uncle start a new business." If you did any work for money during a gap, list yourself as "self-employed." Did your activities during an employment gap relate in any way to the job you want? If so, present the skills you used and the accomplishments you achieved that support your job objective.

TIP: You can downplay a gap by showing the start and finish dates of your employment as complete years. For example, "2005 to 2006" does not show that you were unemployed from January to July 2005.

SKILLS FOR SUCCESS

Respect

Yesterday Miguel overheard a male co-worker talking to other employees about the weekend, and the male co-worker mentioned that he and his boyfriend were going out of town. Later that day, Miguel's boss assigned him to work on a project with this person, and he refused. When his boss asked why, Miguel said he didn't want to talk about it. Is Miguel justified in his refusal?

❋ **Arrest record:** Applications used to ask, "Have you ever been arrested?" Laws today allow an employer to ask only if you have ever been *convicted* of a serious crime, such as a felony. Companies can also inquire about crimes that could affect your ability to do the job. For example, an employer can ask accounting clerks and warehouse workers if they have ever been arrested for theft. And a school can ask applicants if they have ever been arrested for child molesting.

These laws are designed to keep applicants from being screened out of a job for arrests (when they were not found guilty) or for minor crimes that would not affect their work. So, if you were arrested but not convicted of a felony, write "no" on applications.

❋ **Disabilities or physical or emotional problems:** Unless your problem prevents you from doing the job safely, it is probably not an employer's business. You should leave such items blank or write "no" in almost all cases when asked for this information.

❋ **Reason for leaving last job:** Give the reason for leaving your last job, and make it sound positive. Don't write "fired" if you were laid off because of a business slowdown or similar situation. If you didn't leave on the best of terms but didn't do anything illegal, it is often best to list a legitimate excuse. Use something neutral, such as "returned to school" or "decided on a career change." You can always explain the details in an interview.

❋ **Too little experience:** If you don't have much experience for the job you want, emphasize your other strengths. Present volunteer jobs in the Work section and leave the Wages Paid section blank. You can also give lots of details for related training, education, and skills used in other jobs.

❋ **Pay and position desired:** Don't list a specific pay rate. It is often best to write "open" or "negotiable." This approach will not get you screened out.

If possible, list a broad career field. For example, write down "general office" rather than a specific title such as "file clerk." Titles and duties are rarely the same from place to place. Listing a narrow job title may keep you from being considered for other jobs you could do.

❋ **Too much or too little education:** If you are overqualified or your credentials are strong but in another field, consider leaving out some of your unrelated education. If a job usually requires a degree but you did not graduate, write that you "attended" certain institutions. Don't say whether you graduated. You can explain the details in the interview.

Let Your Conscience Be Your Guide

Some people are tempted to lie on an application, but that's not a good idea. Many employers will later fire you if they find out that you lied on your application. A better approach is to leave a sensitive question blank. If you have a serious problem that an application would reveal, you're better off looking for job openings that don't require an application.

Remember that an application is more likely to do you harm than good. When you fill one out, be sure that it is truthful but also as positive as you can make it. Include nothing on your application that could get you screened out. Remember that your goal is to get interviews, not complete applications.

THE WORKING WORLD

What Does Commuting Really Cost?

One consideration for any job—and not a minor one—is how long it takes to get to work. According to the U.S. Census Bureau, the average American spends 100 hours a year commuting to and from work, and the average daily commute is 25 minutes. While it's true that a good job might be only 45 minutes away, it might not be worth it if it means less family or leisure time. And don't forget the price and availability of gas. In fact, your commute may be a concern for a potential employer as well.

Information That an Employer Should Probably Not Require

The following list was compiled by a law firm specializing in employment issues. To comply with antidiscrimination laws, this list includes items that an employer is advised not to ask for on an application or in an interview.

* Age or date of birth

* Previous address

* The length of time at present residence or whether it is rented or owned

* Race, religion, or name of clergy

* Father's or mother's surname

* Maiden name and marital status

* The number of children, their ages, and who will care for them

* Spouse's name, place of employment, and residence

* Parents' names, employment, or residence

* Loans, financial obligations, wage attachments, and personal bankruptcies

* Arrest record (unless related to the job or felony conviction)

* Legal convictions, unless relevant to the job

* Services in a foreign armed service, languages spoken, unless a job requirement

* Social organization memberships

* Dates of education

* Attitudes toward geographic location, unless a job requirement

* Citizenship and birthplace

* Military discharge status

* Height, weight, and gender

* Questions about health, physical and mental conditions, or disabilities

As you are completing applications (or in an interview), remember that asking for the preceding information is illegal.

Employment Tests and Background Checks

Some employers may ask you to take one or more tests as part of the application process. The tests can be paper-and-pencil or computerized. Some tests are designed to measure how honest you are. Others measure your personality, friendliness, and likelihood of getting along with co-workers and supervisors. They can also measure how quickly you work and other job-related skills. Before you are employed, some employers may require you to take a drug test or go to a medical screening. Some tests have been found to be illegal, but others can be used by employers to help them select employees. If you want the job and the employer requires you to take a test, you will probably have to do so. Do your best on whatever tests you are asked to complete.

Many employers will ask you to sign an agreement that will let them check your background. This agreement is sometimes included at the end of an application. A background check will usually allow an employer to check your criminal and credit history, collect information from previous employers, and verify your education, training, or other details presented on your application. Again, if you want the job, you will probably have to cooperate.

SAMPLE APPLICATIONS

I've included two sample applications in this chapter. One is a blank traditional application that shows most of the details you'll see on real applications. For practice, use a pencil or erasable pen to fill in the blank application. Complete it as carefully and as neatly as you can. Make sure all your dates, addresses, and other information are complete and correct. When you are done, you can tear out the finished application and take it with you on your job search. You can then refer to it when filling in applications.

The second application is a computer-based one. I include it to give you familiarity with that type of application. It looks much easier than the first application but can be intimidating if you're required to complete it onsite. The noise and people all around you can be distracting.

If you are completing the computer-based application onsite, be aware that company officials may be observing you and monitoring your answers. If your appearance and answers meet their requirements, they may interview you on the spot, and you may walk out with a job.

MONEY MATTERS

Borrowing Basics

Job applications aren't the only kind of application you will need to fill out to get ahead in life. It's nearly impossible to get through life without borrowing money at some point or another. In fact, borrowing money—and paying off the debt—is the only way to establish a credit history. Whether you are borrowing to pay for a car, a house, a college education, or to start your own business, the basics behind the loan are the same. The key to borrowing is understanding exactly how much you will have to pay back, over what period, and in what increments—that is, what your monthly payment will be. It's important to be a smart consumer when shopping for loans. Compare interest rates to get the best one possible, and always read the fine print.

Sample Printed Application for Employment

APPLICATION
FOR EMPLOYMENT

_____ / / _____
Date of Application

As an equal opportunity employer, this company does not discriminate in hiring or terms and conditions of employment because of an individual's race, creed, color, sex, age, disability, religion, or national origin.

AVAILABILITY

Position Applying for:_____ Date Available to Start:_____

Salary Desired:_____

Desired Schedule: Check Days Available: ☐ Sun ☐ Mon ☐ Tue ☐ Wed ☐ Thur ☐ Fri ☐ Sat

☐ Full-Time ☐ Part-Time ☐ Temporary   Hours Available Each Day: ____ ____ ____ ____ ____ ____ ____

PERSONAL INFORMATION

Last Name	First Name	Middle Name

Present Street Address	City	State	Zip

Previous Street Address	City	State	Zip

Daytime Telephone No. ( )	Evening Telephone No. ( )	Social Security Number	Are you over 18?

EMPLOYMENT HISTORY

List employment starting with your *most recent* position. Account for any time during this period in which you were unemployed by stating the nature of your activities. If you have no prior employment history, include personal references to be contacted.

May we contact your present employer? ☐ YES ☐ NO

Employer	Dates From / To	Position/Title
Address		Duties Performed
City State Telephone ( )		
Supervisor	Hourly Rate/Salary Starting / Final	
Reason for Leaving		

Employer	Dates From / To	Position/Title
Address		Duties Performed
City State Telephone ( )		
Supervisor	Hourly Rate/Salary Starting / Final	
Reason for Leaving		

Employer	Dates From / To	Position/Title
Address		Duties Performed
City State Telephone ( )		
Supervisor	Hourly Rate/Salary Starting / Final	
Reason for Leaving		

Employer	Dates From / To	Position/Title
Address		Duties Performed
City State Telephone ( )		
Supervisor	Hourly Rate/Salary Starting / Final	
Reason for Leaving		

(continued)

(continued)

EDUCATION

Type of School	Name and Location of School		Degree / Area of Study	Number of Years Completed	Graduated? (check one)
High School	Name				☐ Yes ☐ No
	City	State			GPA_____
College	Name				☐ Yes ☐ No
	City	State			GPA_____
Other	Name				☐ Yes ☐ No
	City	State			GPA_____

SPECIAL SKILLS

☐ Typing ☐ Lotus ☐ Word Processing ☐ 10 Key (by touch) Applicable Skills or Equipment Operated:

_____wpm _____keystrokes _____

ACADEMIC AND PROFESSIONAL ACTIVITIES AND ACHIEVEMENTS

Academic and Professional Activities and Achievements, Awards, Publications, or Technical-Professional Societies. Indicate type or name. Exclude organizations which indicate race, creed, color, sex, age, religion, disability, or national origin of its members.	Date Awarded

MISCELLANEOUS

Is there any additional information involving a change of your name or assumed name that will permit us to check your record? If yes, please explain.

Have you ever been employed by this company or any of its divisions? ☐ Yes ☐ No	Dates Employed	Which Division?	Supervisor	Position

List names of friends or relatives now employed by this company.

Have you ever been convicted of a crime? ☐ Yes ☐ No (conviction of a crime does not automatically disqualify an applicant from consideration) If yes, please explain:

Are there any jobs for which you do not wish to be considered? Please explain.

PERSON TO CONTACT IN CASE OF EMERGENCY

This information is to facilitate contact in the event of an emergency and is not used in the selection process.

Full Name	Address	Phone	Relationship to you?
Place of Employment	Address	Phone	

PLEASE READ THIS STATEMENT CAREFULLY

I hereby affirm that the information given by me on this application for employment is complete and accurate. I understand that any falsification will be immediate grounds for dismissal. I authorize a thorough investigation to be made in connection with this application concerning my character, general reputation, personal characteristics, employment, educational background, and criminal record, whichever may be applicable. I understand that this investigation may include personal interviews with third parties such as family members, business associates, financial sources, friends, neighbors, and others with whom I am acquainted.

It is my understanding that as a prerequisite to consideration for employment, I must agree to submit to any post-employment examinations, physical or other, as the Company may lawfully require. The Company will pay the reasonable cost of any such examination which may be required.

I understand and agree that any falsification or omission either on this form or in my response to questions asked during any interview or other examination process is grounds for immediate termination of my employment no matter when the falsification or omission is discovered.

If I am hired, I agree that my employment and compensation can be terminated with or without cause and without notice at any time, at the option of this company or myself. I understand that no representative of this company other than a Vice President has authority to enter into any agreement for any specified period of time or to make any agreement contrary to the foregoing. I further understand that I have the right to make a written request within a reasonable period of time for a complete and accurate disclosure of the nature and scope of the investigation.

I have read and affirm as my own the above statements. Signature_____ Date_____

APPLICANTS IN THE STATE OF MARYLAND ONLY

Under Maryland law an employer may not require or demand any applicant for employment or prospective employment or any employee to submit to or take a polygraph, lie detector, or similar test or examination as a condition of employment or continued employment. Any employer who violates this provision is guilty of a misdemeanor and subject to a fine not to exceed $100.

Signature_____ Date_____

APPLICANTS IN THE STATE OF MASSACHUSETTS ONLY

It is unlawful in Massachusetts to require or administer a lie detector test as a condition of employment or continued employment. An employer who violates this law shall be subject to criminal penalties and civil liability.

Signature_____ Date_____

Computer-Based Application for Employment

Employment Application

Qualified applicants receive equal consideration. No question is asked for the purpose of excluding any applicant due to race, creed, color, national origin, religion, age, sex, handicap, veteran status, marital status, sexual orientation, or any other characteristic protected by law. We are an equal opportunity employer.

The field descriptions in BLUE text are required.

First Name:	Last Name:
Address:	
City:	State:
Zip:	Phone:
E-mail:	
Desired Position:	Select... Click here to view descriptions
If Other:	

Attach resume:
ACCEPTABLE FORMATS: .doc, .wpd, .txt, .wks, .pdf   [Browse...]

CASE STUDY: SKILLS OVERCOME AN EMPLOYMENT GAP

Gaps in employment are actually quite common. Andrea took five years off from work to be with her small children while her husband worked. When her youngest child enrolled in kindergarten, she began searching for a job.

Andrea jokes that filling out job applications is easier when you haven't worked in a while—after all, it's less you have to write. But it also requires more thought. "You have to stress your skills and your personality over your experience," she says. In her applications, Andrea would often list the school and community activities she had been involved in, stressing her people skills and the work ethic that comes from raising children. Ultimately, she began a career that put those communication skills and family values to work.

chapter 9

Write Effective Resumes, E-mail, and Cover Letters

Many resume books and job search "experts" tell you that a good resume is important. They say that a well-done resume will help you get an interview over others whose resumes are not as good. Many Web sites encourage you to post your resume for "thousands" of employers to view. But resumes by themselves don't get job offers—people do.

WHY EVEN A "GREAT" RESUME PROBABLY WON'T GET YOU A JOB

While it is true that a poorly done resume can get you screened out, a resume alone is usually not a good tool for getting an interview. The best way to get an interview is through direct contact with people. As you learned in earlier chapters, most people find their jobs through one of two techniques. They get leads from people they know (warm contacts) or by making direct contacts with employers (cold contacts).

E-mailing or mailing out lots of resumes is not an effective way to get a job. Posting your resume on job-related Internet sites may not get you much response either—unless your skills are very much in demand. While almost any job search technique works for some people, the odds are not in your favor. Mass distribution of your resume often delays direct contact with potential employers. Your resume is put on a pile or into a database of other resumes from people who are competing for the same job. Even with a good resume, you are far more likely to be screened out or overlooked in such circumstances.

> *Where is there dignity unless there is honesty?*
>
> *Cicero*

Resume experts who tell you to create a great resume and then post it on Web sites or to send it to lots of people are giving ineffective advice. They assume that the way to get a job is to deal with human resources offices, go after publicly advertised jobs, and use passive job search methods. Instead, this book teaches you to use techniques that are effective with large as well as small employers (that may not have a human resources office), to go after the hidden market of jobs that are not advertised (where most jobs are found), and to use active techniques.

WHY YOU MUST HAVE A RESUME

While a resume may not be the best tool to get you an interview, you need one for several reasons:

* Employers expect you to have one.

* A good resume will help you present what you have to offer an employer.

* Using the Internet in your job search requires one.

Employers use resumes to find out about your credentials and experience. Covering these details in an interview is not the best use of that valuable time. A well-written resume forces you to summarize the highlights of your experience. Once you've done this, you are better able to talk about yourself during the interview. If you want to use the Internet to help you look for a job, you need a resume in an electronic format to e-mail to employers and to post in searchable databases.

While many books continue to tell job seekers to send out lots of resumes or to post resumes on the Internet in hopes of getting interviews, the following section offers better advice.

The Five Most Effective Ways to Use a Resume

Even an excellent resume won't get you interviews unless you use it effectively. Following are some details on how to best use your resume to get more interviews.

1. **Get the interview first:** It is almost always better to contact employers by phone, by e-mail, or in person before you send a resume. If possible, get a referral from someone you know. Or make a cold contact directly to the employer. In either case, ask for an interview. If no opening is available now, ask to come in and discuss the possibility of future openings.

2. **Then send your resume:** Whenever possible, send or e-mail your resume after you schedule an interview so that the employer can read about you before your meeting. Valuable interview time can then be spent discussing your skills rather than details that are best presented in a resume.

3. **Follow up with a thank-you note:** Immediately after an interview, send a thank-you note. Even if you use e-mail to communicate with employers, most appreciate a mailed thank-you note. A mailed note also allows you to enclose your JIST Card® or another copy of your resume. (JIST Cards are a mini-resume that I cover in Chapter 10, "Use JIST Cards to Get Interviews.")

THE WORKING WORLD

Does Your Resume Match Your Background?

According to a recent survey by the Preemployment Services Directory, as many as 80 percent of companies perform background checks on potential employees. These preemployment checks only reinforce the need to be truthful with prospective employers right from the start. After all, they're bound to find out anyway, and they will appreciate your honesty.

---

4. **Send your resume and JIST Card to everyone in your growing job search network:** This is an excellent way for people in your network to help you find unadvertised leads. They can pass or e-mail your resume and JIST Card to others who might be interested in a person who has your skills.

5. **Send your resume in the traditional way if you can't make direct contact:** In some situations, you can't easily make personal contact with an employer. For example, if you post your resume on the Internet, an employer may contact you first. Or if you respond to a want ad that provides only a post office box number, there is no way to reach an individual. Go ahead and use those methods, but plan to use more active job search methods, too.

Seven Tips on Writing a Resume

There are no firm rules for writing a good resume. Every resume is different. But here are some tips that I have learned are important in writing any resume:

✳ **Write it yourself:** Look at the sample resumes in this book and elsewhere, but don't use their content in your resume. If you do, your resume will sound like someone else's. Many employers will guess you didn't write it—and that will not help you.

✳ **Make every word count:** Most resumes should be limited to one or two pages. After you have written a first draft, edit it at least two more times. If a word or phrase does not support your ability to do the job, cut it. Shorter is often better.

✳ **Make it error free:** Just one error on your resume can create a negative impression that could be enough to get you screened out. Ask someone else to check your resume for grammar and spelling errors. Check each word again before you print a final version. You can't be too careful.

✳ **Make it look good:** Appearance, as you know, makes a lasting impression. For this reason, your resume must look good, with good design and format. Later in this chapter, I give you more tips on producing a good-looking resume in paper and electronic forms.

✳ **Stress your accomplishments:** A resume is no place to be humble. Emphasize results. Give facts and numbers to support your accomplishments. Instead of saying that you are good with people, say "I supervised and trained five staffers and increased their productivity by 30 percent." The sample resumes and JIST Cards often include numbers. They make a difference.

* **Create a simple resume first:** Don't delay your job search while working on a "better" resume! Many job seekers spend time improving their resume when they should be out looking for a job. A better approach is to quickly do a simple, error-free resume and then actively look for a job. You can work on a better version at night and on weekends.

* **Keep it lively:** Keep your resume short and interesting. Use action verbs and brief sentences.

THE FOUR BASIC TYPES OF RESUMES

There are a variety of resume styles, but the two most common are chronological and skills resumes. I will show you how to develop these types and provide samples. I will also include samples of a third resume type, the combination resume, which combines parts of the chronological and the skills resumes. Each resume style has advantages and disadvantages. The best resume type for you depends on your situation.

Let's look at each resume type and learn more about its advantages and disadvantages for different situations.

The Chronological Resume

Chronology refers to time. A chronological resume begins with your most recent work or other experiences and moves back in time. Two sample resumes for the same person follow. Both use a chronological format.

Look at the first resume, a simple one. Notice the job objective and how the job seeker's experience is organized. While this resume could be improved, it presents the facts and would be an acceptable resume for many employers.

This resume works well because David is looking for a job in his present career field. He has a good job history plus related training. Note that he has moved up in responsibility. He emphasizes the skills and experience that will assist him in continuing to move up. This resume also includes an "Applicable Skills" section. Here David lists some of his computer strengths, which are often not included in a resume. This resume would work fine for most job search needs—and it could be completed in about an hour.

This same resume is improved in the second example. The improved resume features a prominent job objective and sections for "Sales & Marketing Experience," "Education & Training," and "Computer Skills." Notice the impact that the added numbers creates. Note, for example, "international sales force of 500," "Delivered 27% sales growth," "Doubled individual sales volume from $149,000 to $312,000," and "Increased territory sales 30% to rank #1." This resume will take an extra hour or two to write. The first resume is fine, but most employers will like the additional positive information in the improved resume.

A Basic Chronological Resume Example

David D. Dillingham
4321 South Johnstone Boulevard
Laguna Niguel, CA 92321
(714) 555-5555

PUBLISHING WORK EXPERIENCE:

International Publishing - Los Angeles, CA
Careers Division, Marketing Manager XXXX to Present
Young Adult Division Field Sales Representative XXXX to XXXX

- ▶ Responsible for Marketing Twenty-five Million Dollar Careers List
- ▶ Maintain Correspondence Between Authors, Editors, and Sales Force
- ▶ Hire, Train, and Manage Marketing Assistants
- ▶ Develop Marketing Materials, Sales Tools, and Advertisements for Sales Force and Consumers
- ▶ Service Universities, State Colleges, Community Colleges, Proprietary Schools, Postsecondary Vocational Technical Schools, and Bookstores
- ▶ Demonstrate Product Through Personal Visits, Book Fairs, and Trade Shows
- ▶ Plan Travel Itineraries, Yearly Budgets, and Forecasting of Sales Goals
- ▶ Develop, Maintain, and Service Accounts
- ▶ Annually Obtained and Increased Sales Goals

Eastern Publishing Company - New York NY
Field Sales Representative XXXX to XXXX

- ▶ Represented Mathematics List to Universities, State Colleges, and Retail Bookstores
- ▶ Set Appointments, Processed Orders, and Provided Customer Service
- ▶ Responsible for Administrative Tasks, Filing, and Documentation of all Data
- ▶ Prepared Mailings, Handled all Correspondence

Harcourt Publishing Company - San Francisco, CA
Inside Sales Representative XXXX to XXXX

- ▶ Sold Computer Science, Physics, Mathematics, Science, and Nursing Textbooks
- ▶ Contacted Accounts via Telemarketing
- ▶ Uncovered Potential Reviewers and Authors
- ▶ Increased Territory 30%

EDUCATION:

BS Degree in Political Science, University of California-Berkeley, XXXX
AA Degree, The Community College, El Cajon, CA

APPLICABLE SKILLS:

Microsoft Office PowerPoint, Word, Access, Excel, WordPerfect, Lotus Notes, Internet Explorer, Employee Appraiser, Professional Selling Skills Training (PSS), Los Angeles County Aids Project Volunteer

This resume is adapted from Résumé Magic *by Susan Britton Whitcomb (published by JIST Publishing).*

An Improved Chronological Resume Example

DAVID D. DILLINGHAM

4321 South Johnstone Boulevard
Laguna Niguel, CA 92321

(714) 555-5555
david.dillingham@gmail.com

SALES & MARKETING
PUBLISHING INDUSTRY

SALES & MARKETING EXPERIENCE

MARKETING MANAGER International Publishing, Los Angeles, CA   XXXX to Present

Manage marketing for $25 million careers list. Develop product strategies, marketing materials, sales tools, and advertisements for international sales force of 500. Hire, train, and manage marketing assistants. Forecast and manage operating budgets and sales goals. Personally sell to and service universities and retail booksellers. Promote product at trade shows and book fairs.

- Delivered 27% sales growth through development of innovative international marketing strategies.
- Doubled individual sales volume from $149,000 to $312,000, an unprecedented increase for territory.
- Led region of 10 reps in sales volume, achieving 22% above goal (well above company average of 8%).
- Initially challenged with turnaround of product line that had not been serviced in over a year; successfully converted key clients from primary competitor and captured new nationwide sales.

FIELD SALES REPRESENTATIVE Eastern Publishing, San Francisco, CA   XXXX TO XXXX

Generated sales for mathematics division in seven western states and three Canadian provinces.

- Gained access to prestigious clients, such as Stanford University and UC Berkeley (previously banning sales presentations).
- Increased sales in territory that had a several-year history of stagnant sales.

INSIDE SALES REPRESENTATIVE Harcourt Publishing, San Francisco, CA   XXXX TO XXXX

Promoted 100+ item catalog of computer science, physics, mathematics, science, and nursing textbooks to college bookstore market in California, Nevada, and Oregon.

- Increased territory sales 30% to rank #1 in division (with no prior industry knowledge).
- Researched and uncovered potential reviewers and authors.

EDUCATION & TRAINING

BACHELOR OF SCIENCE, POLITICAL SCIENCE University of California, Berkeley   XXXX

PROFESSIONAL SELLING SKILLS (PSS) TRAINING

COMPUTER SKILLS

Microsoft Office (PowerPoint, Word, Access, Excel), WordPerfect, Lotus Notes, MSIE, Employee Appraiser

This resume is adapted from Résumé Magic *by Susan Britton Whitcomb (published by JIST Publishing).*

Sample JIST Card

DAVID D. DILLINGHAM

CELL: (714) 555-5555   E-MAIL: DAVID.DILLINGHAM@GMAIL.COM

Job Objective:
Sales and marketing in publishing industry

Experience:
Marketing manager for International Publishing in Los Angeles. Managed $25 million careers list and delivered 27% sales growth through development of innovative international marketing strategies. Doubled sales volume from $149,000 to $312,000. Led region of 10 reps in sales volume, achieving 22% above goal.

Results-oriented, self-motivated, good problem-solving skills, energetic.

Here is an example of a JIST Card, a type of mini resume that fits on a 3-by-5-inch format. It is based on David's background and includes only information that an employer most needs. JIST Cards are used in addition to a resume and will be covered in more detail in Chapter 10.

Advantages and Disadvantages of a Chronological Resume

The chronological resume format has both advantages and disadvantages.

* **Advantages:** A chronological resume is the simplest and quickest one to write. Many employers want to know details about where you have worked, including dates employed. This is a good resume style to use if you have a solid work history in jobs similar to those you want now.

* **Disadvantages:** A chronological resume may display your weaknesses. It quickly shows an employer your employment gaps, frequent job changes, lack of work experience related to your job objective, recent graduation, and other potential negatives. If you are in one or more of these situations, a traditional chronological resume may not be best for you.

TIP: Here's a humble suggestion. A chronological resume is simple and quick to do. For this reason, I suggest you create a simple chronological resume before making a "better" one. Then use this resume in your job search without delay. You might even get a job offer before you finish an improved version.

The Skills Resume

The skills resume is sometimes called a functional resume. In this format, your experience is organized under key skills. A well-done skills resume emphasizes skills that your job objective requires. These should also be the same skills that you are good at and want to use in your next job.

Look at the sample skills resume that follows, and notice how it emphasizes strengths and abilities. Juanita is a recent high school graduate, and all of her work experience is in part-time and summer jobs. The skills format allows her to emphasize what she has to offer. It allows her to present her job-related training and experience in a positive way.

A Skills Resume Example

Juanita Shepherd

Cashier/Customer Service/Warehouse

5523 East 42nd Street, Apt. A
Oakland, CA 94606
(510) 484-2345
jshepherd@hotmail.com

Customer service–conscious assistant who helps build and sustain a loyal customer base. Committed to assisting management in providing impeccable service and products. Dedicated to offering friendly, professional, and resourceful service in a timely manner to diverse customer base.

Strengths and Abilities

Customer Case/Cashier

- Accurately handle cash transactions and balance cash drawer with efficiency.
- Quickly answer customer questions and complaints and repeatedly solicit customer feedback, all to ensure high-quality service.
- Train new employees in product knowledge, customer service, and operation of cash registers.

Warehouse

- With careful detail, conduct inventory of total stock and perform inventory restocking.
- Able to meticulously sort cargo for quality control. Strictly adhere to company policies for disposing of damaged goods.
- Capable of retrieving requested merchandise and loading on forklift.
- Cooperatively and efficiently work to store and remove merchandise, ensuring proper storage and safe handling.

Work Experience

Taco Bell, Hayward, CA   **XXXX–Present**

Cashier
Work as cashier for drive-through and restaurant counter. Accurately take orders, register payments, and return correct change. Deliver food efficiently and pleasantly. Restock supplies and perform other tasks as needed.

Additional Information and Excellent References Available Upon Request

This resume, submitted by Leatha Jones, is adapted from Same-Day Resume: Write an Effective Resume in an Hour *by Michael Farr (published by JIST Publishing).*

Advantages and Disadvantages of a Skills Resume

As with a chronological resume, the skills resume has good and not-so-good points.

* **Advantages:** A skills resume allows you to present accomplishments from all your life experiences. It is a good format when you need to hide problems that a chronological resume might show. For example, Juanita's resume does a good job of presenting what she can do, without making it obvious that her work experience is limited to part-time and summer jobs. It also doesn't say that she is a recent graduate. A well-written skills resume presents your strengths and avoids showing your weaknesses. It can hide limited paid work experience and gaps in your job history.

* **Disadvantages:** Because a skills resume can hide details that can be used to screen people out, some employers don't like them. A skills resume can also be harder to write than a chronological resume.

Resumes as Screening Tools

A survey taken by the Association of Job Search Trainers uncovered the following findings about resumes and the screening process:

* 80% of screening happens at the resume level.
* Individuals with less than five years of experience should keep their resume to one page.
* Errors in grammar and spelling or other typos leave the highest negative impression on prospective employers.
* More than 85% of employers believe a cover letter is important.

The Combination Resume

A combination resume includes elements of both the chronological and skills formats. For example, a new graduate might use the combination style to first list key skills and related school, work, and life experiences. The resume would then give a brief chronological list of jobs.

A combination resume like the one that follows allows you to use resume features that fit your situation best. I also include several samples of this resume type at the end of this chapter. Look over those resumes for ideas to use in your own resume.

MONEY MATTERS

Retirement Reality

Part of getting the job you really want is imagining the time when you won't need a job (or a resume) at all. Unfortunately, the prospect of retirement grows more complicated each year. Longer life expectancies and rising medical costs only increase the need for a healthy retirement savings. Also, the security blanket of Social Security doesn't cover as much as it once did. Companies that offer retirement packages, like matching 401(k)s or stock options, should receive more of your attention than those that don't. Though it may seem a long way off, it's never too early to start planning.

A Combination Resume Example

Peter J. McDonald

1922 Oak Lane, Manchester, MI 48158
pjmcd@rr.com

Residence: 734-555-9832
Cell: 734-345-6789

AUTOMOTIVE TECHNICIAN

Highlights of Qualifications

- ► Knowledgeable about automotive procedures.
- ► Skilled in diagnosing and repairing problems within a short period of time.
- ► Experienced in the use of Ford Techno terminals and equipment as well as Tech 1/Tech 2 service equipment.
- ► Willing to learn new tasks, take on new responsibilities, and meet new challenges.

Education and Training

Washtenaw Community College, Ypsilanti, MI   XXXX–XXXX
  Associate Degree, Automotive Service Educational Program
  Included on-the-job training and partnering with mentor

Ford Motor Company   Ongoing
  Service Technology Group courses (complete list available on request)

Certifications

State of Michigan Motor Vehicle Mechanic Certification
  Braking Systems
  Suspension Systems

A.S.E. certification pending completion of exam in May XXXX

Employment History

University Ford, Ann Arbor, MI   XXXX–Present
Automotive Technician
Diagnose and repair mechanical and electrical problems.

Fabricore, Dexter, MI   XXXX–XXXX
Quality Control Inspector
Inspected automobile front fascias for imperfections occurring during paint application process.

Lear Manufacturing, Milan, MI   XXXX–XXXX
Assembler
Assembled anti-lock braking modules for 4-WAL and R-WAL vehicles.

References available on request

This resume, submitted by Janet L. Beckstrom, is adapted from Same-Day Resume: Write an Effective Resume in an Hour *by Michael Farr (published by JIST Publishing).*

The Electronic Resume

E-mailing your resume as an attached file is the best way to keep your careful format and design. But most resume-posting Web sites want a resume with no formatting, just words. This allows them to put your resume in a database so that employers can search for keywords. A sample electronic resume and tips for writing one are provided later in this chapter. The best approach is to create a standard resume and then modify it as needed for electronic submissions.

WRITING YOUR RESUME

Whatever type of resume you choose, you can do many things to make it stand out. The following sections give tips on writing your resume and designing and producing it.

Ten Tips for Writing Each Section of Your Resume

Use the following tips to write any style of resume. As you look over the sample resumes later in this chapter for ideas, notice how each resume handles these issues.

* **Your name and address:** It is often best to use your formal name instead of a nickname. In your address, avoid abbreviations, and include your ZIP code. If you might move, arrange with the post office to forward your mail to your new address, or use a relative's address on your resume.

* **Phone numbers and e-mail address:** It's important for employers to be able to reach you, even if only to leave messages. Always include one or more phone numbers where you can be reached. Include your area code, and make certain your answering machine or voice mail message sounds professional. Most employers will try to reach you by e-mail, so include your e-mail address. If you don't have good access to e-mail, get an address from a provider such as Yahoo.com and use a library computer to check your messages on a regular basis. And make certain your e-mail address sounds professional!

* **Job objective:** Include your job objective in all but the most basic resume. Look at the examples to see how others have handled this. Notice that David Dillingham's resume didn't narrow his options by using a specific job title or by using terms such as "supervisor," which might keep him out of the running for more responsible jobs.

* **Education and training:** List job-related training and education, including military training. If your education and training are recent or important parts of your credentials, put them at the top. However, people with five or more years of work experience usually place education and training information at the end of their resumes.

* **Previous experience:** List your most recent job first, and then work your way back. Show promotions as separate jobs. Cluster jobs held long ago or not related to your present objective. These could include the part-time jobs you had while going to school. If you

have little work experience, list unpaid work, such as helping with the family business, and volunteer jobs. Always emphasize the skills you used in these experiences that will help you in the job you want now. There is no need to mention that this work was unpaid.

* **Job gaps:** Your list of work experiences may have gaps. You may have been going to school, having a child, working for yourself, or had other reasons for not being traditionally employed. Present this time positively. Saying "self-employed" or "returned to school to improve my business skills" is better than saying "unemployed."

You can avoid showing that you did not have a job at certain times by listing years or seasons. For example, if you didn't work from late January to early March, write your years of employment and not the months. No one will be able to tell that you had a two-month hiatus between jobs. For example: Job A. 2007–2008; Job B. 2008–2009.

* **Job titles:** Many people have more responsibilities than their job titles suggest. Some titles are unusual and won't mean much to most people. In these cases, use a title that more accurately tells what you did. For example, say "shift manager" rather than "waiter" if you were in charge of things. Of course, make sure that you don't misrepresent your responsibilities.

* **Accomplishments:** An employer wants to know about the work you did well and other experiences you had. As you would in an interview, describe some of your best accomplishments. Emphasize the number of people you served, units produced, staff trained, sales increased, and other measurable achievements. You should include special activities or accomplishments from other life activities, such as your school club roles.

TIP: You can customize your resume for specific employers by changing your job objective and emphasizing certain experiences and skills. This can make sense when you're applying for a specific job that is particularly important to you or when you're seeking jobs in different industries.

* **Personal data:** This information is optional. Who cares how tall you are or that you like to read romance novels? Include personal details only if they support your job objective.

* **References:** Don't list references on your resume. If employers want them, they will ask. Saying "References available on request" at the end of your resume adds nothing that an employer does not know. If you have good references, you can say something like "Excellent references from previous employers are available." This sentence can be in the "Personal" section.

A Few Words on Honesty

A good resume presents your strengths and not your weaknesses. But this does not mean that you should misrepresent yourself. Do not claim you have skills you do not have, a degree or other credential you did not earn, or any other claim that is not true. Besides not being the right thing to do, many employers will fire you for lying, should they find out.

Three Tips for Designing and Producing a Resume

What you say in your resume is important, but so is how you present it. Here are some brief tips that will help you create a superior resume after the writing is done.

* **Make your resume look good:** Make sure your resume looks good. Word-processing software and good printers allow you to create a professional-looking resume. All major word processors have resume-writing templates and wizards that make designing your resume simple.

   If you don't have access to a computer and a high-quality printer, many libraries provide free use of their computers for a certain period. Also, most small print shops and resume-writing services can produce a professional-looking resume for a modest cost. Unless you need help in writing your resume, they should charge no more than $50 to format a one- or two-page resume.

* **Get lots of copies:** Earlier in this book, you learned how you can develop hundreds of job leads through networking and cold contacts. It is to your advantage to give each contact one or more copies of your resume and JIST Card. So plan on having lots of copies available. You may go through several hundred before you land your job.

   If you don't have regular access to a computer system or photocopy machine, you can get good photocopies made at most quick-print shops. Look in the yellow pages for listings.

* **Use good paper and matching envelopes:** Most office supply stores and print shops have quality paper and matching envelopes for use with resumes and cover letters. The best paper has a rich look and texture. It costs more but is worth every penny. Ivory, white, and off-white are conservative colors that look professional. Don't use anything that looks gaudy or flashy. It could make your resume stand out in a bad way.

SUBMITTING RESUMES ELECTRONICALLY

During your job search, you will probably want or need to e-mail your resume to an employer or other contact. You will likely also want to post your resume on one or more employment sites. This section will give you some suggestions on how to increase the effectiveness of your resume in these uses.

E-mailing Your Resume

E-mail has taken the place of the telephone for many employers as the preferred way to communicate. If you are sending your resume to them, it is best if you have been referred to them by someone they know or contacted them by e-mail or phone first. If it makes sense to e-mail your resume, attach it as a word-processing or PDF file so that they can print it without losing your formatting. Give your attached file a clear name, such as "David Dillingham resume" so there is no confusion about what it contains.

Employers who don't know you from a previous contact often won't open a file that is attached to an e-mail. That's because many viruses are sent in attachments. Screening software may also simply delete an attachment or send it to the junk e-mail folder.

For these reasons, it can make sense to cut and paste your resume into the e-mail text rather than include it as a separate attachment. Paste it as formatted (RTF) text into your e-mail; then make format changes as needed to make it look acceptable in that format.

Your Resume and Searchable Databases

If you want to submit your resume to Web sites for employers to search, your standard resume should be modified for this use. That's because your resume will go into a database with thousands of others. Employers will then search this database using keywords or phrases to exclude resumes without those words or phrases. For example, if employers use the name of specific accounting software they use as one of their key phrases, your resume will not be selected unless it contains that software name. Because electronic resumes are used differently from those on paper, it is important to understand how you can increase their effectiveness.

TIP: As electronic resumes and scanning increase, it makes sense to have two resumes—one on paper that looks good to humans and another that scans and e-mails well. Having both, for use in different situations, gives you a competitive edge.

Using Resume Web Sites

There are many resume Web sites, and each has its own way of accepting a resume in electronic format. Some smaller sites are simple, asking you to enter information in just a few fields and then cut and paste your resume text into a text box. Others are more complex, requiring you to complete many fields of information and multiple options for submitting your resume text. For this reason, I strongly suggest that you go to several of the more frequently used resume-posting sites to see what they require.

For example, the most used resume-posting site, Monster.com, requires you to set up a personal account (free) with a password, address, job title sought, and other basic information. Then it offers you multiple ways to submit your resume. You can use Monster's resume-creation software to build your resume field by field, which they prefer. Or you can fill out some required fields and then cut and paste your resume text into their text box or upload your resume text, which must be in Microsoft Word format.

Many employers, particularly larger ones, will also ask you to submit your resume to them in electronic format. Here are the somewhat unfriendly instructions I found to submit your resume on one large employer's site. I deleted references to who this employer is.

We are employing an electronic applicant tracking system that allows us to receive your resume by e-mail, direct line fax, or hard copy. This system will enhance your exposure to a wider variety of employment opportunities at all sites within our company. The one-time submission of your resume makes you eligible for consideration of any openings for which you meet the minimum qualifications.

As your resume is input into our system, you receive an acknowledgment, and your resume is kept active in our database for one year. As openings occur, our recruiters search the database for individuals whose qualifications and skills match the criteria needed for the open positions. If a match occurs, you receive further notification regarding the specific opening.

To increase the effectiveness of your resume, be sure to clearly state your skills and experiences, educational background, work history, and specific salary information. In addition, please follow these directions when preparing your resume:

* *Prepare your resume on white or light-colored 8½-by-11 paper (for hard copy or faxing).*

* *Use a standard paper weight so that the system will produce a quality image (for hard copy or faxing).*

* *Avoid fancy treatments such as italics, underlining, and shadowing. Bold-faced type and capital letters are acceptable.*

* *Place your name at the top of the page on its own line, use a standard address format below your name, and list each phone number or e-mail address on a separate line.*

You may submit your resume by one of the following methods:

* *Electronic mail: The e-mail address is resume@bigcompany.com. You must put the word "resume" in the subject or reference line when e-mailing and submit it in ASCII text format. All information must be contained in the body of the message. We cannot accept attachments into this system.*

* *FAX: You may fax your information to 866-244-3325 (too-big-deal). Please fax in fine mode.*

* *Postal mail: You may mail a hard copy of your resume to Corporate Recruitment, Big Company, Corporate Center, Big City, ST 90214.*

TIP: Here is an odd bit of advice: Because so many resumes are being e-mailed or submitted in electronic formats now, some employers may actually pay less attention to them than in the past. Some employers say that they are more likely to actually look at resumes sent in old-fashioned ways, such as via mail or in person.

SKILLS FOR SUCCESS

Honesty

For the past few weeks, you've noticed Belinda, your co-worker, leaving 10 minutes early, and just yesterday you saw her take supplies out of the cabinet on her way out the door. Your boss asks you if you've noticed Belinda doing anything dishonest. What do you say?

The Most-Used Resume-Posting Sites

There are thousands of career-related sites that will post your resume, but here are the ones that are most often used at the time of this writing:

* **Most used overall:** Monster.com; CareerBuilder.com; HotJobs.com
* **For college graduates:** CollegeGrad.com; eRecruiting.com; NACELink.com
* **Managers and executives:** TheLadders.com; CareerJournal.com; 6FigureJobs.com
* **Diversity:** LatPro.com; iHispano.com; DiversityWorking.com
* **Specialty:** Dice.com; jobsinthemoney.com; eFinancialCareers.com
* **International:** JobsDB.com; naukri.com; JobStreet.com

Most Electronic Submissions Will Not Get You Good Results

Resumes submitted via e-mail to employers and others you contacted previously make sense. But submitting your unsolicited resume to Web sites and employer sites is not likely to result in the response you hope for. Unless you have highly sought-after skills or credentials, you are likely to hear either nothing at all or get weak responses from employers wanting to hire telemarketers or other hard-to-fill positions.

I am not against submitting your resume to resume database sites; I just ask you to use other more active methods as well. Some job seekers do get good interviews from resume database sites, but most are disappointed.

What should be clear to you is that you should *not* submit your resume to any Web site without first preparing one specifically for it. Understand that these sites will convert your carefully formatted resume into a simple text file based on keywords and phrases. Because your resume will be used in a different way, you need to prepare your resume for this use.

A Simple Design Is Best

The database that your resume goes into accepts only text, not design, because a basic format introduces fewer errors. What this means is that you need to remove your careful format and design elements and reduce your resume to the simplest text format, following these guidelines:

* No graphics
* No tab indentations
* No lines
* No line or paragraph indents
* No bold, italic, or other text variations
* No centering
* Only one easy-to-scan font

Reducing your resume to a text-only format may be discouraging, but it's the way it is.

Steps to Reformatting Your Print Resume

Fortunately, you can easily take your existing resume and reformat it for electronic submission. Here are some quick steps for doing so:

1. Cut and paste your resume text into a new file in your word processor.

2. Eliminate any graphics elements such as lines or images.

3. Limit your margins to no more than 65 characters wide.

4. Use an easy-to-scan font, such as Courier, Arial, Helvetica, or Times Roman. Eliminate bold, italic, and other font styles.

5. Introduce major sections with words in all-uppercase letters rather than in bold or a different font.

6. Keep all text aligned to the left, and eliminate centering unless you use the Spacebar key to center text.

7. Instead of using bullets, use a standard keyboard character such as the asterisk.

8. Instead of using the tab key or paragraph indents, use the space key to indent.

9. When you're done, click the File menu, choose the Save As command, and select the Plain Text, ASCII (American Standard Code for Information Interchange), or Text Only option if the formats appear in the Save as Type box. Name the file, click Save or OK, and then close the document. Then reopen the file to see how it looks. Make additional format changes as needed.

While this reformatting for electronic submission may undermine your creative side, think of it as making mashed potatoes from sauté potatoes Provençale: The result can be very good if you do it right.

Include Lots of Keywords and Phrases

Employers that are searching resume databases search for keywords in resumes. So, the more keywords you include, the more likely your resume will be selected. Keywords are words and phrases that are specific to the job you want. Here are some ways to find and handle keywords on your resume:

* **Add a keyword section:** A simple technique is to add a section to your resume titled "Key Skills." You can then add keywords that are not included elsewhere in your resume.

* **Include all your important skill words:** Include the key skills you identified in earlier chapters of this book. Chapters 3, "Develop Your Skills Language," and 5, "Consider Important Preferences in Your Career Planning," are good places to review these words and phrases.

* **Think like a prospective employer:** List the jobs you want. Then think of the keywords that employers are likely to use when searching for people who best qualify for these jobs.

* **Review job descriptions:** Carefully review descriptions for jobs you seek in major print references like the *Occupational Outlook Handbook* and the *O*NET Dictionary of Occupational Titles*. Most large Web sites that list job openings have lots of employer job postings and job descriptions that you can review for ideas. Corporate Web sites often post information on job openings, so they're another source of keywords. Make a list of keywords and phrases in descriptions of interest, and include them in your resume.

* **Be specific:** List certifications and licenses, name any software and machines you can operate, and include jargon, abbreviations, or special terms that an employer may use to find resumes for the jobs you want.

The sample resume on page 130 has been created for submission to a resume database. It has a plain format and lots of keywords and phrases that increase its chances of being selected when an employer searches a database.

Keywords That Work

Use powerful keywords in your applications, cover letters, and resumes to describe yourself and your abilities. Make yourself look and sound as good as you can without being deceptive or misleading.

Achieved	Decreased	Implemented	Planned	Serviced
Adapted	Delegated	Improved	Prepared	Set
Administered	Demonstrated	Increased	Presented	Shaped
Advised	Designed	Initiated	Prioritized	Simplified
Advocated	Developed	Inspired	Processed	Sold
Analyzed	Diagnosed	Installed	Procured	Solicited
Appraised	Directed	Instituted	Produced	Solved
Assembled	Discovered	Instructed	Promoted	Staffed
Assessed	Dispersed	Integrated	Provided	Started
Assigned	Edited	Interpreted	Publicized	Structured
Assisted	Educated	Interviewed	Published	Succeeded
Audited	Enabled	Invented	Received	Suggested
Balanced	Ensured	Investigated	Recommended	Summarized
Budgeted	Equipped	Led	Recruited	Supervised
Built	Established	Managed	Redesigned	Supported
Calculated	Examined	Mapped	Reduced	Surpassed
Collaborated	Exceeded	Marketed	Refined	Synthesized
Communicated	Executed	Mediated	Reorganized	Systematized
Compiled	Expanded	Mobilized	Repaired	Taught
Completed	Expedited	Monitored	Replaced	Trained
Composed	Facilitated	Motivated	Represented	Transported
Computed	Formulated	Obtained	Reproduced	Traveled
Conducted	Founded	Operated	Researched	Updated
Consolidated	Funded	Organized	Restored	Utilized
Contributed	Generated	Originated	Restructured	Validated
Controlled	Guided	Participated	Revitalized	Verified
Coordinated	Hired	Performed	Selected	Visualized
Created	Identified	Persuaded	Served	Wrote

A Sample Electronic Resume

```
SAMUEL FEINMAN
489 Smithfield Road
Salem, OR 97301
503.491.3033
samfine@earthlink.net

= = = = = = = = = = = = = = = = = = = = =

SALES PROFESSIONAL

Dynamic, motivated, award-winning sales professional with extensive
experience. Troubleshooter and problem-solver. Team player who can
motivate self and others. Excellent management and training skills.

= = = = = = = = = = = = = = = = = = = =

RELATED EXPERIENCE

Jackson Chevrolet, Springfield, OR
GENERAL MANAGER, XXXX-Present
* Consistently achieve top-ten volume dealer in the Northwest.
* Manage all dealership operations including computer systems, sales,
parts, service, and administration.
* Profitably operate dealership through difficult economic times.
* Meet or exceed customer service, parts, sales, and car service
objectives.
* Maintain high-profile used-car operation.

Afford-A-Ford, Albany, OR
ASSISTANT GENERAL MANAGER, XXXX-XXXX
* Consistently in top five for sales in district; met or exceeded sales
objectives.
* Supervised and trained staff of 90.
* Helped to convert a consistently money-losing store into a profitable
operation by end of first year.
* Focused on customer satisfaction through employee satisfaction and
training.
* Built strong parts and service business, managing excellent
interaction among parts, service, and sales.
* Instituted fleet-sales department and became top fleet-sales dealer
three years running.
* Built lease portfolio from virtually none to 31% of retail.

WetWater Pool Products, Salem, OR
SALES/CUSTOMER SERVICE, XXXX-XXXX
* Advised customers to purchase products that best met their needs while
focusing attention on products more profitable to company.
* Troubleshot and solved customer problems, identifying rapid solutions
and emphasizing customer satisfaction and retention.
* Oversaw shipping and receiving staff.

= = = = = = = = = = = = = = = = = = = = =

ADDITIONAL EXPERIENCE

State of Oregon, Salem, OR
COMPUTER TECHNICIAN INTERN, XXXX-XXXX
* Built customized computers for state offices.
* Worked with team on installation of computer systems.

= = = = = = = = = = = = = = = = = = = = =

EDUCATION

AS, Oregon Community College, Troy, OR
Major: Business studies

= = = = = = = = = = = = = = = = = = = = =

REFERENCES AVAILABLE ON REQUEST
```

This resume is adapted from Expert Resumes for People Returning to Work *by Wendy S. Enelow and Louise M. Kursmark (published by JIST Publishing).*

A FEW FINAL WORDS ON RESUMES

Before you write and use your resume, here is some advice that applies to both paper and electronic resumes.

* **Even the best of resumes will not get you a job:** You have to do that yourself. To do so, you have to get interviews and do well in them. Interviews are where the job search action is, not resumes.

* **Don't trust everyone's resume advice:** If you ask 10 people for advice on your resume, they will all be willing to give it—yet no 2 will agree. You have to make up your own mind about your resume. Feel free to break any "rules" if you have a good reason. It's your resume.

* **Don't avoid the job search by worrying about your resume:** Write a simple and error-free resume, and then go out and get lots of interviews. Later, you can write a better resume—if you want or need to.

* **Look over the sample resumes:** I include several sample resumes in this chapter. Some break "rules," and none is perfect. However, all are based on real resumes written by real people, although the names and other details have been changed. So look them over, learn from them, and then write your own.

  Some resumes were submitted by professional resume writers, and their names are noted. You can find professional resume writers in your area through the Professional Association of Resume Writers at www.parw.com and the National Resume Writers' Association at www.nrwa.com.

If you want to see more cover letters and resumes, many good books and Web sites provide samples. JIST publishes excellent collections written by professional resume writers. And I've written several books that provide lots of examples.

Use a Career Portfolio to Support Your Resume

Another way you can show prospective employers evidence of who you are and what you can do is with a career portfolio. What is a career portfolio? Unlike a resume, a career portfolio is a collection of documents placed in a binder or folder. It can include any of the following items:

* Resume
* School transcripts
* Summary of skills
* Credentials, such as diplomas and certificates of recognition
* Reference letters from school officials and instructors, former employers, or co-workers
* Examples of your work, such as samples of your writing, art, or business reports

Place each item on a separate page when you assemble your career portfolio.

You also might want to create a digital career portfolio. A digital portfolio contains all the information from your career portfolio but in an electronic format. This material is then copied onto a CD-ROM or published on a Web site. One advantage of a digital portfolio is that it can present your skills to a greater number of people than your paper career portfolio can.

Sample Chronological Resume Stresses Technical Credentials

This resume emphasizes the candidate's technical qualifications. The "Technical Skills Summary" section highlights skill statements and lists that do not fit into a traditional chronological form.

KAULANI MAKINO
507 Bedford Drive, Camarillo, California 93010
Home: (805) 555-1212 | makinopc@hotmail.com

Systems engineer/network administrator/analyst with more than 10 years of experience in secure wired/wireless secure networks. Computer degree and multiple certifications.

PROFESSIONAL EXPERIENCE

SYSTEMS ENGINEER/NETWORK SECURITY CONSULTANT   XXXX–XXXX
COMPUTER SCIENCES CORPORATION, INDUSTRY SERVICES GROUP, El Segundo, CA

Key technology advisor to health-industry clients during their wireless LAN migrations. Produced life-cycle cost and security analyses involving system requirements determination, modeling, and trade-off studies; baseline configuration; and test plan, criteria, and procedures development.

➤ Collaboratively designed and set up a secure IP broadband-based satellite system that delivered global communications and positioning (GPS) to more than 50 corporate enterprise partners and 10,000 employees.

NETWORK ADMINISTRATOR/ANALYST   XXXX–XXXX
CONCURRENT COMPUTER CORPORATION, Laguna Hills, CA

Charged with providing secure networking solutions and technical support to industries including academic, aerospace, and scientific. Performed advanced analysis and optimization of network, server, and workstation performance.

➤ Reengineered the company's archaic backup system, replacing it with super-sized shared-disk arrays and pooled devices connected within a secure storage-area network (SAN). The results were reduced backup costs, zero data loss, and a 30% cut in overtime labor.

SYSTEMS ENGINEER I   XXXX–XXXX
ELECTRONIC DATA SYSTEMS CORPORATION (EDS), Folsom, CA

Performed wireless network feasibility studies for government-specific applications.

➤ Baselined a local prison's wired/wireless network infrastructure. This baseline became the backbone of a bid for a multiyear, multimillion-dollar state prison communications network.

TECHNICAL SKILLS SUMMARY

CORE STRENGTHS: Project planning and management for wired/wireless connectivity (e-mail/groupware/ Internet/intranet); hardware/software configuration; RSA-compliant security/firewalls

PLATFORMS: Windows NT/2000/XP, Exchange, Active Directory, Linux, UNIX (Solaris, HP-UX, IRIX), Banyan VINES, Macintosh, OS/2/WARP, Cisco, Novell NetWare

SECURITY SOLUTIONS: Norton Internet Security Corporate, McAfee Enterprise, Sun Identity Server, Oracle Application Server, Citrix Metaframe Password Manager, Datakey CIP, IBM Client Security, Cisco Secure Access Control

EDUCATION and CERTIFICATIONS

University of California at Los Angeles   XXXX
   Bachelor of Science in Computer Science (BSCS)
Microsoft Certified Systems Engineer (MCSE)   XXXX
Cisco Certified Internetwork Expert (CCIE), Security+   XXXX
Certified Information Systems Security Professional (CISSP)   XXXX

This resume, written by Roleta Fowler Vasquez, is adapted from Expert Resumes for Computer and Web Jobs *by Wendy S. Enelow and Louise M. Kursmark (published by JIST Publishing).*

Sample Chronological Resume Emphasizes Results

A simple format focuses on accomplishments through the use of numbers. While Elaine Marshall's resume does not say so, it is obvious that she works hard and that she gets results.

ELAINE MARSHALL

(813) 555-1234   4004 Carroll Wood Circle, Tampa, Florida 33625   emarshall@yahoo.com

Registered Nurse

U.S. Air Force, XXXX–Present — **U.S. Army,** XXXX–XXXX

Level III Clinical Nurse, XXXX–Present

    Plan and implement nursing care for acute and critically ill patients. Provide immediate post-anesthesia recovery for postoperative patients. Orient and train new personnel. Supervise two medical technicians. Serve as trauma unit nurse specializing in liver and kidney transplant in Level 1 Trauma Center.

Triage Telephone Nurse, XXXX–XXXX

    Facilitated referrals for 140 primary-care providers, specialists, and community resources. Documented patient and nurse interaction and issued advice per established unit protocols. Acted as triage nurse in the Emergency Department. Identified patient classification range from emergency to non-urgent. Worked as the team coordinator. Formulated and planned care for patient's optimal health, ranging from physiological to psychosocial.

Nurse Manager, XXXX–XXXX

    Supervised three telephone triage nurses and ten appointment clerks. Planned, organized, and directed activities to enhance accessibility and ensure quality patient care for 90,000 enrolled beneficiaries, including retirees and families.

Staff Nurse, XXXX–XXXX

    Provided care to critically ill patients requiring complex computerized cardiac hemodynamic monitoring and mechanical ventilation. Supervised five nurses and three medical technicians.

Education & Training

MS, Community Health Administration and Wellness Promotion: College of Health Science, Chicago, IL, XXXX
BS, Nursing: Salve Regina College, Newport, RI, XXXX
Licensed Vocational Nurse, Salve Regina College, Newport, RI, XXXX

RECENT TRAINING:

Telephone Nursing Triage	XXXX	Trauma Nursing Core Course, Emergency Nurse	XXXX
Advanced Cardiovascular Life Support	XXXX	Nursing Service Fundamentals	XXXX
Basic Life Support	XXXX	Senior Leadership Training	XXXX
Pediatric Advanced Life Support	XXXX	Indoctrination for Medical Services Officers	XXXX
Nursing Service Management	XXXX	Casualty Care	XXXX
Aerospace Medicine School of Flight Nursing	XXXX	Critical Care Nursing	XXXX

ANNUAL TRAINING:

Code Procedures	Age-Specific Care
Medical Ethics	Standards of Conduct
Patient Rights	Mentoring for Supervisors
Management of Abused Patients	Putting Prevention into Practice
Infection Control	Anthrax Training
Staff Rights	Family Advocacy
Cultural Diversity	Fire Safety
Sexual Harassment	Electrical Safety
Suicide Awareness	Security Awareness
Anti-Terrorism Measures	

This resume, written by Peter S. Marx, is adapted from Expert Resumes for Health Care Careers *by Wendy S. Enelow and Louise M. Kursmark (published by JIST Publishing).*

Sample Skills Resume for Someone with Limited Work Experience

This sample is for a college student whose only work experience has been as an intern. She's applying for another internship, hoping that it will become a full-time position.

Erica C. Herman

School Address		**Permanent Address**
4444 Alder Avenue		8888 N.W. 15th Place
Eugene, OR 97401		Beaverton, OR 97229
(555) 444-4444	ericaherman@aol.com	(333) 555-5555

GOAL

A Public Relations Internship

RELEVANT QUALIFICATIONS

♦ Fully capable of handling assignments that require research, creativity, and decision-making skills. Deadline-oriented; can produce under pressure.
♦ Exceptional language skills, good interviewer, creative writer, able to express thoughts clearly and effectively both verbally and in writing.
♦ Extensive knowledge of and experience with PageMaker, Photoshop, Microsoft Office applications, and Internet communication.
♦ Achiever with an outgoing, enthusiastic personality; comfortable with individuals of all ages and professional levels.
♦ Bilingual: fluent in Spanish.
♦ Editor, high school newspaper.

EDUCATION

University of Oregon, Eugene, OR   Fall XXXX–Present
Major: Journalism   Concentration: Public Relations   Cumulative GPA: 3.5
Minor: Spanish

Activities
• Chi Omega Sorority—Marketing/Public Relations Director
• Vice President, National Honor Society
• Public Relations Student Society of America
• Order of Omega

University of Georgia, Athens, GA   Fall XXXX–Spring XXXX
Major: Pre-Public Relations   Dean s List honors
Minor: Spanish   Cumulative GPA: 3.5

RELATED EXPERIENCE

Media Services Intern   Jan. XXXX–Present
University of Oregon Athletic Media Services, Eugene, OR
Research and develop press releases covering various collegiate athletic events. Regularly update the media with information on all UO home athletic events. Write copy for team media guides; manipulate photos for media and public use. Post releases and team results on *www.goducks.com*.

Public Relations Intern   June XXXX–Aug. XXXX
Portland Art Museum, Portland, OR
As key media contact, coordinated media interviews for staff, curators, and directors; fielded inquiries regarding current exhibitions; and assisted in coordinating and staffing special events to gain the public s interest and participation. Researched and produced press releases, public service announcements, and copy for the PAM newsletter. Created exhibition press kits.

Continued....

ERICA C. HERMAN   Page 2

RELATED EXPERIENCE
Continued

Oregon Public Affairs Intern   Dec. XXXX–Aug. XXXX
XYZ Corporation, Hillsboro, OR
Participated in coordinating community and media relations events. Wrote for worldwide PA newsletter on an Internet Web site; monitored correspondence between the corporation and Oregon legislators. Assisted with the Strategic Investment Program.

HONORS & AWARDS

National Society of Collegiate Scholars
Ancient Order of Druids Honor Society
Outstanding Freshman in PRSSA, XXXX–XXXX
PRSA Codispoti Technology Section Grant, XXXX
Erik Elder Memorial Journalism Scholarship, XXXX
Outstanding Junior: service and performance in journalism, XXXX

COMMUNITY SERVICE

American Cancer Society administrative volunteer
Oregon Humane Society foster family member
Oregon Public Broadcasting telethon volunteer
Spanish tutor for mentally handicapped student
Make-A-Wish Foundation contributor

This adapted resume is a resume written by Karen L. Conway in Gallery of Best Resumes for People Without a Four-Year Degree *by David F. Noble (published by JIST Publishing).*

Sample Combination Resume for a Career Changer

This job seeker has no actual work experience in the field. His resume emphasizes his relevant education, projects completed as group assignments, volunteer work with local bands, and transferable skills.

Alex Standish

4429 Del Mar Avenue, Chula Vista, CA 91915
Home 619-451-0904 ▶ Mobile 619-204-1121
audio-alex@aol.com

GOAL	**Audio/Video Production Assistant**
QUALIFICATION HIGHLIGHTS	▶ Current training in traditional and state-of-the-art audio and video production. ▶ History of bringing projects to successful conclusion, on time and on budget. ▶ Track record of leadership and achievement in customer-focused jobs. ▶ Proven ability to quickly learn and train others in new processes and systems. ▶ Positive attitude and strong work ethic.
EDUCATION	**Associate of Applied Science, Audio/Video Production** COASTAL COLLEGE OF TECHNOLOGY, San Diego, CA, December XXXX
SKILLS	**Production Management** ▶ Script breakdowns ▶ Schedules ▶ Budgets ▶ Shot logs **Production** ▶ DVC and DVCPro cameras ▶ AVID editing system ▶ Production aesthetics **Lighting** ▶ Studio, chroma-key, and product lighting ▶ 3-point lighting ▶ Diffusion **Audio** ▶ Microphone setup ▶ Location audio ▶ Pro Tools audio tools ▶ Analog recording ▶ Foley miking ▶ Foley editing ▶ Signal flow and patching on audio ▶ 24-track linear tape ▶ Non-linear Digital Audio Workstation
PROJECTS	Repeatedly elected as **Production Manager** of 5–8 person project teams because of excellent organizational skills. Brought all projects in on time and within assigned budget without compromising quality. Highlights include ▶ **6 start-to-finish commercial filming projects.** Participated in hands-on project work (planning and setup of audio, camera, and microphones; studio filming; extensive editing). Prepared scripts, budgets, and timing sheets. ▶ **3 audio recording projects.** Prepared demo tapes for local bands via live studio sessions. Participated in studio setup, track mixing, level setting, and CD burning. ▶ **Lighting, analog recording, Foley editing projects.** Performed all facets of audio/video work.
ADDITIONAL EXPERIENCE	**Project Manager/Landscaper:** BAYSIDE NURSERIES, San Diego, CA, XXXX–XXXX ▶ Independently managed assigned accounts, both residential and commercial; designed, installed, and maintained visually appealing landscape projects. ▶ Managed equipment, tools, and project schedules; quickly resolved on-site problems. ▶ Based on reliability and performance, selected to remain for year-round greenhouse position when seasonal work ended. **Customer Service Representative:** AL'S GARDEN CENTER, Chula Vista, CA, XXXX–XXXX ▶ Hired as first cashier prior to new store opening; rapidly promoted to customer-service desk based on ability to quickly and resourcefully resolve customer questions. ▶ Used computerized inventory program. ▶ Chosen to train new employees in store procedures and customer-service skills.
COMPUTER SKILLS	▶ Microsoft Word, Excel, and Publisher. ▶ Solid foundation of computer knowledge gained during 13 months of full-time studies in computer science (University of California at San Diego, XXXX–XXXX).

This resume, adapted from a resume written by Louise M. Kursmark, is from Expert Resumes for Career Changers *by Wendy S. Enelow and Louise M. Kursmark (published by JIST Publishing).*

Sample Combination Resume in a Two-Page Format

This resume for a person wanting to change careers—from education to not-for-profit—emphasizes applicable education and skills and relates all sections back to the applicant's job objective. Key self-management, adaptive, and transferable skills are highlighted throughout.

FRANKLIN HARRIS

84 Park Boulevard • East Syracuse, NY 13900
315-999-5555 • fharris@myemail.com

SUMMARY

- Diverse professional experience gained in human services, local and state government, academic settings, and not-for-profits in addition to extensive community involvement as a volunteer
- Skills in project/program development and implementation; strategic planning; and the management of human, financial, and other resources—with a solid record of accomplishments and contributions
- Extensive hands-on involvement in the creation, update, and execution of procedures and policies
- Well-developed interpersonal, communication, and problem-solving capabilities
- Successful achievement of individual goals and service as an effective team member

HIGHLIGHTS OF ACCOMPLISHMENTS

Program and Operations Management
- Held eighteen-year career with the NYS Division of Parole, beginning as a parole officer based at a state prison facility and promoted several times, most recently serving as senior parole officer.
  - ◇ Managed personal caseloads as well as multiple parole offices and teams of parole officers. In last position, directed six officers, overseeing approximately 450 parolees in an urban area.
  - ◇ Represented Syracuse field operations on citywide task force to target homicide reduction.
  - ◇ Selected for committee involvement, assigned projects, and sought out for advice relative to criminal justice and parole operations knowledge.
- Transitioned Cayuga County's Child Protection Services when state law refocused the agency's purpose.
- Doubled Junior Achievement involvement during tenure as director of Cayuga County operations.
- Held several newly created positions.

Project/Program Development and Implementation
- Designed and implemented the Cease Fire Program in conjunction with the City of Syracuse's task force on homicide reduction. The program was deterrent-focused and targeted at parolees.
- Developed a home/school liaison program for an area public school and served as the first home/school coordinator for that district.
- Created and launched an innovative program for at-risk children in the foster care program. Authored new operating procedures and manuals for staff as well as foster-home parents.

Financial Management
- As director of two agencies, guided fiscal decision making and planning.
- As a school board president, served as financial officer for that school. Involved in bargaining contracts for superintendent and principals.
- Reorganized a nonprofit agency's accounting system to achieve better financial control.

Teaching/Training
- Developed and delivered course curriculum at the university/college level for a variety of learners.
- Assessed training needs for organizations.
- Drove the creation of the Institute for Child Abuse Training.

(continued)

(continued)

GOVERNMENT & HUMAN SERVICES EXPERIENCE

NEW YORK STATE, DIVISION OF PAROLE   XXXX–XXXX
Senior Parole Officer, Field Operations (Syracuse, NY & Onondaga County)
Managed six parole officers, five overseeing 400+ parolees in the Main Street section of the City of
Syracuse and the sixth supervising 30 individuals in the electronic monitoring/home confinement program
throughout Syracuse. Reviewed and made determinations on requests for parolee arrest warrants.
Facility Parole Officer 2, Cayuga Correctional Facility
Facility Parole Officer 2, Auburn Incarceration Facility
Managed the activities of these parole offices, facilitating the prisoner release process from case assessment
to inmates' interviews, release orientation, and presentation to parole board, as well as postrelease support
coordination. Supervised seven staff members. Cayuga's medium-security prison houses 850 inmates, and
the Auburn behavior-modification program services 300 inmates.
Field Parole Officer, Syracuse, NY & Parole Officer, Cayuga Correctional Facility

CAYUGA COUNTY DEPARTMENT OF SOCIAL SERVICES—Auburn, NY   XXXX–XXXX
Cluster Home Coordinator
Successfully created and implemented a program for at-risk children, which maintained children's ties with
their families/communities while providing services at a reduced cost compared to institutional care.

CAYUGA COUNTY DEPARTMENT OF SOCIAL SERVICES—Auburn, NY   XXXX–XXXX
Supervisor of Child Protection Services/Case Worker
As first supervisor of Child Protection Services in this county, oversaw the transition from a broad focus on
child welfare to Child Protection Services as regulated by a 1973 New York State law. Directed five case
workers and three home aides in the management of an average of 100 cases.

EDUCATION & NONPROFIT EXPERIENCE

AUBURN COMMUNITY COLLEGE—Auburn, NY   XXXX
Instructor, Sociology Department (at Cayuga Correctional Facility)

SYRACUSE UNIVERSITY—Syracuse, NY   XXXX–XXXX
Adjunct Professor
Provided Human Services Development training to social workers throughout New York State. Performed
an assessment of New York City's Bureau of Children's Services to identify staff development needs.
Collaborated in the creation of a video illustrating family communication, which was marketed and sold.
Instructor/Program Development
Working via the New York State Research Foundation in conjunction with Cornell University and Syracuse
University, contributed to curriculum development of social worker training. Delivered training across the
state. Instrumental in the creation of the Institute for Child Abuse Training now based at Cornell.

NORTH SYRACUSE CENTRAL SCHOOL DISTRICT—North Syracuse, NY   XXXX
Home/School Coordinator
Developed, implemented, and managed a home/school liaison program to improve communication between
school and home for the benefit of students with educational and/or behavioral issues.

ONONDAGA COMMUNITY COUNSELING SERVICES & SPECIAL FRIENDS
PROGRAM—DeWitt, NY   XXXX
Executive Director

JUNIOR ACHIEVEMENT OF CAYUGA COUNTY—Auburn, NY   XXXX–XXXX
Director

FRANKLIN HARRIS—PAGE 2

This resume, written by Salome A. Farraro, appears in Gallery of Best Resumes: A Collection of Quality Resumes
by Professional Resume Writers *by David F. Noble (published by JIST Publishing).*

Sample Combination Resume with a Matching JIST Card

This resume showcases the job seeker's substantial work experience. She emphasizes skills related to her job objective in the first section and then includes her work history in chronological form later. I include Denise's JIST Card here to show you how these two job search tools can relate to each other effectively.

DENISE A. WOLFE

7102 Dalewood Court — Nashville, Tennessee 37207 — (615) 860-2922 — dawolfe@dawolfe.com

SUMMARY OF QUALIFICATIONS

- **REGISTERED DENTAL ASSISTANT** with ten years' experience assisting with direct patient care. Special interest in pediatric patient care, with the desire and willingness to learn other areas of dentistry.

- Graduate of Dental Assistant program at Volunteer State Community College. Continuing dental education in Coronal Polishing. CPR certified.

- Special expertise in patient management and making patients of all ages feel as relaxed and comfortable as possible, relieving any anxiety or tension they might have. Skilled working with handicapped and other special-needs patients.

- Sound knowledge of clinical procedures and dental/medical terminology.

DENTAL HEALTH CARE EXPERIENCE

DENTAL ASSISTANT ....XXXX to XXXX
David A. Lambert, D.D.S. — Montgomery, Alabama

- Performed general chairside duties (four-handed dentistry) and assisted with all types of procedures, including extraction, crowns, pulpotomy, and composites. Monitored nitrous oxide and applied topical anesthetics.
- Prepared patients (children, adolescents, young adults, handicapped, special needs) for treatment, making them as comfortable and at ease as possible. Assisted with in-hospital visits and procedures.
- Performed coronal polishing, oral examinations, and charting.
- Sterilized instruments and equipment. Prepared tray setups for procedures.
- Mixed amalgams, cements, and other dental materials. Took and poured impressions.
- Took, processed, and mounted X rays. Used intraoral camera equipment.
- Scheduled and confirmed appointments. Ordered dental supplies and maintained inventory levels.

DENTAL ASSISTANT ....XXXX to XXXX
Timothy J. Koeppel, D.M.D. — Hendersonville, Tennessee

- Took impressions, poured and trimmed models, and made night guards.
- Took and processed panorex and cephalometric X rays.
- Instructed and encouraged patients to develop good oral-hygiene habits.

EDUCATION AND TRAINING

Coronal Polishing — Continuing Dental Education — XXXX
University of Tennessee, Memphis College of Dentistry

Dental Assistant Certificate of Proficiency — XXXX
Volunteer State Community College — Gallatin, Tennessee

Certified in CPR through American Heart Association — XXXX to Present

---

This resume is from Expert Resumes for Health Care Careers *by Wendy S. Enelow and Louise M. Kursmark (published by JIST Publishing).*

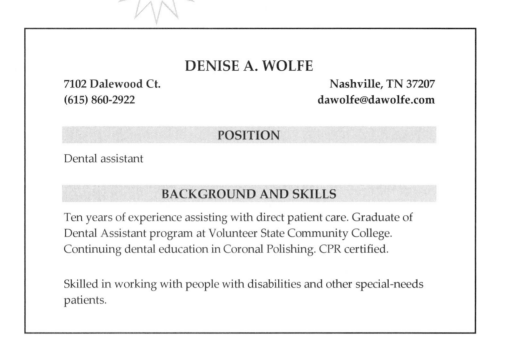

DENISE A. WOLFE

7102 Dalewood Ct.   Nashville, TN 37207
(615) 860-2922   dawolfe@dawolfe.com

POSITION

Dental assistant

BACKGROUND AND SKILLS

Ten years of experience assisting with direct patient care. Graduate of
Dental Assistant program at Volunteer State Community College.
Continuing dental education in Coronal Polishing. CPR certified.

Skilled in working with people with disabilities and other special-needs
patients.

E-MAIL AND COVER LETTERS

Before e-mail was common, most resumes were mailed with a letter or note that "covered" the
resume. Now you are more likely to send an e-mail message with your resume as an attached
file—and no formal cover letter. A less formal business climate in some organizations also permits
your brief comments to be made on a simple note or Post-it note attached to your mailed resume.
Again, no formal cover letter would be needed in this situation. These less formal styles are even
more acceptable if you have already made contact with the employer and are following up.

You may find that you don't need to send many formal cover letters. Job seekers using the
approaches I recommend get by with informal thank-you notes sent with resumes and JIST
Cards. But certain types of jobs and some organizations require a more formal approach, so use
your judgment.

While formal cover letters have become less important over time, there are a variety of situations
where using them makes sense. E-mail sent to an employer must also be done more carefully
than normal e-mail because being too informal or using incorrect spelling or grammar will create
a negative impression.

Seven Tips for Creating More Effective E-mail, Cover Letters, and Employer Contacts

While you may not use many cover letters in your job search, you should know the basics of
how to write them and will need to know what to say in e-mail messages and notes that have
similar functions. So here are some brief tips to help you create more effective e-mail, cover letters, and employer contacts:

* **Send your message or letter and resume to someone by name:** Get the name of the person who is most likely to supervise you. Call or e-mail that person first to get an interview. Then send your message and resume.

* **Get it right:** Make sure you get the person's name, organization name, and address right. Include the contact's correct job title. Make sure that your e-mail or letter does not contain grammar and other errors, because that creates a poor impression.

* **Be clear about what you want:** If you want an interview, ask for it. If you are interested in the organization, say so. Give clear reasons why the employer should consider you for a job.

* **Be friendly and professional:** A professional but simple style is usually best. Avoid a hard-sell "hire me now!" approach. No one likes to be pushed.

* **Make it look good:** Just as with a resume, correspondence to an employer must look good. Take time to format your correspondence so that it looks professional. For mailed correspondence, use nice paper and matching envelopes. A standard business format is good for most letters.

* **Mention your reason for contacting or source of information:** Typical reasons for sending an e-mail or cover letter include responding to an ad, preparing an employer for an interview (the best reason!), and following up after a phone call or interview. Each of these situations is different, and samples for handling each are included in the sample letters that follow.

* **Follow up:** Remember that contacting an employer directly is much more effective than sending an unsolicited e-mail message or letter. Don't expect these passive approaches to get you many interviews. They are best used to follow up after you have contacted the employer.

Sample Cover Letters

The samples that follow give you content, style, and format ideas for cover letters. You can easily adapt their content for use in e-mails.

Space limited the number of samples I could provide here, so the ones I include are pretty basic. Even so, the samples will give you ideas on how to handle typical situations in your job search.

Contents of a Great Cover Letter

A great cover letter will have this structure:

* **An introductory paragraph** that gets the reader's attention and tells why you are writing and which position you are applying for.
* **A body** that builds a connection between your skills and the organization's needs.
* **A concluding paragraph** that states your interest in working for the organization and closes by thanking the reader for his or her time and consideration.

Sample Cover Letter for a Specific Opening

This new graduate called first and arranged an interview—the best approach of all. In her letter, she mentions specifically how she changed procedures for a business and saved the company money. Note how she includes skills such as working hard and dealing with deadlines.

113 S. Meridian Street
Greenwich, CT 11721

March 10, XXXX

Ms. Willa Brown
Connecticut Water Company
604 Waterway Boulevard
Parien, CT 11716

Dear Ms. Brown:

I am following up on the brief chat we had today by phone. After getting the details on the position you have open, I am certain that it is the kind of job I have been looking for. My enclosed JIST Card and resume provide more details on my background. I hope you have a chance to review them before we meet next week.

My special interest has long been in the large-volume order processing systems that your organization has developed so well. While in school, I researched the flow of order processing work for a large corporation as part of a class assignment. With some simple and inexpensive procedural changes I recommended, check-processing time was reduced by an average of three days. For the number of checks and the amount of money involved, this one change resulted in an estimated increase in interest revenues of more than $135,000 per year.

Although I have just recently graduated from business school, I have considerable experience for a person of my age. I have worked in a variety of jobs dealing with large numbers of people and deadline pressures. My studies have also been far more hands-on and practical than those of most schools, so I have a good working knowledge of current business systems and procedures. This includes a good understanding of various computer spreadsheet and application programs, the use of automation, and experience with cutting costs and increasing profits. I am also a hard worker and realize I will need to apply myself to get established in my career.

I am most interested in the position you have available and am excited about the potential it offers. I look forward to seeing you next week.

Sincerely,

Caroline Presson

Enclosures: JIST Card
             Resume

Sample Cover Letter After an Interview

In this situation, the applicant uncovered a problem during her interview. She is writing to offer to solve the problem even though no job exists. Many job seekers never think of scheduling an interview when there is no job opening, but many jobs are created this way to accommodate a good person.

6254 South Hawthorn Drive
Dunwoody, GA 21599

April 10, XXXX

Mr. Christopher Massey
Import Distributors, Inc.
417 East Main Street
Atlanta, GA 21649

Dear Mr. Massey:

I know you have a busy schedule, so I was pleasantly surprised when you arranged a time for me to see you. While you do not have a position open now, your organization is just the sort of place where I would like to work. As we discussed, I like to be busy with a variety of duties, and the active pace I saw at your company is what I seek.

Your ideas on increasing business sound creative. I have thought about the customer service problem and would like to discuss a possible solution. It would involve a simple system of color-coded files that could prioritize correspondence to give older requests priority status. The handling of complaints could also be speeded up through the use of simple form letters similar to those you mentioned. I have some thoughts on how this might be done, and I will work out a draft of procedures and sample letters if you are interested. It can be done on the computers your staff already uses and would not require any additional cost to implement.

Regardless of whether you have a position for me in the future, I appreciate the time you have given me. An extra copy of my JIST Card and resume are enclosed for your files or to pass on to someone else.

Let me know if you want to discuss the ideas I presented earlier in this letter. I can be reached at any time on my cell phone at (942) 267-1103. I will call you next week, as you suggested, to keep you informed of my progress.

Sincerely,

Sandra Zaremba

Enclosures: JIST Card
             Zaremba Resume

Sample E-mail Message from a Network Contact

This job seeker uses names from a professional association to conduct a long-distance job search. In his e-mail message, he explains the end of his old job, indicates certain skills, and mentions the availability of positive references.

File Edit View Create Actions Text Help

Welcome | Request from Fellow NSCA Member × *notes*

Forward   Send   Send and File   Save As Draft   Address...   Delivery Options...   Tools

To: pramirez@centralsatellites.com

cc:

bcc:

Subject: Request from Fellow NSCA Member

Mr. Ramirez, I obtained your name from the membership directory of the National Satellite Communications Association. I have been a member for over 10 years, and I am very active in the southeast region. In fact, we worked together on the annual national convention-planning committee five years ago. The reason I am writing is to ask for your help. The firm I had been employed with has been bought by a larger corporation. The operations here have been disbanded, leaving me unemployed.

While I like where I live, I know that finding a position at the level of responsibility I seek may require a move. As a center of the communications business, your city is one I have targeted for special attention. A copy of my resume is enclosed for your use. I'd like you to review it and consider where a person with my background would get a good reception in your area. Perhaps you could think of a specific person for me to contact.

I have specialized in fast-growing organizations or ones that have experienced rapid change. My particular strength is in bringing systems under control and then increasing profits. While my resume does not state this, I have excellent references from my former employer and would have remained if a similar position existed at the new owner's location.

As a member of the association, I hope that you can provide some special attention to my request for assistance. I plan to come to your city on a job-hunting trip within the next six weeks. Prior to my trip, I will call you for advice on whom I might contact for interviews. Even if they have no jobs open for me now, perhaps they will know of someone else who does.

My attached resume lists my phone number and other contact information should you want to reach me before I call you. Thanks in advance for your help on this.

Sample E-mail Message Following Up on a Cold Call

This applicant contacted the office manager by phone and set up an interview for his upcoming visit to the area. His message is a follow-up to his call.

File Edit View Create Actions Text Help

Welcome | Marie K Leonardo · Drafts | > RE: Figure Corrections, round 3 | Witte Interview and Resume × *notes*

Forward   Send   Send and File   Save As Draft   Address...   Delivery Options...   Tools

To: kmiller@lendonx2nsears.com

cc:

bcc:

Subject: Witte Interview and Resume

Ms. Miller:

Attached is a copy of my resume that describes my work experience as a legal assistant. I hope this information will be helpful as background for our interview next Monday at 4 p.m.

I appreciate your taking time to describe your requirements so fully. The position sounds like one that could develop into a satisfying career. And my training in accounting—along with experience using a variety of computer programs—seems to match your needs.

Lendon, Lendon, and Sears is a highly respected law firm in New Jersey. I am excited about this opportunity to interview, and I look forward to meeting with you.

Sincerely,

Kyle Witte

CASE STUDY: A RESUME CAUTION

Evan had everything taken care of. He was applying for five teaching jobs: two at the college level and three at the high school level. He researched all five of the schools, wrote individualized cover letters to each, and updated his resume. Attaching his resume to each letter, he prepared the envelopes and put them in his mailbox for pickup.

It wasn't until hours later, as he was applying to another college job, that Evan noticed the "Objectives" statement on the resume template: "Seeking position as a high school English teacher at any grade level for a prestigious private institution." Unfortunately, the mail had already been picked up.

Though Evan did ultimately get calls back from all three of the prestigious private high schools, the two colleges simply sent him form letters informing him that no positions were available.

chapter 10

Use JIST Cards® to Get Interviews

Resumes are a traditional job search tool. They are often necessary for your job search, but, by themselves, they are not very effective in getting interviews. Chapter 9, "Write Effective Resumes, E-mail, and Cover Letters," includes a sample of a mini-resume, called a JIST Card, which often is even more effective than the resume as a job search tool. You will likely need both resumes and JIST Cards for your job search. This chapter will show you why JIST Cards are so useful as well as how to use them. Before we get into the details, let's imagine how a potential employer is likely to respond to them.

Time is the coin of your life. It is the only coin you have, and only you can determine how it will be spent. Be careful lest you let other people spend it for you.

Carl Sandburg

Pretend that you are an employer and are responsible for hiring workers for your auto shop. You may or may not have a job opening now. Read the information in the box below, and then answer the questions that follow it.

Stephen Kijek
Phone Message: (222) 222-2222
E-mail: skijek@yahoo2.com

Position Desired: Auto mechanic

Skills: More than three years of work experience, including one year in a full-time auto mechanic program. Familiar with all hand tools and electronic diagnostic equipment. Can handle tune-ups and common repairs to brakes, exhaust systems, and electrical and mechanical systems. Am a fast and careful worker, resulting in 98% positive customer satisfaction ratings. Have all tools required and can start work immediately.

Prefer full-time work, any shift.

Honest, reliable, good with people.

How Did You React?

Please answer the questions that follow. Answer truthfully, but as if you're in the role of an employer who supervises auto repairs. Base your answers on your reaction to the information in the Kijek JIST Card.

1. Do you feel good about this person—yes or no? _____

2. Would you be willing to interview him if you had an appropriate job opening—yes or no?
   _____ Why?_____
   _____

3. Would you be willing to see him even if you did not have a job opening now—yes or no?
   _____ Why?_____
   _____

JIST CARDS GET RESULTS

Most people who read a JIST Card for the first time say they would be willing to interview that person if they had a job opening. And many would be willing to interview that person for a future opening even if they did not have an opening now. It takes about 30 seconds or less to read a JIST Card, but the card creates a positive impression with most employers. There simply is no other job search tool that can accomplish these results.

Would a resume accomplish the same thing? It might, but a well-done JIST Card will often help you get an interview, where a more detailed resume will not. The reason, I think, is that the JIST Card presents what an employer needs and wants to know, with no extra information that might be used to screen you out.

> *The JIST Card presents what an employer needs and wants to know, with no extra information that might be used to screen you out.*

JIST Cards are often printed on 3-by-5-inch cards, in smaller business card sizes, and in other formats.

Some Uses for Your JIST Card

Your JIST Card can be inexpensively printed on a computer printer or by the hundreds at a quick-print shop. Have plenty of them available, because they work only if you use them. Here are some ways you can use your JIST Card in your job search:

* **Give them to friends and relatives:** Ask them to keep you in mind if they hear of any job openings. Also ask them to give the cards to others who might know of a job opening for you.

* **Attach one to a completed application:** Employers can then separate it from the application and put it on their bulletin board or desk.

* **Send one to an employer before an interview:** You can attach your JIST Card to an e-mail to potential employers, along with your resume, before an interview.

* **Enclose one in your thank-you notes:** By including the JIST Card in your thank-you notes, you are reminding the recipients of both your job search and your qualifications.

* **Give several to people who are willing to give them to others:** Everyone in your network should get copies of your JIST Card. Ask your network contacts to pass them on to others who might know of an opening for you.

* **Attach one to a resume:** The JIST Card acts as a quick summary of your resume.

You may have other ideas on how to use JIST Cards. For example, some people have put them on grocery store bulletin boards and under car windshield wiper blades in parking lots. The more JIST Cards you put into circulation, the better!

BUSINESS ETIQUETTE

Business Card Shuffle

Business cards are an internationally recognized means of exchanging personal and professional information, but the exchange of these cards follows different rules in different countries. In Japan, for example, you should accept business cards with both hands. A few general rules apply across cultures, however. Generally, business cards are given out at the beginning or end of a meeting. Also, you should always make it a point to actually look over a card someone gives you—don't just shove it in your wallet or purse—and ask questions if you have any.

Four Reasons That JIST Cards Work So Well

Employers and other people in your network love JIST Cards. They are an effective tool for several reasons:

* **JIST Cards are different:** People are interested in JIST Cards because they are unique. They attract positive attention and comments—good things to get when you are looking for a job.

* **JIST Cards quickly present the most important information that employers want to know:** They very quickly give a lot of information, including your name, how you can be contacted, the job you want, and the key education, training, skills, and experience you have to support your job objective.

* **JIST Cards are less likely to get lost on a desk than other paperwork:** Resumes and applications tend to be put in piles and buried among other papers. E-mail attachments are often never opened or printed, and then they're stored electronically with other e-mail. But printed JIST Cards tend to get taped on a wall, put on a bulletin board, and left out in the open so that the employer can see them.

* **JIST Cards are great tools for people in your network:** Your friends and relatives may not know much about your skills, training, and experience. JIST Cards give them a tool they can use to better understand your skills and to pass along to others. Many job leads can come from putting hundreds of JIST Cards in use.

Sample JIST Cards

Following are some sample JIST Cards. They are for different jobs, from entry-level to those requiring more experience. Study them, and use any ideas that help you to write your own JIST Card.

Deborah Levy has been working in hotel housekeeping since she was a senior in high school. She has been recognized for her excellence as an employee and believes that she deserves a position in housekeeping management, even though she's still completing her degree in hotel management. Her JIST Card emphasizes her experience, exemplary attitude, and excellent work record.

Deborah Levy
Cell Phone: (333) 333-3333
E-mail: deb21@att.com

Job Objective: Entry-level hotel management

Skills: Three years of experience in hotel housekeeping. Employee of the Month (5 times) for improving productivity and quality. Completed one year toward an associate's degree in hotel management. Approach my work with reliable self-management, excellent communication, and creative problem-solving skills.

Enthusiastic, well organized, detail oriented.

Jamal Washington worked full time as he completed his degree in EET. He uses his JIST Card to point out that he maintained good grades despite the heavy schedule, proving to a potential employer that he is a reliable, motivated, and intelligent person. He calls attention to his broad range of experience by listing medical, consumer, communications, and industrial electronic equipment and applications.

Jamal Washington
Phone: (444) 444-4444   E-mail: jwash@netzero.com

Job Objective: Electronics installation, maintenance, and sales

Experience: Four years' work experience plus two-year AA degree in electronics engineering technology. Managed a $500,000/yr. business while attending school full time, with grades in the top 25 percent. Familiar with all major electronic diagnostic and repair equipment. Hands-on experience with medical, consumer, communications, and industrial electronic equipment and applications. Good problem-solving and customer-service skills.

I do what it takes to get the job done right.

Joyce Neely gained her experience as a systems analyst and designer in the military. Listing her programming language and operating systems competencies on her JIST Card can help potential employers determine whether she has the experience required for the available position. Note that she also mentioned the experience she gained in supervising others on projects, even though she was not given an official management position. She placed the statement of her willingness to relocate in a prominent position because she knew that it would increase her appeal to employers.

Joyce Neely
Cell Phone: (555) 555-5555
E-mail: neelyj@netzero.com

Position: Systems analyst and designer

Experience: Ten years of combined education and experience in database systems and design. Competent in programming in C++, Java, and DHTML, and database management on Windows, Linux, and other computer platforms. Extensive PC and network applications experience. Supervise staff of seven on special projects. Meet deadlines.

Desire career-oriented position. Will relocate.

Dedicated self-starter, creative problem solver.

Keywords are important in Tomas Marrin's JIST Card. He knows that terms like *business management* and *administration, planning, cost management, CPA, consistent, results, communication, budgeting, cost savings,* and *computerized* will catch a potential employer's eye. Adding the personal detail of *energetic* paints a picture of him as a sharp, aggressive businessperson.

TOMAS MARRIN, CPA

PHONE: (777) 777-7777   E-MAIL: TMARRIN@RR.COM

JOB OBJECTIVE
Business management position requiring skills in problem solving, planning, organizing, and cost management.

EXPERIENCE
BS in business administration. Over 10 years of management experience. Progressively responsible positions. Managed staff of as many as 40 and budgets in excess of $6 million a year. Consistently improving results. Excellent communication skills. Thorough knowledge of budgeting, cost savings, and computerized database and spreadsheet programs.

Results-oriented, self-motivated, good problem-solving skills, energetic.

COMPLETE YOUR OWN JIST CARD

There is more to a well-written JIST Card than meets the eye. Look over the different sections of a JIST Card in the sample and the tips that follow. Then use the lines after each tip to write your own text.

A JIST Card is small, so it can't contain many details, only the information that is most important to employers. For a simple card, consider all that Sonja Zuleyka's sample includes.

Sonja Zuleyka —————————————— Name
Home phone: (333) 333-3333
E-mail: SKZ1128@aol.com —————————— Contact Information

Position: General Office/Clerical ——————————— Position Desired

More than two years of work experience, plus one year of training in office
practices, using computer programs (word processing, spreadsheet, accounting, —— Experience, Education, and Training
database, and graphic design) and the Internet. Accurate at 70 wpm. Efficient
with general ledger and handle payables, receivables, and most accounting —— Job-Related Skills,
tasks. Responsible for daily deposits averaging more than $200,000 monthly. Performance, Results
Accustomed to strict deadlines and intense demands.

—————————————————————————— Special Conditions

Willing to work any hours. Organized, honest, reliable, and hard working. Good —— Good-Worker Traits,
interpersonal skills. Adaptive Skills

Your JIST Card

This worksheet refers to Sonja's JIST Card and then asks you to write sections of your own JIST Card. Read the instructions carefully, and then complete each section as well as you can. Later, you can use this worksheet to write your final JIST Card.

1. **Identification:** Sonja gives her name. What name do you use in business settings?

   Your name: _____

2. **Two ways to make contact:** Sonja lists two ways she can be reached: a home phone number and her e-mail address. Because employers usually won't write a letter, don't give your address. Instead, list two of these: a regular phone number, a cell phone number, or an e-mail address. If you give a phone number, make sure the phone is answered professionally by a person, voice mail, or answering machine.

   Your contact information: _____

   _____

   _____

(continued)

(continued)

3. **Position:** Sonja includes a broad job objective. This will allow her to be considered for many jobs by an employer. Can you state your job objective broadly enough that employers will consider you for many jobs?

   Your job objective: _____

   _____

4. **Experience:** Sonja lists her total length of work experience. Some of this experience was in part-time and volunteer jobs, something she can explain in an interview. How much time have you spent on relevant part-time and volunteer jobs that can therefore be calculated into the total of your work experience?

   Your experience: _____

   _____

   _____

5. **Education and training:** Sonja lists her total time spent in training. How much time have you spent on education and training?

   Your education and training: _____

   _____

6. **Job-related skills, performance, and results:** This section tells a little about what Sonja can do and how well she can do it. She describes important job-related skills for this work. She also mentions the key adaptive and transferable skills that she learned or used in her work and other experiences. Note that she includes several numbers. The first is "70 wpm," which means she word processes quickly at 70 words per minute. She states that she was responsible for $200,000 of cash deposits each month. This tells employers that she can be trusted with substantial responsibility. What details or results can you provide as proof of your skills and performance?

   Your job-related skills, performance, and results: _____

   _____

   _____

   _____

7. **Special conditions:** Sonja mentions that she is willing to work any hours. This shows that she is flexible and willing to work. Do you have special conditions that will impress an employer?

   Your special conditions: _____

   _____

8. **Good-worker traits/adaptive skills:** Sonja lists her key adaptive skills and personality traits that would be important to an employer. Which of your adaptive skills and personality traits will enable an employer to see how valuable you are to an organization?

   Your good-worker traits/adaptive skills: _____

   _____

THE WORKING WORLD

Are You Bilingual?

After the 2000 census revealed that Hispanic Americans comprised 13 percent of the U.S. population, corporate executives began to realize the value of bilingual business. The ability to speak Spanish is highly valued in many sectors of the American workforce. In fact, due to the increasing diversity of the United States and the emphasis on a global economy, being able to speak any language other than English is a valued skill and one that should be highlighted in an interview or on a resume and JIST Card.

Your Final JIST Card

When you finish the worksheet, transfer the information to your JIST Card and revise it until it is in final form. Make sure it has *no* errors, looks good, and includes only details that support your doing the job. Remember that it should fit onto a 3-by-5-inch card like the image that follows, so make every word count.

USE YOUR JIST CARD TO MAKE DIRECT CONTACT WITH EMPLOYERS

Like a resume, JIST Cards are useful throughout the job search. But they are far more effective than resumes in helping you to *get* interviews.

Earlier in this chapter, I listed some of the ways you can use JIST Cards, including attaching them to your resume and applications, including them with thank-you notes and e-mail, and giving them out to friends and acquaintances. Those uses don't need much explanation, but using your JIST Card as the basis for cold contacting by phone and e-mail does.

> *JIST Cards are far more effective than resumes in helping you to get interviews.*

Get Better Results Using JIST Cards with E-mail

There are various ways to use your JIST Card along with e-mail to increase your chances of getting an interview or job offer:

* **In your initial contact:** You can cut and paste your JIST Card into your e-mail as text or as a graphics image so that it keeps its formatting. Ask for an interview, but don't include your resume. The objective is to catch employers' interest and then send them the more detailed resume after they have set up an interview or asked you for more information.

* **Before an interview:** Once you have an interview set up, it's best to mail employers a paper copy of your JIST Card. As explained earlier, a paper copy is hard to file in normal ways and is more likely to be seen and create a positive impression.

* **After an interview:** E-mail a thank-you note, and then consider mailing a JIST Card as well. Enclose several copies of your JIST Card along with the note to allow employers to pass them along to others or to replace the one they misplaced.

Get Better Results Using Phone Contacts Based on Your JIST Card

It may not be obvious, but the content of your JIST Card can be used as the basis for contacting an employer by phone and asking for an interview. Most people are too timid to try this as a cold contact technique, but doing this is a very effective way to develop job leads and get interviews for unadvertised jobs. Following is one example.

Sample Phone Contact Based on JIST Card Content

Remember Stephen Kijek's JIST Card earlier in the chapter? I used it to create the script for a phone call to an employer that Stephen randomly selected from the phone book. As you read the text that follows, imagine that you are an employer who hires people with these skills.

"Hello, my name is Stephen Kijek. I am interested in a position as an auto mechanic. I have over three years of experience, including one year in a full-time auto mechanic's training program. I am familiar with all hand tools and electronic diagnostic equipment, and I can handle common auto repair tasks, such as tune-ups, brakes, exhaust systems, and electrical and mechanical repairs. I work quickly and carefully, receiving a 98 percent positive customer satisfaction rating. I have all the tools needed to start work immediately. I can work any shift and prefer full-time work. I am also honest, reliable, and good with people. When may I come in for an interview?"

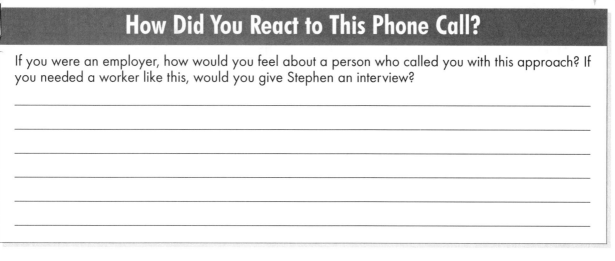

How Did You React to This Phone Call?

If you were an employer, how would you feel about a person who called you with this approach? If you needed a worker like this, would you give Stephen an interview?

_____

_____

_____

_____

_____

_____

Just as with the JIST Card, most people say that they would give Stephen an interview if they had an opening. Some react negatively to his assertive request for an interview, but years of experience have found that this approach works well for obtaining an interview.

While the approach is aggressive when used this way, you can easily adapt it for other situations. For example, you can call people you know to get referrals to employers and then call the employers to request interviews.

BUSINESS ETIQUETTE

Clearly, Voice Mail Messages Help

Voice mail can be an efficient tool or a nuisance, and the person leaving the message is the one who determines which a message is. A clearly stated voice mail can save everyone time, but a garbled, hard-to-hear one can be frustrating. When you leave a message, speak clearly and repeat your name and phone number twice. You will give the recipient of your call the gift of time and freedom from frustration.

Practicing Making Phone Calls Will Improve Your Interview Skills

Even if you don't make cold calls based on your JIST Card's content, practicing such phone calls will accomplish several other important goals that will help you in your interviewing and job search.

* **Practicing phone calls will make you comfortable when saying positive things about yourself:** Few people are comfortable saying positive things about themselves. It sounds like "bragging" even if it is true, so we train ourselves to avoid doing this. We may not even have the language to describe ourselves in positive ways. This is one of the major reasons employer surveys find that most job seekers are unable to express the skills they have for the job they say they want.

* **Practicing phone calls will focus on the most important things you offer an employer:** There are hundreds of things you might say in an interview, but some are far more important than others. Repeating the content of your JIST Card in a spoken format will help you get comfortable with it, preparing you to respond to a wide variety of interview questions by going back to this content.

* **Practicing phone calls will help you answer problem interview questions:** The truth is that you will find some interviewers intimidating. And some questions will be hard to answer well. While I will cover interviewing skills in a later chapter, it is very helpful if you have practiced making phone calls as a way to prepare for the interview. Doing so will help you handle the anxiety of the interview, give you some things you can say, and aid you in overcoming employer resistance.

Three Tips for Writing an Effective Phone Script

To help you write your phone script, I provide a worksheet beginning on page 158. Before you begin, read the following tips carefully. Then use the information on your JIST Card to help you fill in each section of your phone script. Write with a pencil or erasable pen so that you can rewrite or make changes easily.

* **Write exactly what you will say on the phone:** A written script will help you present yourself effectively and keep you from stumbling for the right words.

* **Keep your phone script short:** Present just the information that an employer would want to know about you, and ask for an interview. A good phone script can be read aloud in about 30 seconds or less. This is about the same time it takes to read a JIST Card.

* **Write your script the way you talk:** Because you have completed your JIST Card, use it as the basis for your phone script. However, your JIST Card uses short sentences and phrases, and you probably wouldn't talk that way. So add some words to your script to make it sound natural when you say it aloud.

MONEY MATTERS

Identity Theft

Identity theft, a federal crime, occurs when one person's identification (which can include name, Social Security number, or any account number) is used or transferred by another person for unlawful activities. You can take four steps to protect your identification:

* Don't keep personal identification numbers (PINs) near your checkbook, ATM card, or debit card.
* Shred any papers with confidential information before you throw them out—even the junk mail. (Anything with your name or an account number can be used in identity theft.)
* Carry as few cards with identification and personal information as possible in your purse or wallet.
* Be very cautious when giving out any personal information over the phone.

Anatomy of a Phone Script

Here is a phone script for a person who has more experience and formal education than the previous example. This one is a bit longer than the other sample but still can be read in about 30 seconds.

Like a JIST Card, your phone script is comprised of five sections. The five parts of a phone script are pointed out in the sample that follows.

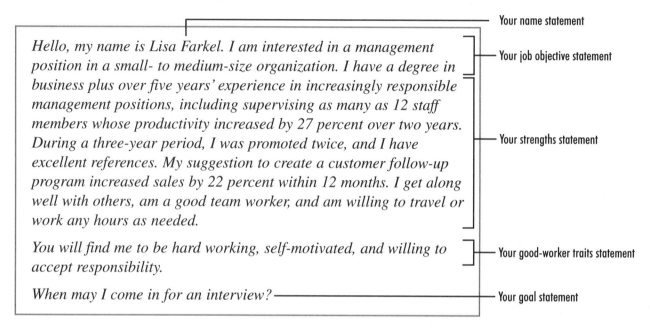

Your name statement

Your job objective statement

Hello, my name is Lisa Farkel. I am interested in a management position in a small- to medium-size organization. I have a degree in business plus over five years' experience in increasingly responsible management positions, including supervising as many as 12 staff members whose productivity increased by 27 percent over two years. During a three-year period, I was promoted twice, and I have excellent references. My suggestion to create a customer follow-up program increased sales by 22 percent within 12 months. I get along well with others, am a good team worker, and am willing to travel or work any hours as needed.

Your strengths statement

You will find me to be hard working, self-motivated, and willing to accept responsibility.

Your good-worker traits statement

When may I come in for an interview?

Your goal statement

COMPLETE YOUR PHONE SCRIPT

The following sections offer tips for writing the parts of a phone script. Read the tips and then complete the worksheet. You may want to refer to your JIST Card as you complete the worksheets.

The Introduction

To begin a conversation with a stranger, you often tell the person who you are. The phone script is no different. Simply say who you are.

Always begin your statement with, "I am interested in a position as..." If you say you are "looking for a job" or something similar, you often will be interrupted and told there are no openings. If the job objective from your JIST Card sounds good when you say it aloud, write it here. If it doesn't, change it around a bit. For example, if your JIST Card says you want a clerical/general office position, your phone script might say "I am interested in a clerical or general office position."

Beginning Your Phone Script

Complete the following two sections of the script:

1. Your name statement: This one is easy. Just fill in the blank.

   Hello, my name is _____

2. Your job objective statement:

   I am interested in a position as _____

   _____

The Strengths Statements

The experience and skills sections of your JIST Card list your length of experience, training, education, special skills related to the job, and accomplishments. Your phone script will use much of that same content.

Rewriting the content from these parts of your JIST Card may take some time because your script must sound natural. You may find it helpful to write and edit this section on a separate piece of paper before completing the worksheet.

For your good-worker traits, take the last lines from your JIST Card and make these key adaptive skills into a sentence. For example, "reliable, hard working, learn quickly" from a JIST Card might be written in a phone script as "I am reliable and hard working, and I learn quickly."

Your Strengths Statements

Answer the following questions. Use your JIST Card to help you word your answers.

1. **Your strengths statement:** What are your strengths?

   _____

   _____

   _____

   _____

   _____

   _____

2. **Your good-worker traits statement:** What are your strengths as a person?

   _____

   _____

   _____

   _____

   _____

The Goal Statement

Your goal is to get an interview. If you ask, "May I come in for an interview?" the employer could reply, "No," and you don't want to make it easy for an employer to say no! The worksheet gives the answer.

Your Goal Statement

The closing statement has been filled in for you because it works!

Your goal statement: _"When may I come in for an interview?"_

Your Final Phone Script

Use what you have written in the worksheets to write or word-process your final phone script on a separate sheet. It may take several edits before it sounds right, and you may want to read it aloud to several people and ask for their suggestions. Your final draft should be written exactly as you would say it and should take no more than 30 seconds to read aloud.

MAKE EFFECTIVE PHONE CONTACTS

Your objective with making a phone contact is to get an interview. Here are some tips to increase your success rate:

* **Get to the hiring authority:** You need to get directly to the person who is most likely to hire or supervise you. Do not ask to speak with someone in human resources unless you want to work in the human resources department. If you don't know a contact name in advance, ask for the name of the person who is in charge of the department you are most likely to work. In a small business, ask to speak to the manager or person in charge. Get the correct spelling of the name and write it down right away. Then use that name in the conversation and in any future correspondence.

* **Get the direct phone number and e-mail address to avoid getting screened out:** In some cases, a receptionist or other staff will try to screen out your call. If this person finds out you are looking for a job, he or she may transfer you to the human resources department or ask you to e-mail a resume, complete an application, or use some other approach intended to keep you from making direct contact with the employer.

Ways to Avoid Being Screened Out

Here are some things you can do to keep from getting screened out:

* **Get information from an employer's Web site:** Many organizations have contact information listed on their Web sites, including names and e-mail addresses of department heads. If not, send an e-mail to the Webmaster and ask for the information you want.

---

* **Call back:** If you are screened out the first time, call back a day later and say you are getting ready to send an e-mail or other correspondence to the manager of the department that interests you. This is true, because you will be sending the manager something soon. Say you want to use the person's correct name, title, and e-mail address. This approach usually results in getting you the information you need. Say thank you and call back in a day or so. Then ask for the supervisor or manager by name—you will usually get through to the person.

* **Call when the screener is out:** You are likely to get right through if you call when the regular receptionist is out to lunch. Other good times are just before and after normal work hours. Less-experienced staff members are likely to give you the information you seek or put you through.

* **Get past voice mail:** If a voice mail system blocks you from getting through, you can usually reach someone by pressing "0" or holding on the line. If you get the voice mail of the person in charge, try calling back later.

The Best Approach: Be Referred by Someone the Employer Knows

It is almost always better to be referred by someone the employer knows. If this is the case, immediately give the name of the person who suggested that you call. For example:

> *"Hello, Ms. Beetle. Joan Bugsby suggested that I give you a call."*

If the receptionist asks why you are calling, say,

> *"A friend of Ms. Beetle suggested that I give her a call about a personal matter."*

When a friend of the employer recommends that you call, you usually get right through. It's that simple.

Adapt Your Basic Phone Script as Needed

Sometimes using the phone script on your worksheet will not make sense. For example, if you are calling someone you know, you would begin with some friendly conversation before getting to your call's purpose. Then you could use your phone script by saying something like this:

> *"I called to let you know I am looking for a job, and I thought you might be able to help. Let me tell you a few things about myself. I am looking for a position as..."*

(and then continue with your phone script.)

You will encounter other situations that require you to adjust your script. Use your judgment. With practice, it becomes easier!

Ask for an Interview or Referral, and Then Follow Up

When using JIST Cards, making contacts, or using any job search tool or technique, remember that you have two primary objectives:

* To get an interview.

* To get the name of someone else who might have a job opening.

After you make the contact, always follow up by doing what you promise, including sending a thank-you note or e-mail message. You will catch the employer off guard. So few people take those extra steps that you're sure to make a positive impression.

USE THESE TWO POWERFUL JOB SEARCH TECHNIQUES—JIST CARDS AND DIRECT CONTACTS

This chapter has given you a few more techniques to use in your job search, and I encourage you to use them. JIST Cards and direct contacts based on them *will* increase your results, but only if you use them. So plan on getting lots of printed JIST Cards into circulation, send out thank-you notes and e-mails (with JIST Cards enclosed or attached) to your contacts, and stay in regular contact with anyone who can help you in your job search.

CASE STUDY: A JIST CARD SUCCESS STORY

Though Mike didn't know it when he got the call, getting the job he really wanted happened because of a card. As part of his last job search, Mike had his wife pass out his personalized business card to her co-workers. It was a simple card explaining his skills and experience as an automotive technician.

Three weeks later, Mike got a phone call from a man he had never even heard of. His automotive technician card had been passed along to this man by the wife of one of Mike's wife's co-workers. The employer was looking for an automotive technician for his company, liked the professionalism of Mike's card, and wanted to meet with him. Six days later, Mike was hired. Mike says he made sure to thank his wife, her co-worker, and the co-worker's wife. He stresses that keeping in contact and sending thank-you notes is necessary to maintain his network.

chapter 11

The Seven Phases of an Interview—and How to Succeed in Each

Interviewing is one of the hardest parts of the job search, and you may be a bit nervous about it. You may have had a bad interview experience, and you don't look forward to another. The fact is that interviewing most often results in rejection, and most people just don't like that.

But it doesn't have to be that way. You know what sort of job you want. You have the skills, experience, and training to do it. All you have to do is convince the employer that you can do the job. This chapter and the next will show you how.

WHAT EMPLOYERS REALLY WANT TO KNOW

Employers use the interview to evaluate you. Will you be able to do the job? Will you be a good employee? If they don't believe you are qualified and willing to work hard, you won't get a job offer. If you do meet their expectations, you may get an offer. You need to know what to do and say in a job interview. You need to meet an employer's expectations.

> *Real integrity is doing the right thing, knowing that nobody's going to know whether you did it or not.*
>
> *Oprah Winfrey*

You looked at employer expectations in Chapter 2, "Meet Your Employer's Expectations," in a section titled "What Employers Look For." These same expectations are very important to an employer in an interview. For this reason, I review these expectations here and add a few details that relate to interviewing.

Expectation 1: First Impressions

The first impression you make in an interview is *very* important. If an employer has a negative first impression, it is not likely to change later, and you are not likely to get a job offer. Here are some things that make the most difference in those first few minutes:

* **Personal appearance and grooming:** Do you look like the right person for the job?

* **Manner and social skills:** Are you friendly and appropriate when you first meet?

* **Preinterview contacts:** Did your e-mail, resume, JIST Card®, phone calls, or other correspondence or personal contact before the interview create a good impression?

Expectation 2: "Soft Skills," Especially Dependability and Other Personality Traits

The employer wants to know if he or she can count on you. Anything in the interview that you say or do will help or hurt you. Here are some questions the interviewer is trying to answer about you:

* Will you come in on time and not abuse days off?

* Can you be trusted?

* Will you get things done on time?

* Do you get along well with others?

* Are you productive and hard working?

Expectation 3: Job-Related Skills, Experience, and Training

Can you do the job? The employer will want to find out if you have the needed background. Following are some of the points that an employer will want to know. Do you have the following:

* Enough work experience to do this job

* The needed education and training

* Interests and hobbies related to this job

* Other life experiences to support your interest in this job

* A record of achievement in school, work, or other activities

* The ability to do this job, if given the chance

In one way or another, the interviewer must find out all these things. At every point in the interview process, you are being evaluated, even when you least expect it.

To help you do well in interviews, I've broken the process into seven parts or phases. As you learn to handle each one, you will be better able to meet an employer's expectations. When you do, you will be much more likely to get a job offer!

At every point in the interview process, you are being evaluated, even when you least expect it.

> **SKILLS FOR SUCCESS**
>
> **Professionalism**
>
> Robert is at an important business lunch with some potential customers. Suddenly, he remembers a hilarious joke he heard on TV last night about three popes standing outside the pearly gates. He's tempted to put up his hand, interrupting one of the customers in the middle of a question, and say, "Stop me if you've heard this one..." What will be the ramifications if he does?

THE SEVEN PHASES OF AN INTERVIEW

No two interviews are alike, but there are similarities. If you look closely at the interview process, you can see separate phases. Looking at each phase will help you learn how to handle interviews well. Here are the seven phases of an interview:

1. Preparing for the interview

2. Staying poised during the opening moves

3. Succeeding in the interview itself

4. Closing the interview

5. Following up

6. Negotiating salary

7. Making a final decision

Every phase is important. The information that follows shows you why and gives you tips for handling each one.

Phase 1: Preparing for the Interview

Before you even meet, the interviewer can form an impression of you.

How First Impressions Are Made Before an Interview

Write at least two ways you can make a good or a bad first impression before you even get to the interview.

1. _____

2. _____

An interviewer can make judgments about you in many ways before you meet. For example, you may have sent the interviewer an e-mail or spoken to him or her on the phone. You may have sent a resume, or someone may have told the employer about you. Be careful in all your early contacts with an employer, and do everything possible to create a good impression. Because your first impression is so important, consider the following points before an interview.

Dress and Groom Carefully

On a normal workday, you may not dress like the boss, but you should on the day you interview. Of course, different jobs and organizations require different styles of dress. For example, a person looking for a job as an auto mechanic would dress differently from one looking for an office job. You will have to make your own decisions about what is right for the jobs that interest you. Here is my rule for interview dress and grooming: Dress (and groom) like the interviewer is likely to be dressed—but better.

> *Dress (and groom) like the interviewer is likely to be dressed—but better.*

Nine Tips for Dressing and Grooming

Not only are there many dress and grooming differences for different jobs, but there are also differences in geographical areas of the country. You will need to use good judgment in how to dress and groom for your situation. The following tips can help you:

* **Use care in grooming:** Get those hands and nails extra clean and manicured. Eliminate stray facial hairs. Get a simple hairstyle. Pay attention to the small details of your grooming. Employers notice.

* **Don't use much cologne, aftershave, makeup, or jewelry:** Be conservative. Keep your grooming simple, and avoid too much of anything. Use perfume or cologne lightly or not at all.

* **Don't wear jeans, tank tops, shorts, or other casual clothes:** Some clothing, even if it looks good on you, isn't good for a serious interview. If you are in doubt about anything you're thinking of wearing, don't wear it.

* **Be conservative in what you wear:** An interview is not a good time to be trendy. Dressing in a conservative style is usually important for office jobs in both large, formal organizations and small ones. Employers want their staff to dress conservatively to create a positive image with customers.

* **Consider an interview "uniform":** Some styles are almost always acceptable in certain jobs. For men who are working in an office, a conservative approach might include slacks, a sports jacket, a solid-color shirt, and a conservative tie. Women have more alternatives, but a simple tailored skirt, matching jacket, and white blouse are safe choices.

* **Dress up, not down:** Many jobs—even many office jobs—don't require formal dress. But, for your interview, plan to dress a few notches above the clothing you might normally wear in that job. You can, of course, overdress for an interview, too.

* **Know that details count:** One study found that employers reacted to the condition and style of a job seeker's shoes! Dirty or old shoes were an indication, they felt, of someone who was sloppy and would not work hard. Little things do count, so pay attention to everything you wear.

* **Spend some money if necessary:** You don't need to spend a lot of money to dress well for an interview. Get your hair styled. Look a bit sharper than you usually do. If you have a limited budget, borrow something that looks good on you, or find quality used outfits at a thrift shop. Make sure you have at least one interview outfit that fits well and looks good. It's important.

* **Ask for advice:** If you are not sure how to dress and groom for an interview, discuss proper interview dress and grooming with friends and family members who have a good sense of style before you finally decide for yourself.

Your Interview Outfit

After you've thought about it, write how you plan to dress and groom for an interview in the space that follows.

_____

_____

_____

_____

_____

Research the Employer Before the Interview

Learn as much as you can about the organization and the interviewer before an important interview. This will help you make a good impression! For example, knowing that the organization is expanding will help you emphasize the skills that entails. Or knowing the interviewer's hobby will help you make conversation at the interview's beginning. If the company has a Web site, check it out. Or search the Web and online news sources for information about the company and the interviewer's name. A good research librarian can also help you get information from online databases, news stories, and other information sources. People who work for the company or who refer you to the employer are also excellent sources of inside information. You should try to find out the following points:

* **The organization**

    * What is the company size, and how many employees work there?

    * What are the major products or services?

    * Who are the competitors, and what is the competitive environment?

    * Have there been any major changes in policies or status?

    * What is the company's reputation, and what are its values?

    * What are the company's major weaknesses or opportunities?

* **The interviewer**

    * What is the interviewer's level and area of responsibility?

    * Does the interviewer have special work-related projects, interests, or accomplishments?

    * What are the interviewer's personal interests (family, hobbies, and so on)?

    * What sort of boss is the interviewer?

    * What is his or her management style?

* **The position**

    * Does an opening or a similar job exist now?

    * What happened to others in similar positions?

    * What is the salary range, and what are the benefits?

    * What are the duties and responsibilities?

BUSINESS ETIQUETTE

Just in Time

Punctuality is especially important in business situations. Whether it's a formal interview or a business lunch, you should always plan to be there on time, if not a little early.

Arriving more than five minutes early could make you appear overzealous, but what should you do if you are running late?

If you can, contact those you will be meeting with and let them know. When you arrive, apologize for your late arrival, but do not waste time with long excuses about why you were late.

Other Things That Create a Positive First Impression

You want to do everything you can to help an employer envision you as a reliable, effective employee. The following points can create a positive impression.

* **Get there early:** Allow plenty of time to get to the interview at least a few minutes early. Get directions from a site such as www.mapquest.com, or call the receptionist for directions.

* **Check your grooming and other details:** Before you go in for the interview, stop in a restroom. Look at yourself in a mirror, and make any final adjustments to your hair and clothing. Get relaxed and mentally prepared. Check for extra resumes, JIST Cards, and a pen.

* **Remember that the receptionist's opinion of you matters:** Go out of your way to be polite and friendly to any employee who greets you. If you spoke to the receptionist on the phone, mention that and express appreciation for any help you were offered. Assume that interviewers will hear about everything you do in the waiting room. The interviewer may ask the receptionist how you conducted yourself.

* **Consider yourself fortunate if the interviewer is late:** He or she will probably feel bad about making you wait and may give you better-than-average treatment to make up for it. If you have to wait more than 20 minutes or so, ask to reschedule your appointment. You don't want to act as if you have nothing to do. Again, the interviewer will probably make it up to you later.

Some Self-Improvement Notes

Consider what you have learned about Phase 1 of an interview, and note specific ideas to improve your performance in this phase.

_____

_____

_____

_____

_____

Phase 2: Staying Poised During the Opening Moves

The first few minutes of an interview are very important. Research indicates that employers quickly form a good or bad impression during those minutes. If you make a bad impression during the first five minutes of an interview, you probably won't be able to change it.

Once Again, First Impressions Count

You already know how important your dress and grooming are. What else do interviewers react to? List three things that would affect an interviewer's impression of you when you first meet.

1. _____

2. _____

3. _____

What Interviewers React to in the First Few Minutes

Interviewers react to many things you say and do during the first few minutes of an interview. Here are some points they mention most often:

* **Initial greeting:** Be ready for a friendly greeting! Show that you are happy to be there. Although this is a business meeting, your social skills will be considered. A firm but not crushing handshake is needed unless the interviewer does not offer to shake hands. Use the interviewer's last name in your greeting if possible, as in, "It's good to meet you, Ms. Kelly." Ask the receptionist in advance how to pronounce the interviewer's name and how the interviewer likes to be addressed.

✻ **Posture:** How you stand and sit can make a difference. You look more interested if you lean forward in your chair when talking or listening. If you lean back, you may look too relaxed.

✻ **Voice:** You may be nervous, but try to sound enthusiastic and friendly. Your voice should be neither too soft nor too loud. Practice sounding confident.

✻ **Eye contact:** People who don't look others in the eye are considered shy, insecure, and even dishonest. Although you should never stare, you appear more confident when you make eye contact while you listen or speak.

✻ **Distracting habits:** You may have nervous habits that you don't notice, and some interviewers might find such habits annoying. For example, do you play with your hair or clothing? Do you say something like "You know?" or "Uhh" over and over? *("Uhh, you know what I mean?")* The best way to see yourself as others do is to have someone videotape you while you role-play an interview. If that is not possible, become aware of how others see you, and then try to change your negative behavior. Your friends and relatives can help you notice habits that could bother an interviewer.

THE WORKING WORLD

How Well Did You Begin and End the Interview?

Psychological studies have found that individuals remember what comes first and what comes last but often forget the middle part. This is known as the *primacy-recency effect*, and it's true of interviews as well. An employer with several interviews will generally remember her first impression and last impression of each candidate. Thus, even if you struggle with some questions in the middle, be sure you start and end strong.

Use the First Few Minutes to Establish the Relationship

Almost all interviews begin with informal conversation. Common subjects are the weather, whether you had trouble getting to the office, and similar topics. This informal talk seems to have nothing to do with the interview, but it does. These first few minutes allow an interviewer to find out how well you relate to others socially. Here are some suggestions from experienced interviewers to improve your performance in the first few minutes of an interview.

✻ **Allow things to happen:** Relax. Don't feel you have to start a serious interview right away. Follow the employer's lead.

✻ **Smile:** Look and sound happy to be there and to meet the interviewer.

✻ **Use the interviewer's name in a formal way:** Use "Mr. Rogers" or "Ms. Evans" unless you are asked to use another name. Say his or her name as often as you can in your conversation.

✻ **Compliment something in the interviewer's office, or look for something you have in common with the interviewer:** Most offices have photographs or decorations you can comment on. Say how cute the interviewer's kids are or that you like the decorations in the office.

✳ **Ask some opening questions:** If the interviewer doesn't begin the interview after a few minutes of friendly talk, you could ask a question to get things started. For example: "I'd like to know more about what your organization does. Would you mind telling me?" Or, "I have a background in _____, and I'm interested in how these skills might best be used in an organization such as yours."

Some Self-Improvement Notes

Consider what you have learned about Phase 2 of an interview, and note any specific ideas to improve your interview performance.

_____

_____

_____

_____

_____

Phase 3: Succeeding in the Interview Itself

Phase 3 is the most complicated part of the interview. This is when the interviewer tries to discover your strengths and weaknesses. Phase 3 can last from 15 minutes to 45 or more.

Interviewers may ask you almost anything during this time. They are looking for any problems you may have. They also want to be convinced that you have the skills, experience, and personality to do a good job. If you have made a good impression during the earlier phases of an interview, you can use this phase to talk about your qualifications for the job.

Key Steps You Can Take in This Phase

There are several key steps you can taking during this phase:

✳ **Know your key skills:** Select key skills you have to support doing the job the employer is trying to fill. Then emphasize these skills in the interview.

✳ **Answer problem interview questions:** Every interviewer will ask you difficult questions. Be ready to answer them! In one survey, employers said that most of the people they interviewed could not answer one or more problem questions. More than 80 percent could not explain the skills they had for the job. Obviously, not being able to give good answers to basic interview questions is a big problem for most job seekers. The good news is that you can learn to answer most interview questions, and that can make all the difference in getting a job offer. I'll give you some tips to answer these interview questions in the next chapter.

* **Know something about the job:** Look up a description of the job in a reference such as the *Occupational Outlook Handbook* (available from most libraries and online at www.bls.gov/oco/home.htm), and then emphasize why you are prepared to do that job well.

* **Ask good questions:** List points you want to know before you go to the interview. They may include information on job responsibilities, who you would report to, and office hours. Then ask these questions in the interview.

* **Show support documents:** Take extra copies of your resume, JIST Card, and letters of reference. If you have a portfolio with samples of your work and other useful items, have it on hand as well.

* **Give the employer a reason to hire you over someone else:** If you want the job, this is the most important point of all. Think about it in advance, and give the employer one or more good reasons to hire you!

The Ten Most Frequently Asked Interview Questions

There are thousands of possible interview questions. That's too many to prepare for, so I've developed the top 10 questions here. Although these questions may be asked in different ways, they represent the problem questions you are most likely to face during interviews. If you can learn to give good answers to these questions, you will be able to handle most others.

The next chapter shows you how to answer these and other difficult interview questions.

The Ten Most Frequently Asked Interview Questions

1. Why don't you tell me about yourself?
2. Why should I hire you?
3. What are your major strengths?
4. What are your major weaknesses?
5. What sort of pay do you expect to receive?
6. How does your previous experience relate to the jobs we have here?
7. What are your plans for the future?
8. What will your former employers (or references) say about you?
9. Why are you looking for this sort of position, and why here?
10. Why don't you tell me about your personal situation?

Note: Some of these questions may seem inappropriate for an employer to ask, but the questions are based on research that studied the information employers that want, even if they don't ask the questions as clearly as those in this list.

Some Self-Improvement Notes

Consider what you have learned about Phase 3 of an interview, and note any specific ideas to improve your interview performance.

_____

_____

_____

_____

_____

Phase 4: Closing the Interview

While techniques for ending an interview are often overlooked, how you end it can make a big difference.

Three Tips for the Closing

Use the following tips to leave the employer confidently:

* **Summarize at the end:** As an interview is about to close, take a few minutes to summarize your key strengths. Point out to the employer the strengths you have for the job and why you believe you can do it well. If any problems or weaknesses came up in the interview, state why they will not keep you from doing a good job.

* **If you want the job, ask for it:** If you are interested in the job, say so! If you want the job, ask for it! Many employers will hire one person over another simply because one candidate really wants it and says so.

* **Use the call-back close technique:** This technique can end the interview to your advantage. You may not be comfortable with the technique at first since it takes some practice to use it, but it works!

Use the Call-Back Close Technique

Use the following four steps to create a call-back close:

1. Thank the interviewer by name.

2. Express your interest in the job and organization.

3. Arrange a reason and a time to contact the employer again.

4. Say good-bye.

Here's an example of a call-back interview close:

* **Thank the interviewer by name:** While shaking hands, say, _"Thank you, Mr. Williams, for your time today."_

✳ **Express interest:** Tell the employer that you are interested in the position or organization (or both!). For example, *"The position we discussed today is just what I have been looking for. I am very impressed by your organization and believe I can make a contribution here."*

✳ **Arrange a reason and a time to call back:** If the interviewer has been helpful, he or she won't mind your following up. It's important that you arrange a day and time to contact the interviewer again. Never expect the employer to contact you. Say something like *"I'm sure I'll have other questions. When would be the best time for me to get back to you?"*

✳ **Say good-bye:** After you've set a time and date to contact the interviewer again, thank him or her by name and say good-bye. *"Thank you, Mrs. Mullahy, for the time you gave me today. I will contact you next Tuesday morning, between 9 and 10 o'clock."*

Some Self-Improvement Notes

Consider what you have learned about Phase 4 of an interview, and note any specific ideas to improve your interview performance.

_____

_____

_____

_____

_____

Phase 5: Following Up After the Interview

Once you've left the interview, it's over, right? Not really. You need to follow up! This can make the difference between you and someone else getting the job. Here are some steps you should take:

✳ **Send a thank-you e-mail or note:** As soon as possible after the interview—no later than 24 hours—send a thank-you e-mail or mailed thank-you note. If you do it by mail, enclose another JIST Card or resume or both. If you do it by e-mail, include your JIST Card and resume as an attachment file.

✳ **Make notes:** Write yourself notes about the interview while it is fresh in your mind. This might include key responsibilities, benefits, and other details you may not remember in a week or so.

✳ **Follow up as promised:** If you said you would call back next Tuesday between 9 and 10 o'clock, do it. You will impress the interviewer with how well organized you are.

Following up can make the difference between you and someone else getting the job.

More on the Importance of Sending Thank-You Notes

Sending a thank-you note is a simple act of appreciation. People who receive them do appreciate them. Thank-you notes also have practical benefits because the people who receive your notes are more likely to remember you. Employers say they rarely get thank-you notes. They describe people who send them in positive terms, such as thoughtful, well organized, and thorough.

A thank-you note won't get you a job you're not qualified for, but it will impress many employers. When a job you *are* qualified for opens up, the employer will remember you. People in your job search network will also be more interested in helping you when you thank them.

Seven Tips for Preparing Thank-You Notes

As stated earlier, a paper thank-you note is more likely to be noticed by a busy employer who gets a lot of e-mail. You can also send a paper thank-you note after an e-mail note. Here are some tips for preparing thank-you notes in paper form. Many of these hints apply to e-mail notes as well:

* **Use good paper and envelopes:** You can use note-size paper and smaller envelopes. Notes with a preprinted "Thank You" on the front are available at any stationery or office-supply store and can be used in your computer printer. Use good-quality paper with matching envelopes in white, off-white, or another conservative color.

* **Decide whether you want to use a typed or handwritten note:** Handwritten notes are fine unless your handwriting does not look good. Computer-printed notes are fine, too, as long as they are personalized.

* **Don't use first names in salutations:** Unless you are thanking a friend or relative, don't use first names. Write "Dear Ms. Krenshaw" or "Ms. Krenshaw" rather than "Dear Vera." Include the date.

* **Keep the note short:** Keep your note short and friendly. This is not the place to write, "The reason you should hire me is..." Remember that the note is a thank-you for a person's time and help. Do not make a hard-sell pitch for what you want from the person. As appropriate, be specific about when you will next contact him or her. If a meeting is planned, say that you are looking forward to it and name the date and time. Make certain your e-mail or mailed note looks good and has absolutely no spelling or grammar errors.

* **Be careful with your signature:** Use your first and last name, and avoid initials. Make your signature legible.

* **Promptly send the note:** As stated earlier, send your note no later than 24 hours after your interview. Ideally, you should write it immediately after the interview while the details are fresh in your mind. Always send a note after an interview, even if things did not go well. The interviewer may feel badly, too, and give you another chance.

* **Add an enclosure:** Depending on the situation, a JIST Card is often the ideal enclosure. It's a soft sell that provides your contact information if the person should wish to reach you. ("I can't believe a job just opened up! Who was that person I spoke with last week?") Make sure your note card is at least as big as the JIST Card so you don't have to fold the JIST card.

Sample Thank-You Notes

2244 Riverwood Avenue
Philadelphia, PA 17963
April 16, XXXX

Ms. Helen A. Colstron
Henderson Electronics, Inc.
1801 West Blvd., Suite 1201
Philadelphia, PA 17963

Dear Ms. Colstron:

Thank you for sharing your time with me so generously today. I really appreciated seeing your state-of-the-art electronic equipment.

Your advice has already proven helpful. I have an appointment to meet with Mr. Robert Smith on Friday. As you anticipated, he does intend to add more technicians in the next few months.

In case you think of someone else who might need to hire someone with my skills, I'm enclosing another JIST Card. I will let you know how the interview with Mr. Smith goes.

Sincerely,

Jamal Washington

2244 Riverwood Avenue
Philadelphia, PA 17963
April 16, XXXX

Ms. Helen A. Colstron
Henderson Electronics, Inc.
1801 West Blvd., Suite 1201
Philadelphia, PA 17963

Dear Ms. Colstron:

Thank you for sharing your time with me so generously today. I really appreciated seeing your state-of-the-art electronic equipment.

Your advice has already proven helpful. I have an appointment to meet with Mr. Robert Smith on Friday. As you anticipated, he does intend to add more technicians in the next few months.

In case you think of someone else who might need to hire someone with my skills, I'm enclosing another JIST Card. I will let you know how the interview with Mr. Smith goes.

Sincerely,

Jamal Washington

Jamal Washington

Sample Thank-You Notes and Messages

⚡ Send	📩 Send and File	🔄 Save As Draft	🔲 Address...	🔳 Delivery Options...	🔧 Tools

To:	hcolstron@henderson.com
cc:	
bcc:	
Subject:	Thank You

Dear Ms. Colstron:

Thank you for sharing your time with me so generously today. I really appreciated seeing your state-of-the-art electronic equipment.

Your advice has already proven helpful. I have an appointment to meet with Mr. Robert Smith on Friday. As you anticipated, he does intend to add more technicians in the next few months.

In case you think of someone else who might need to hire someone with my skills, I'm enclosing another JIST Card. I will let you know how the interview with Mr. Smith goes.

Sincerely,

Jamal Washington

Some Self-Improvement Notes

Consider what you have learned about Phase 5 of an interview, and note any specific ideas to improve your interview performance.

_____

_____

_____

_____

_____

_____

_____

_____

_____

_____

Phase 6: Negotiating Salary

Pay attention now. This information could end up being worth much more to you than the price of this book. Imagine that the job you are interviewing for sounds ideal. But you still have to answer some tough questions.

What Would You Say?

Suppose that the interviewer asks, "What do you expect to get paid for this position?" What would you say? Write it here.

_____

_____

_____

_____

_____

Whatever you say, you will probably lose—unless you are prepared. Suppose that the employer was willing to pay $25,000 per year. If you say you will take $23,000, guess what you will be paid? At $200 a second, that may have been the most expensive 10 seconds in your life!

Never discuss salary until you are being offered the job.

There are other ways you can lose, too. The employer may decide not to hire you. He or she may think the company needs a person who is worth $25,000—which leaves you out. Or, you may have asked for $27,000 and hoped you would get it. You could lose here, too. Many employers will assume that you'll be unhappy with the lower salary they had in mind, even if you would have been happy with it. So it is important to know how to answer questions about pay. Here is one important point to remember: Never discuss salary until you are being offered the job.

Many job seekers have trouble answering salary-related questions. But you can learn to do better than most job seekers. You will read more about negotiating salary in the next chapter.

Some Self-Improvement Notes

Consider what you have learned about Phase 6 of an interview, and note any specific ideas to improve your interview performance.

_____

_____

_____

_____

Phase 7: Making a Final Decision

The interview process is not over until you accept a job offer. Taking a job can sometimes be an easy decision. At other times, deciding can be very hard.

The sample chart that follows will help you put the positives and negatives of a difficult decision on paper. People who use this process tend to make better decisions. Research shows that these individuals tend to be happier with their decisions, even if the decision they made did not work out. You can use this example to help you make any important decision.

The sample shows how one person considered a job offer. You can make your own chart on a blank sheet of paper. This form can help you make a good decision.

Sample Decision-Making Chart

Option Considered: _To Accept or Reject the Job Offer_

Positives	**Negatives**
More money	Pressure to succeed
Work I enjoy	Long hours
An office of my own	Less job security
Better benefits	Boss has a temper
Impressive title	Stressful

Some Self-Improvement Notes

Consider what you have learned about Phase 7 of an interview, and note any specific ideas to improve your interview performance.

_____

_____

_____

_____

_____

PRACTICE FOR SUCCESSFUL INTERVIEWS

You have now learned about the seven phases of an interview. I hope this information helps you understand and improve your interview performance. In the next chapter, you will learn to answer problem interview questions. Knowing how to answer these questions will help you get the job you want!

CASE STUDY: POISE PAYS OFF

While interview success stories have happy endings, the interviews themselves are often uneventful. It's the bad interviews that stand out. One horror story comes from Kent, who was interviewing to be a public relations manager for a pharmaceutical company. As he was going to the interview, an unexpected rain totally drenched him.

Kent will always remember that interview as one of the most embarrassing moments of his life. Though he doesn't know how many times he apologized for dripping water all over the building, he does remember his interview's response: "It's a good thing we're not hiring you as a model in our promotions."

Proving that you can recover from anything, Kent composed himself and sailed through the rest of the interview, regaining his confidence and hiding his embarrassment. He was offered the position, though he says his "drenched rat" incident is still a constant source of company humor.

Answering Problem Interview Questions

In the previous chapter, you learned that an interview has seven phases. The third phase is the interview itself, and it's often the most complicated part. It can last 15 minutes to 45 or more.

No one can make you feel inferior without your consent.

Eleanor Roosevelt

DON'T BE CAUGHT BY SURPRISE

Interviewers can ask you almost anything during interviews. They are trying to find out about your strengths and weaknesses. They are looking for any problems you may have that would keep them from making you a job offer. If you are not screened out, they will also want to be convinced that you have the skills, experience, and personality to do a good job.

You *Must* Be Prepared to Answer Problem Questions

The biggest challenge that job seekers face in an interview is how to answer one or more problem questions. A typical problem question follows. Write an answer to this problem question. Try to keep your interview response short and positive.

Interview question: What are your plans for the future? _____

_____

_____

_____

_____

_____

Are you satisfied with what you wrote? Would your answer make a good impression on an interviewer?

If you are like most job seekers, you can learn to do better. As I noted earlier in this book, employers in one survey said that most of the people they interviewed could not answer one or more problem questions. More than 80 percent could not even describe the skills they had for the job. This is a serious problem for most job seekers because it keeps them from getting good jobs.

The following list shows 10 questions that you are most likely to be asked during an interview. This is the same list you saw in Chapter 11, "The Seven Phases of an Interview—and How to Succeed in Each."

1. Why don't you tell me about yourself?

2. Why should I hire you?

3. What are your major strengths?

4. What are your major weaknesses?

5. What sort of pay do you expect to receive?

6. How does your previous experience relate to the jobs we have here?

7. What are your plans for the future?

8. What will your former employers (or references) say about you?

9. Why are you looking for this sort of position, and why here?

10. Why don't you tell me about your personal situation?

It's important to remember that few employers will ask these questions so directly. Employers will use language that sounds less forceful. For example, instead of asking, "Why don't you tell me about your personal situation?" they may find out what they want during informal conversation. Or instead of asking, "What are your major strengths?" they may say, "Tell me about a conflict you had with a boss or co-worker and how you resolved it." The questions in the list are examples of the type of questions you will be asked, even if they are asked in other ways.

These 10 questions cover most of the types of questions that employers have, but there are many other questions an employer might ask. Because there are too many potential questions to prepare for in advance, it is more important to learn a technique for answering any question than to memorize good responses to a small number of questions. Let's take some time now to learn a technique for answering all kinds of difficult questions.

SKILLS FOR SUCCESS

Adaptable

A manager from another department comes to Sandra and asks if she can help him generate an important report because his own assistant is out for the week. Unfortunately, he says, the report has to be ready by the end of the day. Sandra's job description clearly states her duties, and assisting managers from other departments isn't on there. Plus, she already has all of her own work to do. Should she refuse?

THE THREE-STEP PROCESS TO ANSWERING MOST PROBLEM QUESTIONS

The approach that follows will give you a simple way of understanding each question that you are asked in an interview. With practice, you can use the steps to answer most interview questions.

Step 1: Understand what is really being asked.

Many problem questions are attempts by the employer to find out if you will be dependable or meet other employer expectations. The questions are often along these lines:

* Can we depend on you?

* Are you easy to get along with?

* Are you a good worker?

The question may also relate to another basic employer expectation: Do you have the skills, experience, and training to do the job?

Step 2: Answer the question briefly and in a nondamaging way.

* Acknowledge the facts.

* And present them as advantages, not disadvantages.

Step 3: Answer the real concern by presenting your skills.

Once you know what the question is really asking, answer the question as it is asked. But add the information that will help you most:

* Mention one or more of your key skills, as listed on your JIST Card® or key skills list developed earlier in this book.

* Give specific examples to support your skills statements.

Let me give you an example of how to use the three-step process to answer an interview question. One of the 10 questions you are likely to be asked in an interview is, "What are your plans for the future?" How would you answer this? Let's use the three-step process to see how you could give an honest answer that meets an employer's expectations.

Reminder: Know What an Employer Expects

To provide good answers to problem questions, it is essential to know what an employer expects. This was covered in Chapter 2, "Meet Your Employer's Expectations," but it includes the following:

Expectation 1: First impressions

Expectation 2: "Soft skills," especially dependability and other personality traits

Expectation 3: Job-related skills, experience, and training

Step 1: Understand What Is Really Being Asked

What does the interviewer really want to know? Look at the three-step process described earlier, and decide what the employer is looking for with this question.

Write what you think is really being asked. _____
_____
_____

In this case, the interviewer probably wants to know if you are going to remain on the job long enough. And he or she probably wants to know that you *want* this particular kind of job in this type of organization. Saying that you hope to travel around the world may be interesting, but it would not be a good response.

Step 2: Answer the Question Briefly and in a Nondamaging Way

First, answer the question as it is asked. For example, you could say,

> *"There are many things I want to do over the next five years. One is to get settled into the career I have decided on and learn as much as I can."*

This is a brief answer to the question. It doesn't say much and it doesn't hurt you, but it allows you to begin answering the real question.

Step 3: Answer the Real Concern by Presenting Your Skills

Ask yourself what the employer really wants to know by asking this question. While it may not be obvious, the interviewer probably wants to know if you are dependable. For example, if you are new to the area, the employer may wonder if you plan to leave soon, should a reason to do so come along. Knowing this, here is what you might say:

> *"I've had a number of jobs (or had one job, been unemployed, or had other experiences), and I have learned to value a good, stable position. My variety of experiences is an asset because I have learned so many things I can now apply to this position. I am looking for a position where I can get totally involved, work hard, and do well."*

Depending on your situation, there are many other things you could say. This response emphasizes your stability. As brief as it is, this answer meets one of the major employer's expectations.

Early in this chapter, you wrote an answer to the interview question, "What are your plans for the future?" Look at what you wrote there. Then use the three-step process to write a better answer.

Interview question: What are your plans for the future?

_____

_____

_____

GOOD ANSWERS TO THE TEN MOST FREQUENTLY ASKED INTERVIEW QUESTIONS

Now, let's look at some tips for answering the top 10 interview questions. Your responses will be different from the examples I give here. But if you use the three-step process to answer problem questions, you can learn how to answer these questions effectively. Then you'll be ready to do better than most of the job seekers who are competing with you.

Question 1: Why Don't You Tell Me About Yourself?

The interviewer does not want to know your life history! Instead, he or she wants you to explain how your background relates to doing the job. Following is how one person might respond:

> _"I grew up in the Southwest, and my parents and one sister still live there. I always did well in school, and by the time I graduated from high school, I knew I wanted to work in a business setting. I had taken computer and other business classes and had done well in them. The jobs I've had while going to school have taught me how many small businesses are run. In one of these jobs, I was given complete responsibility for the night operations of a wholesale grocery business that grossed over two million dollars a year. I learned how to supervise others and solve problems under pressure."_

This answer gives a brief personal history and then gets right into the job seeker's skills and experiences. A different job would require you to stress different skills. Your personal history is unique, but you can still use the three-step process to answer the question for yourself.

Your Answer to Problem Question 1

How would you answer problem question 1 in an interview? Use the three-step process to write your own answer here.

_____

_____

_____

_____

_____

_____

_____

> **BUSINESS ETIQUETTE**
>
> **Table Manners**
>
> Interviews and meetings that involve meals may feel more informal or chatty, but you should still be professional. Order food that is easy to eat (no chicken on the bone), avoid alcohol if possible, and use the manners that you would during a fine dining experience. (That is, put your napkin in your lap, keep your elbows off the table, and use the proper silverware.) Wait until the meal is over to exchange business cards.

Question 2: Why Should I Hire You?

This is the most important question of all! If you don't have a good reason for someone hiring you, why will anyone? This question is not often asked so clearly, but it is "the" question behind many other interview questions.

The best answer shows how you can solve a problem for the employer, help the business make more money, or provide something else of value that the organization needs. Think about the most valuable thing you can do for an organization, and try to include that information in your answer. Here is a sample response from a person who has recent training but little work experience:

"I have over two years of training in this field and know about all the latest equipment and methods. That means I can get to work and be productive almost right away. I am also willing to work hard to learn new things. During the entire time I went to school, I held a full-time job to help earn the tuition and support myself. I learned to work hard and concentrate on what was important. I expect to do the same thing here. Because I won't be going to school now, I plan on putting in extra time after regular work hours to learn anything this job needs."

Your Answer to Problem Question 2

Now think about the job you want. What strengths can you bring to that job? Write your answer to the question here.

_____

_____

_____

_____

_____

Question 3: What Are Your Major Strengths?

This is a direct question with little hidden meaning. Answer it by emphasizing the adaptive skills you defined in Chapter 3, "Develop Your Skills Language." These are the skills that employers are most concerned about. Here is one answer from a person who had little prior work experience:

"I think one of my strengths is that you can depend on me. I work very hard to meet deadlines and don't need a lot of supervision in doing so. If I don't know what to do, I don't mind asking. In high school, I got a solid B-plus average even though I was very involved in sports. I always got my assignments in on time and somehow found the time to do extra credit work, too."

Your Answer to Problem Question 3

Review Chapter 3 and use at least two of your top adaptive skills in answering this question.

_____

_____

_____

_____

_____

_____

Question 4: What Are Your Major Weaknesses?

This is a trick question. Most job seekers don't handle this one well. If you discuss what you don't do well, you may not get the job. If you say you have no weaknesses, the interviewer won't believe you. Ask yourself what the interviewer really wants to know. He or she wants to know that you are aware of your weaknesses and that you have learned to overcome them so that they don't affect your work. Using the second step of the three-step process would result in a response like this:

"I do have some weaknesses. For example, in previous jobs, I would get annoyed with co-workers who didn't seem to take their job seriously. I sometimes said so to them, and several times I refused to do their work when they asked me to."

You have answered the question, but the response should not end there! Using step 3 of the three-step process would result in a statement like this:

"But I have learned to deal with this better. I still work hard, but now I let the supervisor deal with another worker's problems. I've also gained some skills as a supervisor. I've learned to motivate others to do more because they want to, not because I want them to."

Did you notice that this weakness isn't such a weakness at all? Many of our strengths begin in failure. We learn from them and get better. Your answer to any interview question should always present your positives. It is important here to admit that you have weaknesses that you have overcome or are working on. If you say you have few or no weaknesses or come across as arrogant, many employers will see this as a negative.

Your Answer to Problem Question 4

List some weaknesses that you could use in your own answer. Then pick one that can be turned into a positive and use it to respond to the question. Remember to use the three steps!

_____

_____

_____

_____

_____

_____

_____

Question 5: What Sort of Pay Do You Expect?

This is another trick question. Knowing how to answer this question could be worth a lot of money! In the previous chapter, you learned that one of the interview phases is negotiating salary. This question deals with that issue. The following rules can help you answer that question.

Farr's Salary Negotiation Rule 1: Never Discuss Salary Until You Are Being Offered the Job

Before you continue, it might be helpful to review why Rule 1 is true. Let's review what I said in the previous chapter to refresh your memory:

Remember that whatever you say, you will probably lose. Suppose that the employer was willing to pay $25,000 per year. If you say you will take $23,000, guess what you will be paid? That may have been the most expensive 10 seconds of your life!

Remember, too, the other ways you can lose. If you proposed $23,000, the employer may think the company needs a person who is worth $25,000—which leaves you out. Or, if you asked for $28,000, you could lose here, too. Many employers assume you would be unhappy with the salary they had in mind, even if you would have been happy with it.

Good advice. But you didn't really learn how to answer the salary question. For this question, you need to remember three additional rules, which I share in the following sections.

Farr's Salary Negotiation Rules

Rule 1: Never discuss salary until you are being offered the job.

Rule 2: Know the probable salary range in advance.

Rule 3: Bracket your salary range.

Rule 4: Never say no to a job offer before it is made or until 24 hours have passed.

MONEY MATTERS

Policy Matters

With the rising cost of health care and questions surrounding Social Security, the benefits package that comes with a job has become nearly as important as the salary or hourly wage for most job seekers. According to the Census Bureau, over 45 million Americans go without health insurance each year. Getting insurance—including health, car, homeowners, and life—is crucial to achieving a sound financial future. Most companies offer health insurance plans, often including dental, vision, and life insurance. The total premium (cost) and the percentage you would pay as an employee for you and your family are serious considerations before accepting any job offer.

Farr's Salary Negotiation Rule 2: Know the Probable Salary Range in Advance

Before the interview, you need to know what similar jobs in similar types of organizations pay. The library or the Internet is a good source of salary information. The *Occupational Outlook Handbook* provides average earnings for major jobs, and other career references mentioned in Chapters 4, "Identify Your Job Objective," and 5, "Consider Important Preferences in Your Career Planning," provide earnings for more specialized jobs. Ask people in similar jobs in your area what you should expect. When reviewing pay, keep in mind that those with less than average experience often earn much less than the average for all workers in a field.

Farr's Salary Negotiation Rule 3: Bracket Your Salary Range

If you think that the employer pays between $25,000 and $30,000 per year, state your range as "mid-twenties to low thirties." That covers the amount the employer probably had in mind and gives you room to get more. Bracketing will not get you screened out, and it leaves open the possibility of getting more than your minimum.

Look over the examples that follow. The principles apply for any salary range, so simply translate the concept, and apply it to the salary range that makes sense for you.

Some Examples of Salary Brackets

If the Job Pays	You Say	If the Job Pays	You Say
$9/hour	$8 to $11 per hour	$22,000/year	Low to mid twenties
$15,000/year	Mid to upper teens	$27,500/year	Upper twenties to low thirties
$18,000/year	Upper teens to low twenties	$90,000/year	High five-figure to low six-figure

Okay, that last entry was for fun. But I hope you get the idea. Bracketing keeps your options open. It won't get you screened out, and it may allow you to get a higher offer than you might have otherwise. Which brings us to my next rule.

Farr's Salary Negotiation Rule 4: Never Say No to a Job Offer Before It Is Made or Until 24 Hours Have Passed

Remember, the objective of an interview is to get a job offer. Many job seekers get screened out early in the interview by discussing salary. If you give the impression that the job doesn't pay what you had hoped or that it pays more, you could get screened out. The best approach is to avoid discussing salary until you are offered the job. If the money is not what you had in mind, say you want to consider the offer and will call back the next day. You can always turn it down then.

You may also say that if the salary were higher, you would take the position. Perhaps you could be given more responsibility to justify a higher wage. Or you could negotiate an increase after a certain period of time. Do not negotiate like this unless you are willing to give up the job offer. But you just might be able to get a counteroffer that you would accept.

Your Answer to Problem Question 5

Now, using the bracketing technique, answer the salary question.

_____

_____

_____

_____

_____

Question 6: How Does Your Previous Experience Relate to the Jobs We Have Here?

This one requires a direct response. The employer is really asking, "Can you prove that you have the experience and skills to do the job?" The question is directly related to the employer's expectation on skills and training. In some cases, other people with better credentials than yours will want the job you're after. You can even mention this and then explain why you are a better choice. Here is an example of how one person answered this question:

> "As you know, I have over five years of experience in a variety of jobs. While this job is in a different industry, it will also require my skills in managing people and meeting the public. In fact, my daily contact with large numbers of people on previous jobs has taught me how to work under pressure. I know I can deal with pressure and get the job done."

One of the jobs this person had was waitress. She had to learn to handle people under pressure in such a job. By presenting the skills she used in a previous job, her answer tells the employer that she could use the same skills in another job.

Your Answer to Problem Question 6

Be sure to mention any specific skills and training you have that will help you do the job. Include your greatest job-related strengths in your answer.

_____

_____

_____

_____

_____

Question 7: What Are Your Plans for the Future?

As you may recall, I covered this question earlier in this chapter. The interviewer is really asking whether you are likely to remain on the job. But an employer has many concerns, depending on your situation, including these:

* Will you be happy with the salary? (If not, you may leave.)

* Will you leave to raise a family or relocate because of a spouse's job transfer?

* Do you have a history of leaving jobs after a short stay? (If so, it seems likely you will do so again.)

* Are you overqualified? (And likely to be unhappy in this job—and eventually leave?)

Depending on the situation, there may be other concerns, too. You may wish to practice answering this question again. If so, put yourself in an employer's place. Then answer the real question.

Your Answer to Problem Question 7

Try to bring up anything in your life situation that employers might be concerned about. Then write a response to the question that will put them at ease. Of course, whatever you say should be true.

_____

_____

_____

_____

_____

Question 8: What Will Your Former Employers (or References) Say About You?

This question again concerns the employer's expectation regarding dependability and other adaptive skills. Are you easy to get along with? Are you reliable?

Many employers will call your references and former employers. If you are less than honest about problems in previous jobs, you could be caught! If everyone you ever worked for thinks you are great, answering this question will be easy. But many people have had a problem with a past employer. If the interviewer is likely to find out about your problem by checking with previous employers, honesty could be the best policy. Consider telling it like it was, and accept responsibility for being part of the problem. If you learned something from the experience, say so. Many employers have been fired at some point and know that this often has little to do with being a good worker.

In a way, this question is similar to asking about your major weakness. A good answer can help you get the job—even if you have to reveal some negative information. Here is an example:

> *"If you check with my two previous employers, they will tell you that I am a good worker and that I do things right. But you may find out that one of them is not too enthusiastic about me. I really can't explain why we did not get along. I tried to do my best, but she passed me over for merit raises twice.*

> *"She will tell you that I got the work done, but she may also tell you that I was not willing to socialize with the other workers after hours. I had a new baby, and I was working full time. I was very reliable, but it was true that I didn't go out two or three times a week with the others. I felt uncomfortable on that job and eventually left on my own. My next job was with a boss who will say wonderful things about me. But I thought you might want to know."*

It is better to know in advance what a previous employer will say about you. If you expect a problem from a previous employer, try to find out exactly what will be said. If possible, talk it over with the former employer so you know exactly what he or she will say. Sometimes, you can get your past employer to agree to avoid being negative. Ask the employer to write you a letter of reference. Usually it will not be too negative, and your new employer may accept the letter and not call.

TIP: If you know that this employer will give you a negative reference no matter what, think of someone else you worked with closely in the same organization. Ask that person to write you a letter of reference instead.

Some organizations do not allow their supervisors to discuss previous employees because they are afraid of being sued. If someone calls the organization for a reference, managers or human resources staff may give out only your employment dates and nothing else. Since a new employer can't find out about you, he or she may not take a chance on hiring you. This situation makes it even more important for you to get letters of reference from those employers, if they are positive.

Your Answer to Problem Question 8

Answer the question now. Try to address any problems you may have had with previous bosses that will be revealed if your references are checked or past employers are called.

_____

_____

_____

_____

_____

_____

_____

Question 9: Why Are You Looking for This Sort of Position, and Why Here?

Employers know that you will do better in a job you really want. They want to make sure you know what you want. They also want you to tell them what you like about the job and what you like about doing the job in their organization. The closer you come to wanting what they have, the better.

The best answer for this is the truth. You should have a clear idea of the type of job you want before the interview. You should also know the sort of organization and the type of people you want to work with. You gathered all of this information earlier in this book. If you are interviewing for a job you want, in a place where you think you would enjoy working, answering this question should be easy.

Your Answer to Problem Question 9

Consider your reasons for wanting the type of job you're seeking. Select your top two reasons, and include them in your answer. Because you don't yet have a particular employer to respond to, use your imagination to decide what the organization you're interviewing with is like. Then explain what you like about the organization and the job.

_____

_____

_____

_____

_____

_____

_____

Question 10: Why Don't You Tell Me About Your Personal Situation?

Very few interviewers will ask this question so directly. But they want to know the answer and will often try to find out in casual conversation. While you may feel that your personal situation is none of the organization's business, you may not be hired unless the employer feels comfortable about you and your personal situation.

If you follow the three-step process, you should first ask yourself what the employer is really asking. Most often, they want to make sure that your personal situation will not keep you from being a reliable and productive worker. Interviewers will look for signs that you are unstable or unreliable.

Laws restrict the types of questions that employers may directly ask without risk of a lawsuit. Even so, most employers want to know enough about you to feel comfortable.

Following is a list of points related to your personal situation that employers might wonder about. You could argue that interviewers would be unfair and biased if they asked these questions. But you must understand that employers want to know that you can be counted on—even if you just moved here, even if you have kids, even if you are single.

Some Things an Employer Might Wonder About Your Personal Situation

The Question	An Employer's Real Concern
Are you single?	Will you stay?
Are you married?	Will you devote the time needed?
Do you have marital or family problems?	Will you miss work, give poor performance, or have poor interpersonal skills?
How do you handle money or personal problems?	Will you steal, or are you irresponsible?
Have you moved recently?	Will you move again?
How do you spend your free time?	Do you have alcohol or substance abuse problems or other socially unacceptable behavior?
Do you have children?	Will you have child-care problems and require more days off than you're entitled to?

Following are some sample responses to direct or indirect questions about your personal situation. If one or more of these life situations are true for you and they do not limit your ability to work, consider telling the interviewer even if the employer doesn't directly ask.

When answering a question about your personal life, be friendly and positive. The message to give is that your personal situation will not hurt your ability to do a good job. Instead, suggest that your situation could offer some advantage to the employer! The responses that follow are simple, direct, and positive. Each one also allows you to quickly move to presenting the skills you have to do the job.

* **Young children at home:** *"I have two children, both in school. Child care is no problem since they stay with a good friend."*

* **Single head of household:** *"I'm not married and have two children at home. It is very important to me to have a steady income, so child care is not a problem."*

* **Young and single:** *"I'm not married, and if I should marry, that would not change my plans for a full-time career. Because I don't have any distraction now, I can devote my full attention to my career."*

* **Just moved here:** *"I've decided to settle here in Depression Gulch permanently. I've rented an apartment, and the six moving vans are unloading now."*

* **Relatives, childhood:** *"I had a good childhood. Both of my parents still live within an hour's flight from here, and I see them several times a year."*

* **Leisure:** *"For relaxation, I grow worms in my spare time and am a member of the American Worm Growers Association."* Okay, that one may not be the best of responses, so let's try another one. *"My time is family-centered when I'm not working. I'm also active in several community organizations and spend at least some time each week in church activities."*

All these responses give you ideas on how you might answer personal questions, but they should be modified to fit your situation. The responses follow the principles presented in the three-step process for answering problem questions.

Your Answer to Problem Question 10

Think about your personal situation and what an employer might want to know about it. If you have more than one issue to explain, list them here. Then write an answer for each one. Remember, you want an employer to know that you will be a responsible, reliable worker. Keep your response positive, and mention your skills.

_____

_____

_____

_____

_____

_____

_____

_____

_____

_____

_____

> ## THE WORKING WORLD
>
> ### Why Should You Send a Thank-You Note?
>
> Sending a thank-you note after any interview just seems like common courtesy, but studies suggest that less than 10 percent of job seekers actually bother to send them. This is true despite the fact that the vast majority of employers say a thank-you can help an individual's chances of getting a job. There aren't many other opportunities where 10 minutes of your time can put you ahead of 90 percent of your competition, so be sure to take advantage of it.

QUICK ANSWERS TO OTHER "PROBLEM" QUESTIONS

Most people feel that employers will hold one particular point against them. It may be something obvious, like age (being "too old" or "too young"). Or it may be something not so obvious, like not having certain training or work experience.

But employers are people, too. They generally try to be fair. And as employers, they are very interested in getting a good worker.

Your job is to make it easy for an interviewer to find out you *can* do the job. The problem is that many interviewers may *assume* you have a problem. They may not ask you directly if their assumption is true for you. And you won't have a chance to tell them that, in your case, their assumption is not true.

For example, if you are more than a little overweight, some employers may feel you will be sick often or be slow in your work. The interviewer will probably not bring it up. But this assumption can affect the employer's opinion, unless you convince him or her that you are healthy, reliable, and quick. You can bring up your weight or not. It's up to you. But it would be wise, if you do not bring it up directly, to emphasize that you do not fit any stereotype.

In almost all cases, the employer's assumptions have to do with his or her expectation of dependability. Employers need to know that they can count on you to do the job. If they don't ask and you don't tell them, who will?

Here are sample statements and recommendations covering typical "problems" that may concern an employer. Some are not fair or accurate assumptions. As a job seeker, though, you need to deal with what is real. Once you have the job, you can show the employer what is true for you.

* **Too old:** *"I am a very stable worker requiring little training. I have been dependable all my life, and I am at a point in my career where I don't plan to change jobs. I still have 10 years of work until I plan to retire, which is probably longer than the average young person stays in a position these days."* (This last statement is quite true, as most employers know.)

* **Too young:** *"I don't have any bad work habits to break, so I can be quickly trained to do things the way you want. I plan to work hard to get established. I'll also work for less money than a more experienced worker. I will prove that I am worth more than I am paid."*

* **Prison or arrest record:** *"You need to know that I've spent time in jail. I learned my lesson and paid my debt to society for a mistake I have not repeated. While there, I studied hard and earned a certificate in this trade. I was in the top one-third of my class."*

* **Unemployed:** *"I've been between jobs now for three months. During that time, I've carefully researched what I want to do, and now I'm certain. Let me explain."*

* **Overweight:** *"You may have noticed that I am a tad overweight. Some people think that overweight people are slow, won't work hard, or will be absent frequently. But let me tell you about myself."*

* **Gender:** *"Not many women (or men) are interested in these kinds of positions, so let me tell you why I am."*

* **Race:** Race should not be an issue. Present your skills, do your best, rest your case, and send a thank-you note. This advice is the same for all job seekers.

* **National origin:** A lack of English language skills is a real limitation in getting many jobs. If you are not a citizen of this country, employers will be concerned about your stability on the job—and they may be legally restricted in their ability to hire you. These are specialized problems where you may need help from the agencies who provide assistance to immigrants. Even so, many employers will consider hiring you if you can present a good argument.

* **Physical limitations or disability:** Don't be defensive or clinical. If your disability is obvious, consider mentioning it in a matter-of-fact way. People will want to know that your disability will not be a problem, so explain why it won't be. Then emphasize why you can do the job better than the next job seeker. For example: *"Thank you for the job offer. Before I accept, you should know that I have a minor physical limitation, but it will not affect my performance on the job."*

THE WORKING WORLD

How Well Do You Use the Halo Effect?

Interviewers are human beings and thus are prone to the same biases as the rest of us. For example, someone viewed as being attractive will generally be considered to be more skilled or have a better personality even if that isn't actually the case. Psychologists call this the *halo effect*. Use the halo effect to your advantage by dressing professionally and paying attention to your grooming.

ILLEGAL QUESTIONS

Some people argue that certain questions in the previous section are illegal for an employer to ask. I agree that these questions would be in poor taste. But this is a free country, and anyone can ask anything he or she wants. It is what an interviewer *does* with the information that can be a problem. Hiring or not hiring people based on certain criteria is illegal. A number of laws protect people with certain characteristics from being kept out of jobs for those reasons alone. These laws require that people be considered for their ability to do the job and no other criteria.

For example, a woman should be considered fairly for a job as a carpenter based on her ability, not on her gender. A person in a wheelchair should be considered fairly for a job as an accountant based on his or her accounting skills alone. A manager should be hired on his or her management skills and credentials, without race or ethnic background as an issue. It's our right to be treated fairly.

The problem is that most interviewers will not ask these questions as clearly as they were stated here. But they most likely will wonder how these issues may affect your ability to do the job. You don't have to answer a question if you don't want to. It's a free country for you, too. But you should understand by now that most questions are intended to find out if you will be a good employee. So why not say that, yes, there are good reasons that employers can count on you to do a good job?

Fortunately, most employers are just like you are. They will be sensitive to your feelings and will treat you as an adult. They want to hire someone they believe will do a good job. There is a lot at stake for them, too, in making a hiring decision. So, ultimately, it is your responsibility to convince them you will be a good employee. Do not leave their impressions to chance. Tell them why they should hire you!

Questions That Employers Are Advised Not to Ask

To avoid lawsuits based on discrimination, a law firm suggests that employers avoid questions on these interview topics, unless answers are specifically required for the job. (For example, a firefighter must be able to do strenuous work and be under a specific age.)

* Age or date of birth
* Previous address
* How long at present residence or whether rent or own
* Race, religion, or name of clergy
* Father's or mother's surname
* Maiden name and marital status
* How many children, their ages, and who will care for them
* Spouse's name, place of employment, and residence
* Parents' names, employment, and residence
* Loans, financial obligations, wage attachments, and personal bankruptcies
* Arrest record
* Legal convictions, unless relevant to the job
* Services in a foreign armed service, languages spoken, unless a job requirement
* Social organization memberships
* Dates of education
* Attitudes toward geographic location, unless a job requirement
* Citizenship and birthplace
* Military discharge
* Height, weight, and gender
* Questions about health or physical and mental conditions or disabilities

FIFTY MORE QUESTIONS

Here is a list of 50 interview questions. It came from a survey of 92 professional interviewers who interviewed students for jobs after graduation. Most of the questions are those asked of any adult. Underline the questions you would have trouble answering. These are the ones you need to practice answering! In doing so, remember to use the three-step process.

1. In what school activities have you participated? Why? Which did you enjoy the most?

2. How do you spend your spare time? What are your hobbies?

3. Why do you think you might like to work for our company?

4. What jobs have you held? How were they obtained, and why did you leave?

5. What courses did you like best? Least? Why?

6. Why did you choose your particular field of work?

7. What percentage of your school expense did you earn? How?

8. What do you know about our company?

9. Do you feel that you have received good general training?

10. What qualifications do you have that make you feel that you will be successful in your field?

11. What are your ideas on salary?

12. If you were starting school all over again, what courses would you take?

13. Can you forget your education and start from scratch?

14. How much money do you hope to earn in five years? Ten years?

15. Why did you decide to go to the school you attended?

16. What was your rank in your graduating class in high school? Other schools?

17. Do you think that your extracurricular activities were worth the time you devoted to them? Why?

18. What personal characteristics are necessary for success in your chosen field?

19. Why do you think you would like this particular type of job?

20. Are you looking for a permanent or temporary job?

21. Are you primarily interested in making money, or is serving your fellow human your main concern?

22. Do you prefer working with others or by yourself?

23. Can you take instructions without feeling upset?

24. Tell me a story!

25. What have you learned from some of the jobs you have held?

26. Can you get recommendations from previous employers?

27. What interests you about our product or service?

28. What was your record in the military service?

29. What do you know about opportunities in the field in which you are trained?

30. How long do you expect to work?

31. Have you ever had any difficulty getting along with fellow students and faculty? Fellow workers?

32. Which of your school years was most difficult?

33. Do you like routine work?

34. Is the stability of your employment important to you?

35. What is your major weakness?

36. Define cooperation.

37. Will you fight to get ahead?

38. Do you have an analytical mind?

39. Are you willing to go where the company sends you?

40. What job in our company would you choose if you were free to do so?

41. Have you plans for further education?

42. What jobs have you enjoyed the most? The least? Why?

43. What are your special abilities?

44. What job in our company do you want to work toward?

45. Would you prefer a large or a small company? Why?

46. How do you feel about overtime work?

47. What kind of work interests you?

48. Do you think that employers should consider grades?

49. Are you interested in research?

50. What have you done that shows initiative and willingness to work?

Plus, One More Question

What is the one question that you are most afraid an employer will ask? Write it here. Then use the three-step process to give a positive answer that an employer could accept.

The question: _____

_____

The answer: _____

_____

_____

_____

_____

_____

YOU ARE READY FOR THAT INTERVIEW

There you have it. You are now better prepared for a job interview than most other job seekers. If you do well, you will be considered for jobs over people with better credentials. The more interviews you have, the better you will get at handling them. And you will get job offers. The next chapter looks at organizing your job search and managing your time effectively throughout the process.

CASE STUDY: SILENCE CAN BE GOLDEN

We've all been there—that moment during an interview when you draw a blank. Sometimes even when you have prepared for the question, it happens. Nothing comes to you immediately, so you start to fill in with an answer that you know isn't your best or even close because you are afraid of the silence.

Yet most experts agree that a moment of silence created by gathering your thoughts is much less damaging than a poorly thought-out response. "After all," says Judy Olsen, a human resources department head, "employers don't expect their employees to have an answer instantly ready for a customer or client on every occasion, and they'd much rather you think about it than say something that turns out to be wrong." An interview is no different. Though you won't want to take too long (the silence is uncomfortable for the interviewer, too), it's worth taking a moment to collect your thoughts.

chapter 13

Getting a Job *Is* a Job

I f you've read this book to this point, you now know more about finding a job than most people in North America. But knowing about effective job search methods will not help unless you use what you've learned.

ORGANIZE YOUR TIME TO GET RESULTS

This chapter helps you put these job search methods to work. It helps you organize your time so that you get more interviews, get the job you want, and get it in less time.

Continuous effort, not strength or intelligence, is the key to unlocking our potential.

Liane Cardes

The More Interviews You Get, the Less Time It Takes to Get a Job

The average job seeker gets just a few interviews per week. At that rate, it takes an average of three to four months to find a job. Anything you can do to increase the number of interviews you get is likely to decrease the time it takes to land a job. It's that simple.

Look at the chart that follows. It shows the number of interviews that the average job seeker needs to get a job.

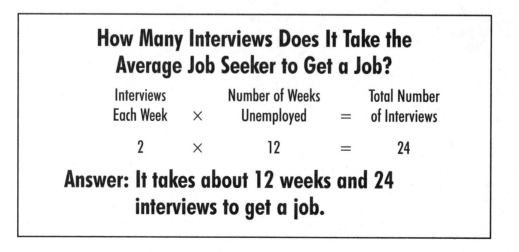

How Many Interviews Does It Take the Average Job Seeker to Get a Job?

Interviews Each Week	×	Number of Weeks Unemployed	=	Total Number of Interviews
2	×	12	=	24

Answer: It takes about 12 weeks and 24 interviews to get a job.

Industriousness

It's already 5:05, and Patrick is just turning his light off to go home when he notices a fellow employee struggling to finish some last-minute filing. Should he sneak out the door or offer to help?

The More Time You Spend Looking, the More Interviews You Are Likely to Get

The average job seeker takes about 12 weeks and 24 interviews to get a job. Many people find jobs in less time, but some take much longer. The average time goes up and down with the unemployment rate. People tend to take longer to find jobs when the unemployment rate is high. But, whatever the unemployment rate, people who get more interviews tend to get their jobs in less than average time.

The key to getting a job in less time is to get more interviews per week. Doing this requires you to work harder and spend more hours on your job search. The average job seeker spends only about 15 hours per week looking for a job and remains unemployed longer than needed. Are you willing to spend more than 15 hours per week looking for your next job? If so, this chapter shows you how to organize your time to get more interviews. It shows you how to turn your job search into a job itself. In a sense, getting a job *is* your job. So let's get to it.

SET UP YOUR JOB SEARCH OFFICE

To organize your job search as if it were a job, you need a place to work. Usually, this is a spot in your home set aside as your job search office. Following are some ideas to help you set up this office.

The Basics

Most offices need these basics:

* **A phone:** A phone is an essential tool for your job search. If you don't have one, ask to set up your office in the home of a friend or relative who does.

* **Basic furniture:** You need a table or desk to write on, a chair, and enough space to store your materials.

* **A quiet place:** As on a job, you must have a place where you can concentrate. If you have children, arrange for someone to care for them during your "office" hours. Ask family or friends not to contact you on personal matters during these hours. It is best to select a place where your materials will be undisturbed.

* **A computer:** Set up your computer and printer, if you have them. More on this later.

Using a Computer to Help Organize Your Job Search

Having access to a computer can be very important in your job search. As you actively look for a job, it will help you create professional-looking cover letters, customize your resume, write thank-you letters, and handle other correspondence. I discuss using the Internet in your job search in earlier chapters and, of course, a computer is essential for that. If you don't have a home computer, you can often find computers at public libraries, at your school, or at a friend's house.

A computer can also help you organize your search. You can use calendar or contact management software to remind you of tasks, appointments, and follow-up activities. If you have one, pocket-sized electronic schedulers and assistants can be of great help in taking notes and setting follow-up times.

If you have access to a computer, use it when it makes sense. But a good schedule book, the simple paper-based techniques presented in this chapter, or any other scheduling system you are used to can also work very well. The point to remember is to use whatever time-management tools work best for you.

Other Items You May Need

Besides the basics, you may need these items:

* Several good blue or black ink pens

* Pencils with erasers

* Lined paper for notes, contact lists, and other uses

* Copy paper (for your printer), cover letter paper, and envelopes

* 3-by-5-inch cards for use as job lead cards, discussed later in this chapter

* 3-by-5-inch card file box with dividers

* Thank-you notes and envelopes

* Copies of your resume and JIST Card®

* Business-sized envelopes

* Stamps

* Yellow pages phone book

* Daily newspaper

* Calendars and planning schedules

* Career references and other books

* A copy of this book, of course

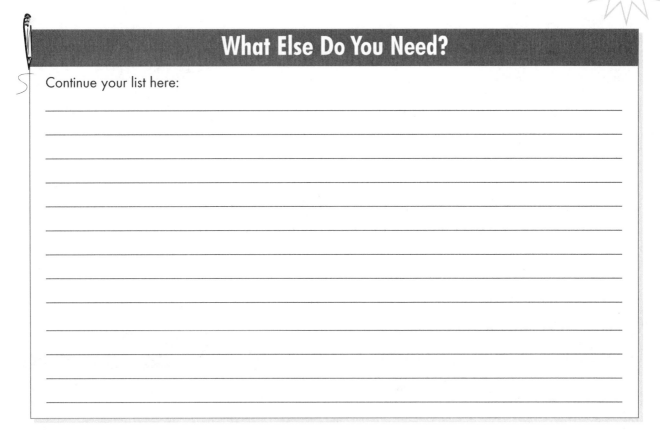

SET UP A JOB SEARCH SCHEDULE

What will you do on the first Tuesday morning of your job search? Do you have a schedule for each day of your job search? Most job seekers don't have a plan, and this is one reason that they don't get much done.

Remember that looking for a job *is* your job. If you want to get a good job in less time, you should make a daily and weekly schedule—and stick to it. Take the following steps to create your own weekly job search plan. It will make a difference.

Step 1: Set the Number of Hours Per Week You Are Willing to Spend on Your Job Search

Think about how many hours per week you are willing to spend looking for a job. I recommend that you spend at least 25 hours per week in your job search. Because the average job seeker spends about 15 hours per week looking for work, 25 hours is much more than the average. People who spend more hours looking are likely to find their jobs before those who spend fewer hours. However many hours you decide to spend is fine—just remember that the more hours you can spend, the more likely you are to find the job you want in less time.

Write the number of hours per week you plan to spend looking for work: _____

If You Can't Look for Work Full Time

This chapter assumes that you will look for work more or less full time. If you already have a job, go to school, and have other responsibilities, this obviously reduces the time you can spend looking for a job. You will have to do the best you can, so adapt the techniques I present here to your situation. And be creative: Tell more people you are looking for a job; get more JIST Cards and resumes in circulation; and set interviews for early mornings, lunch times, and other times you can squeeze into your schedule.

Step 2: Decide on Which Days of the Week You Will Look

Decide which days each week you will use to look for work. Because most organizations are open Monday through Friday, these are usually the best days to conduct your search. In the first column of the following form, check the days you plan to use for your job search. Don't mark in the other columns yet.

Job Search Days, Hours, and Times Planning

✔	Days	Number of Hours	Times
☐	Sunday	_____	From _____ to _____
☐	Monday	_____	From _____ to _____
☐	Tuesday	_____	From _____ to _____
☐	Wednesday	_____	From _____ to _____
☐	Thursday	_____	From _____ to _____
☐	Friday	_____	From _____ to _____
☐	Saturday	_____	From _____ to _____

Total number of hours per week _____

Step 3: Specify the Number of Hours You Will Look Each Day

How many hours will you look for work on each day you have selected? Write the number of hours in the second column of the worksheet. For example, if you selected Monday as a day you would look for work, you may decide to spend six hours looking on that day. You would then write "6" in the "Number of Hours" column. Do this with each day you checked. Total that column at the bottom of the worksheet; it should equal the number of hours you listed in Step 1. It's okay if you decide to spend more hours than you listed in Step 1. If so, go back and change the number of hours you wrote in Step 1.

Step 4: Set the Specific Times You Will Look Each Day

If you plan to look for work for six hours on each Monday, which hours? For example, you may decide to begin at 8:00 a.m. and work until noon (four hours), take an hour off for lunch, and then work from 1:00 to 3:00 p.m. (two hours). Complete the third column with this information for each day you selected.

Step 5: Set Daily Goals, and Record Them in Your Daily Job Search Schedule

Now you have decided which days and hours to spend on your job search. But what activities will you do each day? You need a daily plan to get the most out of each hour. Look at the following "Sample Daily Job Search Schedule." Your schedule may look different, but you should use many of the same ideas in your daily schedule.

Sample Daily Job Search Schedule

This schedule is based on years of research into what gets the best results in the various job search programs I ran. Some schedules had more hours, some less. Some had different activities or times spent on those activities. Those who used this schedule got jobs in less time than any other schedule I tried.

7:00 to 8:00 a.m.	Get up, shower, dress, eat breakfast, get ready to go to work.
8:00 to 8:15 a.m.	Organize my workspace. Review schedule for interviews and promised follow-ups. Update schedule as needed.
8:15 to 9:00 a.m.	Review old leads for follow-up. Develop new leads (want ads, yellow pages, networking lists, Internet exploration, and so on).
9:00 to 10:00 a.m.	Make phone calls, set up interviews.
10:00 to 10:15 a.m.	Take a break.
10:15 to 11:00 a.m.	Create more job-search related e-mails and make more calls. Set up more interviews.
11:00 to noon	Send follow-up e-mails and notes, make follow-up calls.
Noon to 1:00 p.m.	Lunch break.
1:00 to 3:00 p.m.	Go on interviews. Make cold contacts in the field. Research potential employers at the library, on the Internet, and at the local bureau of employment services and other sources.
Evening	Read job search books, send e-mails, and make calls to warm contacts you could not reach during the day, work on a "better" resume, spend time with friends and family, exercise, relax.

Four Daily Job Search Schedule Tips

Your schedule will be more effective if you keep these tips in mind:

* **Set a daily goal for number of interviews:** Use the form later in this chapter to create your job search schedule. I suggest you set a goal of getting at least one or two interviews per day. Many people who use the methods I present in this book get two or more interviews per day. Remember to think of an interview as seeing people who hire people like

you but who don't necessarily have an opening now. Increasing the number of interviews you get is a simple step that can make a big difference in getting a job in less time.

❋ **Expect to be rejected:** It is highly likely that you will be rejected many times before you get a job offer you accept. Most people hate being rejected, but you need to convince yourself that each rejection gets you closer to a job offer. So, as odd as it sounds, you need to go out and *seek* rejection. Keep trying to improve your contact and interview skills as you go. And follow up, in a nice way, even when you have been rejected, because that employer may have another opening for you in the future.

An example of how rejection can work in your favor is making cold phone contacts to set up interviews with people you don't know. Most people fear doing this, but those who do find that making 10–15 such phone calls typically will result in one interview. Most people can make that many calls in an hour, so two hours of calls will often result in two interviews. Making 15 calls to get one interview sounds like a lot of rejection. But the calls that don't get you an interview are often friendly, so the rejection you experience is really no big deal.

Get ready for some rejection. The more the better, because the more you get, the closer you are to your objective.

❋ **Be active, not passive:** You won't get interviews or job offers by reading job search books or working on your resume during the day. Save those activities for other times. During the day, concentrate on active methods that set up interviews!

❋ **Stick to your daily job search schedule:** During your job search, your job is getting your next job. So approach your job search like a job, with specific things you need to get done each day. This is why you should create a daily schedule and stick to it. That way, you are more likely to do the things you don't like to do, such as making cold contacts and following up. If possible, arrange interviews at times other than those you planned to spend in your job search office. Plan to take care of your personal business after your office hours.

Your Daily Interview Goals Add Up!

Getting 1 interview a day equals 20 interviews a month. Getting 2 interviews a day equals 40 interviews a month.

Compare this to the average job seeker, who gets fewer than 8 interviews a month. Getting just 1 interview a day is more than double that average. And getting 2 interviews a day is more than five times what the average job seeker gets. If you get more interviews, you are likely to get a job in less time. And you are more likely to find the job you really want. It is that simple.

Step 6: Create Your Own Job Search Schedule

Now you need to put together your own job search schedule and stick to it. The best way to do this is to document your schedule in advance. The completed "Sample Weekly Job Search Schedule" that follows shows how one person created a daily and weekly schedule that made sense for her. Look it over carefully for ideas on completing your own worksheet or computer schedule.

Sample Weekly Job Search Schedule

Days of the Week

Time	Sunday	Monday	Tuesday	Wednesday	Thursday	Friday	Saturday
8:00		Organize day	⟶				⟶	Day off
9:00	Read want ads	Gather old and new leads	⟶				⟶	
10:00		Make phone contacts	⟶				⟶	
11:00		Follow up. Get two interviews	⟶				⟶	
12:00	Lunch	Write and send follow-up correspondence	⟶				⟶	
1:00	Explore Internet	Plan afternoon. Lunch	⟶				⟶	
2:00	↓		Leave for interview	Drop off resume at printer	Appt. with Lisa at Whitman Co.	Afternoon off!	
3:00		Work on resume	Interview at Fischer Brothers	⟶	Pick up resume	↓	
4:00	↓	↓	Make final revisions on resume	⟶	Drop by state employment office	↓	
5:00	Dinner	⟶				⟶	
6:00	Read job search books	⟶				⟶	↓

Consider what you have learned so far when completing your own "Weekly Job Search Schedule." If you're using the paper worksheet, make copies of the blank worksheet and complete several in advance to cover a month or more of your job search. Or set up your computer scheduler, schedule book, or other calendar system you use to do the same thing.

Weekly Job Search Schedule

Days of the Week

Time	Sunday	Monday	Tuesday	Wednesday	Thursday	Friday	Saturday
8:00							
9:00							
10:00							
11:00							
12:00							
1:00							
2:00							
3:00							
4:00							
5:00							
6:00							

BUSINESS ETIQUETTE

Returning Calls

Knowing when to return phone calls can be confusing. If you're expecting a call from a prospective employer and your caller ID shows that you did indeed receive a call, you may be tempted to return it. However, business etiquette says that returning phone calls is appropriate only when the caller leaves a message requesting that you do so.

MORE FORMS AND FILING SYSTEMS TO HELP YOU ORGANIZE YOUR SEARCH

Here are a few more forms and ideas to help you organize your job search. Use the ideas presented here to create systems and forms that work for you. If you use a computer, electronic scheduler, or schedule book, you can easily adapt the ideas here to work on those systems.

Job Lead Cards

By using the job search methods you have learned in this book, you can develop hundreds of contacts. Keeping track of them is more than any person's memory can handle. Look at the following 3-by-5-inch card. It shows the kind of information you can keep about each person who helps you in your job search. If desired, you can list the same kind of information on your computer or scheduler instead.

Buy a few hundred 3-by-5-inch cards to start with. Create one card for each person who gives you a referral or is a possible employer. Keep brief notes each time you talk with that person to help you remember important details for your next contact. Here is an example of one job lead card. Notice that the notes are brief but contain enough detail to help you remember what happened and when to follow up.

Organization: *Mutual Health Insurance*
Contact person: *Anna Tomey*
Phone number: *(888) 888-8888*
Source of lead: *Aunt Ruth*
Note: *4/10 called. Anna on vacation. Asked me to call back 4/15. 4/15 Interview set for 4/20 at 1:30. 4/20 Anna showed me around. They use the same computers we used in school. Sent thank-you note and JIST Card. To call back on 5/1. 5/1 Second interview for 5/8 at 9 a.m.*

THE WORKING WORLD

Is Getting the Job You Really Want Good for Your Health?

Job burnout. It's that sense that you are barely treading water at work, characterized by feelings of powerlessness, fatigue, frustration, and sometimes depression. The National Institute for Occupational Safety and Health has found that as much of 40 percent of job burnout is due to stress. Job burnout has serious consequences for the company in terms of lost production and even more so for the individual. It has been linked to migraines, depressed immune system, high blood pressure, and heart disease. However, individuals who enjoy what they are doing are much less likely to experience burnout. Thus, getting the job you really want is actually good for your health.

Job Search Follow-Up Box or Some Similar System

Most department and office-supply stores have small file boxes made to hold 3-by-5-inch cards and tabbed dividers for these boxes. Everything you need will cost you about $10.

Set up file box dividers for each day of the month, numbering them 1 through 31. After you're finished, file each completed job lead card under the date you want to follow up on it. Here are three scenarios that illustrate ways you can use this simple follow-up system to get results.

*   **Scenario 1:** You get the name of a person to call, but you can't get to this person right away. Create a job lead card and file it under tomorrow's date.

*   **Scenario 2:** You contact someone from an Internet or yellow pages listing, but she is busy this week. She tells you to call back in two weeks. You file this job lead card under the date for two weeks in the future.

*   **Scenario 3:** You get an interview with a person who doesn't have openings now, and he gives you the name of someone who might have an opening. After you send a thank-you e-mail, note, and JIST Card, you file his job lead card under a date a few weeks in the future.

As you contact more and more people in your job search, the number of cards you file for future follow-up will increase. You will find more and more new leads as you follow up with people you've contacted one or more times in the past. Following up with past contacts is one of the most effective ways of getting a job!

> *Following up with past contacts is one of the most effective ways of getting a job!*

Every Monday, simply review all the job lead cards filed for the week. On your weekly schedule, list any interviews or follow-up contacts you promised to make at a particular date and time. At the start of each day, pull the job lead cards filed under that date. List appointments and contacts you scheduled on your "Daily Job Search Contact Sheet," which is described next.

The job search follow-up box is a simple, inexpensive system that works very well. You can do the same thing with computer scheduling software, an electronic scheduler, a schedule book, or a personal digital assistant, but they don't work any better than the file box.

Are Electronic Scheduling Systems Better Than 3-by-5-Inch Cards?

Maybe not. If you already use scheduling or time management software, go ahead and use it to manage your job search contacts. If you don't use such software now, you will probably be better off trying the card system I suggest. The reason is simple: It works. Instead of spending your time messing with new software, you can go right to work making contacts and getting results.

Daily Job Search Contact Sheet

If you do what I suggest, you will try each day to set up one or two interviews. To accomplish this, you have to contact a lot of people. Some you will contact for the first time; others you will follow up from earlier contacts.

To get you started now, I suggest you begin each day by completing a "Daily Job Search Contact Sheet" or creating a "to-do" list in your computerized system. Use it to list at least 20 people or organizations to call. Use any source to get these leads, including people you know, referrals, yellow page leads, Internet leads, and want ads. Feel free to make copies of the form, or make your own on lined paper. An example of a contact sheet follows.

This is also a good time to review Chapter 6, "Use the Most Effective Job Search Methods," where I cover networking and how to develop lists of people to contact. That chapter also discusses how to use the Internet and the yellow pages to generate contacts. Reviewing this information will remind you how to generate the contacts you need.

Contact Name/ Organization	Referral Source	Job Lead Card	Phone Number/ E-mail Address
1. *Manager/ The Flower Show*	*Yellow pages*	*Yes*	*897-6041*
2. *Manager/ Rainbow Flowers*	*Listed on Rainbow's Web site*	*Yes*	*admin@rainbow flowers.com*
3. *Joyce Wilson/ Hartley Nurseries*	*John Lee*	*Yes*	*892-2224*
4. *John Mullahy/ Roses, Etc.*	*Uncle Jim*	*Yes*	*299-4226*
5. *None/Plants to Go*	*Want ad*	*Yes*	*835-7016*

MONEY MATTERS

Financial Security on Your Computer

While the Internet can make your job search easier, it also can make personal information vulnerable to viruses, hackers, and worms. To secure your computer, use strong passwords and personal firewalls and regularly run updated virus software.

Daily Job Search Contact Record

Contact Name/Organization	Referral Source	Job Lead Card?	Phone Number/ E-mail Address
1.			
2.			
3.			
4.			
5.			
6.			
7.			
8.			
9.			
10.			
11.			
12.			
13.			
14.			
15.			
16.			
17.			
18.			
19.			
20.			

A FEW FINAL WORDS ON BEING ORGANIZED

Most people don't enjoy the job search experience. It's true that lots of rejection is involved. To avoid rejection, people find many ways to avoid looking for work.

Of course, delaying your job search just leaves you unemployed longer than you need to be. Or it keeps you from getting the job you really want. So don't get discouraged. The best way to shorten your job search is to structure your time as if your job search is your job.

Looking for a job is hard work, so take time for breaks, and allow time to take care of yourself. There is a job out there that is just what you are looking for, or very close. And there is someone out there who wants just what you have to offer. But you will not find those opportunities unless you go out and look for them!

CASE STUDY: A DISORGANIZED JOB SEARCH

There is no question that computers have made the job search simpler, but they can also make staying organized harder. During a recent stint of unemployment, Antonio Hastings estimates that he sent out well over 300 resumes through a combined effort of networking, answering classifieds, and submitting resumes online. "I was unemployed for only three weeks, but in that time I was scrambling to find a job—I was applying for just about anything that looked remotely interesting."

That was a year ago. Since then, Antonio has been employed with a company that he is happy with, doing something he enjoys, but he says he still gets calls and e-mails from other companies who have his resume on file. "They send me an e-mail asking me if I am still interested in working for them, and I don't even know what made me interested in the first place." If he had it to do over again, Antonio says a spreadsheet with at least the name of each employer, the position applied for, and the date the resume was sent would be a necessity. Till then, he says, it's nice to see that other employers are interested in him, even though he no longer can remember when or how he contacted them.

chapter 14

Keeping a Job—
and Moving Up—
Is a Job, Too

One of the things you should have learned by now is that getting a job *is* a job. In a similar way, you will need to work at keeping a job and moving ahead in your career. Because you will probably work for 40 or more years, it is important that you think ahead to keep a job you enjoy, advance in your career, or meet other goals. Most people have more control over their career than they realize. For example, what you learn in one job can prepare you to advance to a new job with higher pay or other advantages.

> *Doing well while doing good.*
>
> The JIST Publishing company mission

For this reason, this last chapter presents steps you can take to increase your chances of job satisfaction and success. It also covers how and when to leave a job in a positive way. Whole books have been written on these topics, but the short tips provided here will give you some things to consider as you start a new job and move ahead in your career.

TO GET AHEAD, YOU NEED TO *EXCEED* AN EMPLOYER'S EXPECTATIONS!

In earlier chapters, you learned about the three major employer expectations. These are the things that are most important to an employer in deciding to hire one person over another. In case you don't remember, here are the expectations:

* First impressions

* Soft skills, especially dependability and other personality traits

* Job-related skills, experience, and training

Why People Are Fired

To get ahead on a job, you first have to understand what will get you in trouble. Here is a list of points often mentioned in employer surveys as top reasons for firing workers:

* Refused to or was unable to get along with other workers
* Was dishonest; lied or stole things
* Dressed inappropriately; had poor grooming
* Was unreliable; was late or absent too many times
* Used work time for personal business
* Refused to or was unable to do the work
* Worked too slowly; made too many mistakes
* Would not follow orders; did not get along with supervisor
* Abused alcohol or drugs
* Misrepresented skills, experience, or training
* Had too many accidents; did not follow safety rules

An employer will not hire someone unless that person meets his or her expectations in these areas. But once you have the job, you must *continue* to meet your employer's expectations—and then exceed them to get ahead.

EIGHTEEN WAYS TO SURVIVE AND SUCCEED ON THE JOB

Meeting minimum expectations may keep you from being fired, but to get promotions or increases in your pay, you need to do *more* than the minimum. There are no guarantees of success, but the tips that follow will help. Each tip is followed by space for you to write notes on how you can apply the information to your own situation. (See the response after the first tip for an example.) Use extra paper if needed.

Correct Weaknesses in Your Basic Skills

Employers expect you to have good basic academic skills. If, for example, you don't write well, don't have good language skills, or need to upgrade your computer skills, you might have trouble getting ahead. While the skills needed for different jobs vary, consider any weaknesses you have and decide to make improvements. This may include taking courses or learning and practicing on the job and in other ways.

How might you use this tip in your next job? _____

_____

_____

To give you an example, here is what one person wrote in response to this tip:

I don't write all that well and make mistakes in grammar and spelling. My job now doesn't need much writing, but the technician job I want requires lots of reports sent to customers. I will look into a remedial writing class at the community college and sign up for the next class. I am also using my word processor's spell- and grammar-checking features on everything I write. This helps me see my errors and correct them. I am writing more e-mails to friends at home to practice writing. I plan to keep writing more and get better at it.

Dress and Groom for a Promotion

If you want to get ahead, dress and groom as if you work at the level you hope to reach next. Be clean and well groomed, and wear clothes that fit well and look good on you. Copy the grooming and dress of others in the organization who are successful. Even when you're with co-workers away from work, dress and groom appropriately to present the image you want.

How might you use this tip in your next job? _____
_____
_____

Arrive Early and Stay Late

Get to work a little early each day. Use that time to plan your day's goals. Always be at your workstation at the time work begins so that your co-workers and boss know you are there. At the end of the day, leave a few minutes after quitting time. Let the boss know that you are willing to stay late to meet an important deadline.

Some employers may not want you to work beyond their regular hours. They fear problems with governmental agencies that may force them to pay overtime wages. If this is so, do what your employer wants you to do, but make it clear that you are willing to help in any way needed.

How might you use this tip in your next job? _____
_____
_____

Be Positive and Enthusiastic

Go out of your way to enjoy your job. Tell others—particularly your boss and those you work with—what you like about it. Emphasize those parts of your job that you like and do well. It will help others notice what you do. Enthusiasm also encourages teamwork and can improve how you feel about your work and yourself. Share this enthusiasm with your friends. Being positive will help you overcome problems and be more effective.

How might you use this tip in your next job? _____

_____

_____

Set Clear Goals

Many tips in this section assume that you want to get ahead. It is up to you to set goals in your career and personal life. The clearer your goals, the more likely you will reach them. If, for example, you want to be promoted, you will probably need to supervise others or learn new skills. If your goal is important to you, you are more likely to do what is needed to meet it. So spend some time writing down your key work-related goals; then write down what you have to do to get there.

How might you use this tip in your next job? _____

_____

_____

Ask for More Responsibility

Let the boss know that you want to move up and are willing to take on more responsibility. Ask for advice about what you can do to be more valuable to the organization. As soon as you begin a new job, look for ways to learn new things. Volunteer to help in ways you feel will make you more valuable to the organization. For example, go out of your way to help solve a problem. If you are willing to supervise others, let your boss know.

How might you use this tip in your next job? _____

_____

_____

Ask for Advice in Getting a Pay Increase or Promotion

In your first few weeks on the job, ask your supervisor for about 30 minutes of private time. When you have your boss's attention, say that you want to be more valuable to the organization. Ask what you can do to get a raise within a reasonable time, and make sure you know what you have to do to get the raise. Before you leave the meeting, ask for a specific future date to go over your progress. Ask the boss to give you feedback on your progress from time to time. Don't push too hard for an increase—just letting your boss know about your ambitions can help him or her see you as someone to develop for the future.

How might you use this tip in your next job? _____
_____
_____

Ask for Training

Get as much training as possible! Take any training that is available from your employer. Even if the training is not in your area of responsibility, it may help you gain new skills. Define what training you need to do your job better. If that particular training is not available through your employer, explain to your supervisor how it will help the organization. Ask for help in finding the best training source.

How might you use this tip in your next job? _____
_____
_____

SKILLS FOR SUCCESS

Time Management

Bill has a list of five things he has to get done by the end of the day, and a full eight hours to do it. It all seems easy enough, and he gets the first item checked off in the first two hours. Feeling proud, he takes an hour out to send e-mails, and then he takes a slightly longer lunch than usual. An unexpected phone call puts him at 2:00 with four tasks still on his list. Of course, Bill isn't worried: What he doesn't get done today, he's sure he can get done tomorrow... or maybe next week. Right?

Learn More on Your Own Time

Decide what you need to learn to get ahead in this or a future job you want. Take evening classes instead of watching TV, and read books and magazines on related subjects. Stay up-to-date on your field, and identify skills you need to learn to get ahead. As you learn new skills, look for ways to use them in your present job.

How might you use this tip in your next job? _____

_____

_____

Volunteer for Difficult Projects

You will get positive attention if you do more than is expected. Look for projects you think you can do well and that would benefit the organization in some clear way. Don't promise too much, and keep a low profile while you do the work. If no one expects much, it is easier to be seen as successful—even if your results are not as good as you had hoped. If you succeed, your boss will often appreciate what you did and be more likely to reward you in the future.

How might you use this tip in your next job? _____

_____

_____

Get Measurable Results

Look for some way to measure the results of your work. Keep records of what you do, and compare your results to past performance or the average performance of others in similar situations. If your results look good, send a report to your supervisor. For example, if orders went up 40 percent over the same month last year with no increase in staff, that's a big accomplishment. Look for ways to present what you do in numbers: dollars saved, percent of increased sales, number of persons served, number of units processed, or budget size.

How might you use this tip in your next job? _____

_____

_____

SKILLS FOR SUCCESS

Integrity

Stewart works at a large factory. He recently discovered that the waste disposal team was dumping toxic substances in the river outside of town. He's afraid that if he tells someone—either inside or outside the company—he will lose his job. What should he do?

Emphasize Computer and Technical Skills

With rapid changes in technology, it is essential that you find ways to stay up-to-date with computer and technical skills. Even if your job does not require these skills, don't allow yourself to fall behind. Instead, learn new ways of doing things, and bring them to your job as much as you can. Doing this will put you in a leadership position and make you more valuable to the organization.

How might you use this tip in your next job? _____
_____
_____

Keep Networking

Look for people inside and outside of the organization who can help you in your career. Stay in touch with people you met through your job search, join professional organizations, and look for other networking opportunities. These contacts can help you advance your career with advice, referrals, and other support.

How might you use this tip in your next job? _____
_____
_____

Find a Mentor

A *mentor* is someone you respect who can give you good advice about your career. The person may be a supervisor, manager, or key employee who knows a lot about how things work and is willing to help you advance. Or the mentor may be someone working elsewhere who you respect and who knows a lot about your field or type of job. Ask this person if he or she would be willing to help you advance in your career and, if so, maintain contact with him or her on a regular basis.

How might you use this tip in your next job? _____
_____
_____

Keep Your Personal Life from Affecting Your Work

No excuses here: Don't come in late and blame your kids; spend time on the Web shopping; extend your lunch break; or do other nonwork activities during work time. Talking to friends or family on the phone, planning your vacation, and so many other personal matters are simply not what you are being paid to do. Many employers see spending time on nonwork activities as a form of theft. Real emergencies, of course, require attention. But too many personal problems can be avoided with better planning or just by avoiding inappropriate activities.

How might you use this tip in your next job? _____
_____
_____

Think Long Term

Consider how your attitude and behavior on the job will affect your long-term career plans. If you want an increase in responsibility, for example, are you doing the right things to earn it? Are you learning new things to help you reach your goals? Are you managing your time to be productive and taking on more responsibility? Do things now to prepare for your longer-term career plan.

How might you use this tip in your next job? _____
_____
_____

BUSINESS ETIQUETTE

Cubicle Courtesy

It has been estimated that over 40 million Americans work in cubicles and that each of them loses an hour of work per day due to distractions and other problems. Cubicle etiquette is crucial to maintaining a healthy work environment, following these guidelines:

* Keep your decorations tasteful.
* Keep casual conversations to a minimum, wear headphones when listening to music, and avoid obnoxious ring tones on your cell phone.
* Because your co-workers are so close, be considerate and stay home when you have a cold or the flu.
* Most importantly, take a little time to get to know your neighbors.

Be Productive

It's essential that you do what you were hired to do. Don't become distracted from your primary job responsibilities! Pay attention to the core activities and goals for your job, and do them well.

How might you use this tip in your next job? _____

_____

_____

Promote Yourself

Working hard and doing your job well is important, but it may not be enough to get noticed for career advancement. You have to stand out by doing some of the things I have noted previously. The important thing is to "look" like you are worthy of advancement. So dress the part, inform your boss of your achievements, and ask for a promotion. Along with other things I have suggested, doing these things will help you be noticed in a positive way.

How might you use this tip in your next job? _____

_____

_____

You can take many steps to succeed on the job. The tips I gave you here will help you learn and use many of the skills that employers say are the most important to them. Getting ahead does require some luck, but it also requires hard work. The important point to remember is to plan ahead, set goals, and work toward what you want to accomplish.

The Skills That Employers Want

Way back in Chapter 3, "Develop Your Skills Language," you identified some of your key skills. At the end of that chapter, I included a list of skills that employers said are most important for success on the job. Let's take another look at the skills on that list:

* Learning to learn
* Basic academic skills in reading, writing, and computation
* Listening and oral communication
* Creative thinking and problem solving

* Self-esteem and goal setting
* Personal and career development
* Interpersonal skills, negotiation, and teamwork
* Organizational effectiveness and leadership

Employers say that these skills are most important for success on the job. So make sure you improve these skills to make you more effective and successful in your career.

How Can the Pareto Principle Help You?

The *Pareto Principle*, also known as the 80-20 rule, generally states that 80 percent of all effects can be attributed to 20 percent of the causes. In other words, 80 percent of a company's sales probably comes from 20 percent of its staff, and 80 percent of its profit comes from 20 percent of its products. The rule helps individuals and managers by encouraging them to focus on that most productive 20 percent.

THE RIGHT WAY TO LEAVE A JOB

Too many people leave their jobs for the wrong reasons or in the wrong way. Some jobs just don't work out. It may be that you don't get along with your supervisor or co-workers. Or maybe you don't see a way to advance to a job you want. There are many reasons why you may want to leave a job. But, before you do, consider the tips that follow to help you to decide to stay or leave. If you decide to leave, the tips here will help you do so in a professional way.

Don't Just Quit!

If you quit suddenly and without notice, your boss and co-workers will not have time to cover your job. This can hurt you later, because you will not be able to use them as references to help get another job. While this may not seem important to you now, many employers will not hire you unless they can verify your employment history.

Exceptions: There are some situations where you should leave a job right away. For example, if you feel threatened or harassed by co-workers or a supervisor, you should make a formal complaint to your boss or the human resources staff. If you feel unsafe, you should leave as soon as possible, and then file a formal complaint. If you are asked to do something dishonest or "wrong" and don't think you can safely report this to a supervisor, consider leaving the job as soon as possible. Later, you can file a formal complaint or do whatever you think is best.

If you are thinking about quitting, take some time to write down why you are not satisfied. Doing this will help you know what to avoid in your next job and point out things you might be able to change on your present job.

Clearly Define Why You Are Not Happy

If you are not satisfied in a job, it is important to know why. If you are thinking about quitting, take some time to write down why you are not satisfied. Doing this will help you know what to avoid in your next job and point out things you might be able to change on your present job.

Before You Give Up, Consider Something Different

Once you define why you want to quit, ask yourself if you can change it. Be creative—what do you have to lose? Consider asking for a job change within the organization before you give up. Or be more assertive in asking your boss for more responsibility or different assignments. At this point, you have nothing to lose by trying something different.

Don't Tell Anyone You Are Thinking of Leaving

Many people tell co-workers that they are unhappy and thinking of leaving. The problem is that others—including the boss—often find out. If the boss hears about your plans, he or she may start looking for someone to replace you and then fire you when a replacement is found. Even if the boss doesn't know about your thoughts, others will begin to take you less seriously or not give you the help and training you need to succeed.

Get a New Job Before You Leave Your Old One

The best way to leave a job is to resign to go to a better one. Once you decide to leave a job, start actively looking for a new one. Since you are still working, you will have to use job search methods that don't interfere with your work. For example, use the Internet to post your resume and search for openings (but not at the office). Set up interviews over lunch or outside of regular work hours. Use vacation or personal time as needed.

Stay Positive and Productive

Most people who are unhappy with their jobs develop a negative attitude. They complain more, blame others, and often don't perform as well as they used to. If this keeps up, many employers will notice the poor performance and bad attitude. This can lead to being fired for poor performance, even though the employer never knew that the person wanted to leave. So, if you are looking for another job, it is important to keep a positive attitude and to keep doing your job well. Doing so will allow you to leave on your own terms.

> *Remember that your next employer will want to contact your previous ones, so be as friendly and as productive as possible in your final days on a job.*

Give Plenty of Notice Before You Leave

Once you find a new job, you will need to resign. The best way to do so is in a letter to your supervisor. Keep it positive, say you appreciate your boss's help, and mention other good points about your experience there. Offer to remain on your job for at least two weeks, or more if you can. This will allow the company to find someone to replace you and make a smooth transition.

Leave on Good Terms with Everyone

Remember that your next employer will want to contact your previous ones, so be as friendly and as productive as possible in your final days on a job. Get your projects and work area organized so that someone else can quickly understand what to do. Help train the person who will take over. Say positive things about your experience to co-workers and supervisors.

IN CONCLUSION

This book has come to an end. But, for you, there is so much more to come. The final lessons I can offer are these:

* **Trust yourself:** No one can know you better than you do. So make the best decisions you can, and keep moving ahead in a positive way.

* **Decide to do something worthwhile:** Whether it is raising a family, saving the whales, or being friendly to customers, believe in something you do as special, as lasting, and as valuable.

* **Work well:** All work is worth doing, so put your energy into it and do it as well as you are able.

* **Enjoy life:** It's sort of the same as having fun, but it lasts longer and means more.

* **Say thank you:** Many people will help you throughout your life in large and small ways. Let them know you appreciate them by sending them thank-you notes and e-mails or saying thank you in person. The more you give in life, the more you are likely to get in return.

Thank you for using this book. I wish you good fortune in your job search and your life.

CASE STUDY: EMPLOYERS TAKE NOTICE

Latisha thought she was in trouble. She had been working at this job for only three months, and she felt she had done her best and made positive contributions. She had never once been called into her boss's office—until today. She assumed that something had gone wrong. She started planning her defense, discussing the times she came into work early or the two or three times she had volunteered to take on extra work.

Instead, her boss handed her a piece of paper and pointed to a number on it. It was a raise in acknowledgement for all of her outstanding work. Her concern immediately turned to joy. Says Latisha, "It goes to show that employers do notice a job well done."

index